Bread
Machine

Also by Linda Rehberg and Lois Conway

More Bread Machine Magic
The Bread Machine Magic Book of Helpful Hints

Bread Machine Magic

Revised Edition

138 Exciting Recipes
Created Especially for Use in
All Types of Bread Machines

**LINDA REHBERG
LOIS CONWAY**

Illustrations by Lois Simmons

St. Martin's Griffin
New York

www.stmartins.com

Library of Congress Cataloging-in-Publication Data

Rehberg, Linda.
    Bread machine magic : 138 exciting recipes created especially for use in
all types of bread machines / Linda Rehberg, Lois Conway ; illustrations by
Lois Simmons.—Rev. ed.
        p. cm.
    Includes index (page 247).
    ISBN 0-312-30496-X
    1. Bread. 2. Automatic bread machines. I. Conway, Lois. II. Title.
TX769 .R38 2003
641.8'15—dc21

                                                                2002036891

10   9   8   7   6   5   4   3   2

*To our mothers, Estelle and Dulcinea,
who were with us in spirit every step of the way*

Contents

Acknowledgments

This book could not have been written without the assistance of Cheri Cotton Ginsberg, our associate baker and taster. She's allergic to yeast, so her efforts went far beyond what was asked of her. Cheri, you are incredible!

Putting our ideas on paper was made possible through the computer knowledge and invaluable assistance of Debbie and Rick Carlson. It was such a relief knowing you were only a phone call away! Mega-thanks to you both.

We are indebted to family members who offered their support and many good friends who tasted and critiqued each loaf we made, often several times over until we got it right! Thank you, Madelyn and Bob Robenhymer, Gary and Rita Gottshalk, Dave and Terri Brown, Sue and Steve Garfin, Gil and Carolyn Andrade, DeDe and Shareen Carlson, Susan Schelkun, Bill and Elise Mungovan, Elliot and Sara, Michael, Eric and Janey, Anita, Morris and Evelyn Schaffran, the wonderfully supportive ladies from the North Clairemont Library, the great cooks and connoisseurs of the Wrangler Square Dance Club, the fantastic faculty and staff of Poway High School, the ever-hungry Cosmo Club regulars, the hardworking real estate agents in the Clairemont Coldwell Banker office, coworkers at Smokenders, who had to put up with our incessant bread discussions, and our favorite tester, Briscoe, the Soft-Coated Wheaten Terrier.

We're grateful to Lou Ramsey, Max Hagan, and Janet Swanson for their special contributions to this book. By the way, Lynn Dominguez, you started it all! Most of all we wish to thank some very special friends: Margaret Smith, Lorraine Flora, and Irene Billingsley—a team of coworkers that make each workday a delight. Your enthusiastic support, highly valued opinions, and marvelous senses of humor were an integral part of this project. Our heartfelt appreciation to Marilyn Lauer, who cheered us on from the sidelines. Now that this book is done, Marilyn, we hope you'll bake more than one type of bread in your machine!

Shayna (our "in-house editor"), you were a great help. Even though you're so much smarter than your mom, your gentle spirit prevented you from flaunting it. Thanks, kiddo.

We wish to acknowledge Dr. Nancy Gamble and Lucy Silvay Peluso, both authors, psychologists, and friends who have set an inspiring example through their own successes.

We extend additional expressions of gratitude to two men who helped us through the transition from wishful thinking to reality: Lloyd Billingsley, who gave us sound advice and guidance and a glimpse of the dedication it takes to write full time, and Frank Phillips, a legal consultant extraordinaire—there should be more attorneys like him!

Bread Machine Magic would not be a reality without our editor, Barbara Anderson. Her warmth, wit, and superb editing skills contributed greatly to the fulfillment of our dream. When Barbara retired, we were blessed once again with another very caring and competent editor—Marian Lizzi. Marian has patiently seen us through many panicky phone calls and e-mails over the years, and with much good humor, has been our guide through the intricacies of publishing and promoting a cookbook.

Our husbands, Dennis and Jim, deserve applause. They never flinched as we brought home one bread machine after another. They endured inaccessible phone lines and computers, numerous "courier" runs on their way home from work, nonexistent wives at several social events, and freezers crammed full of frozen breads and rolls instead of their marinated steaks. Pack up the RVs, guys; the book is finally done and it's time to go play!

Introduction

Welcome to the world of bread baking made easy! With an automatic bread machine and 5 minutes of your time, you can create an almost endless variety of delicious, healthful loaves to please your family or shower on friends. You can skip the rolled-up sleeves, clouds of flour, and sticky countertops and go right to the final product—a beautiful, aromatic, incredible-tasting loaf of homemade bread. The 4 or 5 hours once spent tending a rising loaf of bread can now be programmed into the bread machine to suit our busy schedules. Will you be gone all day? No problem . . . just program your machine to bake that loaf 8 hours from now as you walk through the door. Did you forget to bake a bread for dinner? Nowadays, there are machines that bake breads in 1 hour . . . about the time it would take you to kick off your shoes, change clothes, and rustle up a meal for the family. But if you want to know the nicest bonus of all, it's waking up any given morning to the delectable, heady aroma of freshly baked bread. It's as though little elves had been busy during the night to leave you a special treat. How can any day go wrong when it starts like that?

Because freshly baked homemade bread has such a wonderful taste and texture, it's the perfect gift when you want to say a simple "thank you" or when you're invited for dinner and don't know what to bring. It's a gift that's always appreciated. We know a real estate agent who bakes a loaf whenever she meets clients for a listing. It's also a delightful way to greet new neighbors. When you have company over, the bread machine creates a special perfume of its own. Nothing says "come on in" faster than the smell of baking bread.

You probably already own a bread machine and are well aware of its many advantages. But, chances are, you picked up this book for the very same reason we were motivated to write it. For all their advantages, most machines come with just a few rather uninspired recipes. That's a major disappointment for those of us who have grand visions of creating an endless variety of healthful whole-grain breads, unusual fruit and vegetable breads, delicious white breads for sandwiches, European ryes and pumpernickels, luscious sweet rolls and coffee cakes—maybe even a sourdough bread if it isn't too complicated.

With those breads in mind, we tossed out the recipe booklets and set out to create our own masterpieces. What we created, however, were a lot of disasters! We'd never seen so many ugly loaves of bread! How discouraging to discover that "blue ribbon" breads aren't easy to produce, at least for a novice.

We retrieved the recipe booklets and started again from scratch, but we had many questions that went beyond the basic instructions in our bread machine booklets. Since bread machines were still a novelty at that time, and there were no bread machine cookbooks on the market, it was necessary to back up and do a great deal of research on bread-baking techniques to find the answers to all of our questions. We've compiled much of that knowledge and our experiences in the chapter Tips for Baking the Perfect Loaf.

Once we had answers, our next challenge was to adapt all that we had learned to the unique requirements of each of the leading brands of bread machines. That could only be accomplished by purchasing the machines and testing more than one thousand loaves of bread! It's no wonder this book was more than two years in the making! The most trying part of the process was achieving a picture-perfect loaf in several of the machines but seeing it sink in one or two of the others. Our goal was to produce recipes that made consistently acceptable loaves in all the bread machines. We finally realized it was necessary to list the liquid ingredients with an eighth-cup range in order to overcome the idiosyncrasies of each machine. Also, rather than sacrifice a good recipe because one or two of the test loaves failed to meet our standards for height or appearance, we simply made a notation at the beginning of those particular recipes.

As you can imagine, all those loaves of bread needed sampling, too. We enlisted the aid of many valued, opinionated tasters: spouses, children, friends, coworkers, relatives, neighbors, even Lois's dog, Briscoe! Pavlov would have been proud of him. The moment a machine beeped that a loaf was done, Briscoe dashed into the kitchen, screeched to a halt in front of that bread machine, and waited for the first slice, his salivary glands working overtime.

Our cooking backgrounds and food preferences differ dramatically, and this book reflects that broad range of tastes. We both work for Smokenders, although our full-time occupation at the present seems to be bread baking! We have taught numerous bread-baking classes at local gourmet cooking stores. In addition, Linda taught basic cooking skills to both special-education and gifted students. Lois's forte is gourmet cooking. Easily bored, she prefers concocting new recipes. A good part of her weekend is spent in the kitchen creating unique and lavish meals. To Lois, heaven is a slice of crusty French bread topped with sun-dried tomatoes, minced garlic, fresh basil, and some crumbled goat cheese. Linda, on the other hand, is more the down-home, slapdash type of cook. She loves the recipes of her childhood, but if any recipe has more than 6 ingredients, forget it. Cooking at home is done on the run. A BLT on toasted sourdough with home-grown tomatoes is more her version of nirvana.

We are both convinced that in years to come, the automatic bread machine will be found on most kitchen counters. It meets two very modern needs: it's an appliance that is quick and easy to use and it enables us to put healthier, whole-grain and preservative-free breads on our tables.

This cookbook contains more than 130 fabulous new recipes for your bread machine. We know many of them will become family favorites that you'll find yourself baking time and again. Though the recipes for dinner rolls, coffee cakes, and specialty breads require more time and effort, we hope you won't overlook them. We believe many of the best recipes in the book are in those chapters. You'll find most of them take less than an additional 20 minutes to create. Even if you don't consider yourself a baker, we urge you to give them a try. If you've never made homemade cinnamon rolls or pita bread, you're in for a real treat!

With *Bread Machine Magic* in hand, we feel you, too, can strike out on your own, adapting or creating just about any bread recipe you desire. In the next chapter, we discuss the basic ingredients and provide more detailed information on the limitations and capabilities of this marvelous new appliance.

We've had great fun concocting recipes for so many types of breads—even the failures tasted yummy! Now it's your turn. May your days of bread machine baking be filled with miracles and magic!

Tips for Baking the Perfect Loaf

INGREDIENTS

As any good cook or baker will tell you, the secret to success lies in using the best possible ingredients. The same is true for breads. Always try to obtain the most recently milled flours, the freshest vegetables, the ripest fruit, the freshest yeast. You *will* notice a difference! Here are some guidelines that should help:

WHITE FLOURS

Bread flour is now sold in most grocery stores. (Gold Medal packages it as "Better for Bread" flour.) It has a higher gluten content than all-purpose flour. Gluten gives structure and height to each loaf, therefore bread flour will produce a higher loaf of bread (also, one with a coarser texture) and should be used in the recipes where it's indicated.

We switch to **all-purpose flour** (bleached or unbleached) for most dinner rolls, sweet rolls, and specialty breads, as well as for loaves that rise too high with bread flour. Both bleached and unbleached all-purpose white flours are refined; however, bleached flour has also been whitened with an oxidizing or bleaching agent such as chlorine dioxide.

WHOLE-GRAIN FLOURS

Whole wheat flour, unlike white flour, is ground from the complete wheat berry and thus contains the wheat germ as well as the wheat bran. Avoid using stone-ground whole wheat in the bread machine. It is coarser in texture and does not rise as well as regular whole wheat flour in the machine.

Rye flour is a heavy flour milled from the rye grain. It is low in gluten. You will need to combine it with white or whole wheat flour to produce an acceptable-size loaf. A rye dough is also stickier than other doughs.

Barley flour is milled from barley kernels, which are very high in minerals. It contributes a slightly sweet taste and a cakelike texture to the dough.

Buckwheat flour has a strong, tart, and earthy flavor and lends a grayish color to the finished product. We use it in small quantities because a little goes a long way.

Millet flour is ground from whole millet, and when added to bread, gives it a crumbly, dry taste and texture.

Oats have the highest protein and mineral content of all grains. They add that sweet and nutty "country" richness to bread.

Cracked wheat and bulgur are pieces of the wheat kernel. Bulgur is cracked wheat that has been parboiled and dried for faster cooking. It will absorb liquids more readily than cracked wheat.

Bran is the outer covering of the wheat kernel. It is added to bread recipes for texture, flavor, and fiber. Use it sparingly since too much bran (more than ⅓ cup in the small loaf, ½ cup in the medium loaf, or ⅔ cup in the large loaf) can inhibit the yeast's growth. Most supermarkets now carry miller's wheat bran in a box. Check the cereal or health-food section of your market.

Wheat germ is the tiny embryo of the wheat kernel. It contributes texture and a nutty flavor to whole-grain breads. If used in excess (more than ¼ cup per small or medium loaf or more than ½ cup per large loaf), it will inhibit the rising action of the yeast. Normally sold in jars, it's usually located in the cereal or health-food section of your grocery store.

Millet is a yellowish, round grain that resembles a mustard seed. It adds a crunchy texture and extra nutrition to your breads.

We had no difficulty locating the various whole grains used in these recipes at local natural-foods stores. The larger stores offer them both packaged and in open bins. Compare prices and we think you'll discover that buying them in bulk from the bins is a better deal.

Whole-grain breads do not rise as quickly as white-flour breads and are normally shorter, denser loaves when made in a bread machine. Most machines, however, take that fact into account and allow a longer rising period in the whole wheat cycle. Only white, wheat, and rye flours contain gluten; therefore, all whole-grain recipes require white and/or whole wheat flour as a base.

Whole-grain breads also brown faster and have a more robust flavor. If they are too dark for your liking, switch to the Light Crust setting when baking whole-grain breads.

It's important to note that whole-grain flours and wheat germ contain natural oils and will soon go rancid if stored at room temperature. You should always store them in airtight containers in the refrigerator or freezer.

VITAL WHEAT GLUTEN

Vital wheat gluten is an additive that gives bread extra strength and increased height. Vital wheat gluten is not a flour (don't confuse it with something labeled "gluten flour"). It is almost pure gluten, which is the flour's protein, and it is isolated in a long process that involves washing out the starch and then drying, grinding, and packaging the pure gluten that remains. It's especially useful when baking heavy whole-grain breads that need a boost. Use 1 tablespoon per cup of flour.

LIQUIDS

The very best water to use is bottled spring water. It has no chlorine and contains all the minerals the yeast needs to perform at its best. Avoid softened water. It's high in sodium.

When a recipe calls for buttermilk, fresh is best. If you don't use it that often, you can buy a small carton and store it in the freezer. Once defrosted, it will keep in the refrigerator for up to a month. Shake it well before using. Even more convenient is the powdered buttermilk found in cans, usually with the other powdered milks in your grocery or natural-foods store. It's best to store it in the refrigerator. There's no need to mix the buttermilk powder with water before adding it to the mix. Simply replace the buttermilk with water and add 1 tablespoon buttermilk powder to the other dry ingredients for every ¼ cup buttermilk called for in the recipe. For instance, if the recipe calls for ¾ cup buttermilk, substitute ¾ cup water and add 3 tablespoons buttermilk powder to the other dry ingredients.

A similar substitution can be made if you find yourself out of milk. Add ¾ to 1 tablespoon nonfat dry milk powder to the dry ingredients for each ¼ cup fresh milk called for in the recipe.

FATS

Fats add flavor and tenderness, and keep the bread from turning stale rapidly. (Note that the Authentic French Bread, page 26, has no fat in the recipe. As a result, it dries out and loses it fresh flavor in just a matter of hours.)

Margarine is fine to use but avoid the lower fat varieties because they contain more water than regular margarine and will affect the recipe. If you choose butter, select unsalted butter. It is usually fresher. Also, for your convenience, select a brand of butter or margarine that has tablespoon measurements marked on the wrapper.

SWEETENERS

Sweeteners such as granulated sugar, brown sugar, honey, molasses, corn syrup, maple syrup, and fructose add flavor and color to the bread crust and provide food for the yeast.

EGGS

Use only large eggs. One large egg is equivalent to a scant ¼ cup liquid and it will add a golden color and a cakelike texture to the loaf. To eliminate cholesterol, you can substitute ¼ cup water, ¼ cup liquid egg substitute, or 2 egg whites for each whole egg. For vegans, there's a non-animal product called Egg Replacer. Look for it in health-food stores.

SALT

You can omit the salt in recipes if you are on a salt-restricted diet. However, the salt affects both the time it takes the dough to rise and the strength of the gluten formed. Your salt-free loaf will rise more rapidly and probably collapse during baking. Reducing the amount of liquid and yeast slightly might help. If not, try a Rapid Bake setting. Or consider using a "lite salt," such as Morton's, as long as it contains both potassium chloride and sodium. The easiest option of all: Cut the amount of salt in half in the recipes. Your bread will most likely still rise well, not sink too much, and taste almost the same as the original.

YEAST

Yeast is a live fungus that feeds on sugar, ferments it, and produces carbon dioxide. Small bubbles of carbon dioxide are trapped in the gluten, the bread's weblike structure, and when they expand, the bread rises. To avoid killing the yeast, do not use liquids that are extremely cold or hot (over 115° F).

Since the yeast is often the most expensive ingredient in the bread, here's a money-saving tip: Buy your yeast in 1-pound or 2-pound bulk packages at one of those warehouse discount stores, such as Costco or Sam's Club, or at a wholesale restaurant-supply store. The savings are remarkable! Open the brick-hard, vacuum-packed bag of yeast and pour a little into a small, baby food–sized jar. Close the package, seal it well, and store inside a freezer bag in your freezer. It will keep for at least a year that way. Or share it with friends if you don't think you'll be using that much yeast in a year's time.

Not sure your yeast is still active? There's an easy way to test its potency. Place 1 teaspoon yeast and 1 tablespoon sugar in 1 cup warm water (105 to 115° F) and wait 5 minutes. If the mixture doesn't start to foam in that time, it's time to replace your yeast.

Miscellaneous Ingredients

Again, we recommend using only the freshest ingredients. This is especially true when it comes to Parmesan cheese, as noted in the recipe for Anita's Italian Herb Bread on page 34.

Several recipes call for sunflower seeds. We found that the raw unsalted seeds from the natural-food store bins were best. If you use salted seeds, reduce the amount of salt called for in the recipe. Always store seeds and whole grains in the refrigerator or freezer to avoid rancidity.

Potatoes, buttermilk, eggs, and oats add a wonderful rich flavor and moist texture to breads and rolls. Keep them in mind when you want to vary a recipe.

A Note for Those on Special Diets

If you are concerned about your cholesterol intake, you can substitute nonfat milk for whole milk and 2 egg whites or ¼ cup water or ¼ cup liquid egg substitute for each egg.

If you are a vegetarian who eats no dairy products, you can substitute water or soy milk for the milk or buttermilk, ¼ cup water for each egg, and vegetable shortening or oil for the butter or margarine in these recipes.

Measurements

Basic Measurements

1½ teaspoons = ½ tablespoon
3 teaspoons = 1 tablespoon
4 tablespoons = ¼ cup
5⅓ tablespoons = ⅓ cup
16 tablespoons = 1 cup

You'll find that eighth-cup measurements are frequently used for measuring liquids. The measuring cup that came with your machine is probably marked in eighths. If not, use the following equivalents:

⅛ cup = 2 tablespoons

Therefore:

$$\frac{3}{8} \text{ cup} = \frac{1}{4} \text{ cup} + 2 \text{ tablespoons}$$
$$\frac{5}{8} \text{ cup} = \frac{1}{2} \text{ cup} + 2 \text{ tablespoons}$$
$$\frac{7}{8} \text{ cup} = \frac{3}{4} \text{ cup} + 2 \text{ tablespoons}$$
$$1\frac{1}{8} \text{ cups} = 1 \text{ cup} + 2 \text{ tablespoons}$$

TIPS FOR BAKING THE PERFECT LOAF

There are so many things we've learned along the way about bread machines and baking bread. Most are contained in our second book, *The Bread Machine Magic Book of Helpful Hints,* but here are some we'd like to pass along to you now:

GREAT BREADS START WITH THE PROPER DOUGH CONSISTENCY

· Experience will be your best teacher. If you're new at the bread-baking business, take time to look at and touch the dough several times during the mixing/kneading process. You'll soon develop a sense of the proper consistency for the perfect loaf. You're looking for a dough that forms a smooth, pliable ball after about 10 minutes of kneading. It will be slightly tacky to the touch. It shouldn't be crumbly. It shouldn't be sticky. It shouldn't leave traces of dough in the bottom of the pan as the mixing blade rotates. And it shouldn't be so stiff that the bread machine sounds like it's straining to knead it or about to stall. Some doughs can look perfect but have no give to them. Doughs that are stiff will invariably bake up into short, dense loaves. Think sensuous! What you're looking for is a dough that is warm, soft, alive—one that makes you want to pull it out of the machine and work with it for hours because it feels so wonderful.

· Once in a while there are exceptions, when a dough should be wetter than normal or will take quite a while to pull moisture from various ingredients, but we let you know which recipes will produce an atypical dough. Read the "blurbs" at the start of the recipes. By the way, rye bread doughs will normally be on the wet side, so you need to allow for a moister dough in all rye bread recipes.

· If the dough feels too dry or wet during mixing, add more liquid or flour to correct it, 1 tablespoon at a time. Often, all it takes is a tablespoon or two to correct it. If the mixing cycle is almost over, you can make the addition, stop the machine, and then restart it.

Measuring Ingredients

· It's very important to use accurate and proper measuring equipment and techniques. Sometimes as little as 1 tablespoon liquid can make the difference between a great bread and a not-so-great one. Use a dry measuring cup for your flours and grains. They normally come nested in ¼-, ⅓-, ½-, and 1-cup sizes. **Avoid using the measuring cup as a scooper!** This has been the cause of many a short, heavy loaf. To measure your dry ingredients properly, gently spoon them into the cup (do not pack them down with the back of the spoon or tap the side of the cup to settle them), and then level them with a straight-edged knife or spatula. Why be a spooner rather than a scooper? Because, when dipping down into your canister or bag of flour with the measuring cup, you can pack in at least 1 extra tablespoon of flour *per cup,* enough to make a big difference in your final product.

· Use a clear plastic or glass liquid measuring cup for your liquids; set the cup on a flat surface and check the measurement at eye level.

· When a recipe calls for more than 2 tablespoons butter or margarine, cut it into smaller pieces to ensure that it will blend well with the other ingredients.

· If a recipe calls for both oil and honey, measure the oil first. The honey or molasses will then slide easily out of the tablespoon.

· To make use of the last few drops of honey or molasses that coat the sides of the jar, remove the lid and place the jar in the microwave on High for 10 to 15 seconds. It will then pour easily into your measuring spoon.

· Any ingredients that are heated or cooked on the stove should be allowed to cool to room temperature before you add them to the rest of the ingredients; otherwise, they will kill the yeast. We suggest, too, that you add the ingredients to the bread pan in the order listed, adding the yeast last. Avoid adding yeast directly on top of the salt or vice versa. The two don't mix.

Tips for High-Altitude Bakers

· Try any or all of the following suggestions if your breads rise too quickly and deflate when baked due to lower pressure at high altitudes: Reduce the amount of yeast by about one-third, increase the salt by 25%, and add ½ to 1 tablespoon vital wheat gluten per cup of flour. If all else fails, try baking your bread on the Rapid Bake cycle.

STORAGE

· Store all whole-grain flours, bran, cracked wheat, bulgur, wheat germ, and nuts in sealed containers in the freezer or refrigerator to prevent them from turning rancid. They all contain natural oils and do not have a long shelf life.

· If you plan to bake bread several times a week, make it as convenient for yourself as possible. We fill our canister sets with bread flour, sugar, nonfat dry milk powder, and oats. In the cupboard overhead we have containers of salt, honey, molasses, brown sugar, instant potato flakes, raisins, cornmeal, baking soda, herbs, and spices. With that arrangement, it's possible to toss together all the ingredients for a loaf of bread in just 5 minutes.

· If you like to bake a wide variety of breads, we suggest having these ingredients on hand:

FLOURS: Bread, all-purpose (unbleached or regular), whole wheat, rye, barley, buckwheat, millet

LIQUIDS: Milk or nonfat dry milk powder, buttermilk or dry buttermilk powder

WHOLE GRAINS: Oats, wheat bran, wheat germ, cracked wheat or bulgur, millet

SWEETENERS: Granulated sugar, dark and light brown sugar, confectioners' sugar, honey, molasses

FATS: Margarine or unsalted butter, vegetable and olive oil, shortening

MISCELLANEOUS: Yeast, salt, instant potato flakes, eggs, sour cream, sunflower seeds, oranges, raisins, imported Parmesan cheese, various herbs and spices

· Once a loaf is done, remove it from the bread pan as soon as possible. Even with the Cool Down and Keep Warm cycles, bread left to sit in the pan too long will turn damp and soggy on the outside.

· Baked bread and rolls, if allowed to cool completely and wrapped well in plastic, foil, or plastic bags, can be frozen satisfactorily for 1 month. It's best to slice the bread first for convenience sake. We don't recommend refrigerating bread. Bread stales 6 times faster in the refrigerator than when stored at room temperature.

· In a hurry? No time to bake that dough that just came out of the machine? No problem. You can park most doughs in the refrigerator for 2 or 3 days. Place the dough in an oiled, sealed, plastic bag or bowl. You will need to punch it down each day. When ready to use it, simply take it out of the refrigerator and allow it to come to room temperature before shaping it into a loaf or rolls. We do this quite often with pizza dough. Having it handy like that means hot pizza from the oven faster than a delivery boy can get bring one to the door.

TROUBLESHOOTING

· Once in a while you'll have loaves that turn out like miniboulders rather than anything edible. Did you check the dough's consistency during kneading? It probably needed a little more liquid. Did you forget to place the blade securely on the post? Did you forget to add yeast? Did you scoop your flour out with a measuring cup rather than spooning it into the cup? Toss the loaf out (be careful you don't hit anyone with it!) and try again.

· Too much liquid in the dough can produce a wide variety of unsightly results. It will usually cause a whole-grain bread to be coarse and full of holes or very small with a flat or sunken top. If you end up with a tall loaf that is spongy-soft with caved-in sides, or a bread that rose too high and mushroomed over the top of the pan, those are also results of dough that was too wet. Don't forget that ingredients such as fruits, vegetables, sour cream, and cottage cheese add moisture to the dough as well.

· If a loaf consistently rises too fast but looks very deflated after it bakes, that means it had too long a rising period or rose too fast. The gluten strands broke, the gas escaped, and the bread fell during baking. You may need to use the Rapid Bake cycle if this happens often. It can also be the result of omitting salt from the recipe. You can reduce the amount of salt in a recipe, but we don't recommend you leave it out altogether.

· Breads that contain whole grains, cheese, eggs, or extra sugar will often bake up very dark or have a burnt crust. You should switch to a Light Crust setting for those breads.

· The weather can play an important part in your bread-baking efforts. Days when the humidity is either very high or very low, the flour's moisture content changes significantly. Professional bakers get around this by weighing their flour, which takes into account how much moisture the flour has absorbed from the atmosphere and gives them consistent results. If you're not keen on weighing your ingredients, simply adjust your wet or dry ingredients slightly to allow for the change in weather. As the dough mixes, add 1 or 2 more tablespoons flour if it's particularly humid outside, or 1 or 2 teaspoons more liquid if it's unusually dry out. Those are the times when it's especially important to pinch the dough as it mixes to make sure it's wet or dry enough.

· We've noticed that in the horizontal bread pans that bake the more traditionally shaped loaf, flour has a tendency to pile up in the corners and not always get mixed in with the rest of the ingredients. If you have one of those pans, it's always a good idea to clear out the corners with a rubber spatula shortly after the initial mixing cycle begins.

MISCELLANEOUS

· When using the Delayed Baking cycle on your machine, avoid using any ingredients that might spoil if left out at room temperature for any length of time, such as eggs, milk, sour cream, cottage cheese, and buttermilk. Also, make sure the yeast is not sitting in any liquid once you add it at the end.

· A serrated bread knife is invaluable. Make it your first purchase.

· The second purchase, if you bake free-form breads in the oven quite often, is one of those silicone or Teflon baking sheets. They're reusable and you'll never again have to grease a baking sheet. What a godsend!

· Here's a tip from one who learned the hard way: Remember to remove the mixing blade from that special loaf of bread you've baked as a gift. Once the bread is wrapped and given, it's quite embarrassing to ask for the blade back!

· If you're making rolls or specialty breads and the recipe calls for a baking pan or a cake pan, and all you have is a glass baking dish or pie plate, reduce the oven temperature by 25°F to avoid overbrowning.

· Dark pans will produce dark crusts; shiny pans will produce lighter crusts.

· When making sweet rolls that are rolled up jelly-roll fashion and then sliced, here's a nifty trick. Use dental floss to cut each slice. Lightly mark the roll with a knife where you want to slice it. Starting at one end, slide a 12-inch length of dental floss or heavy thread underneath the roll, and at each mark, bring the ends of the floss up and crisscross them on top. Keep pulling in opposite directions and the floss will cut right through the roll with ease.

· When you find your freezer half full of bags containing that one last slice of bread no one will kill off, what do you do with all those odds and ends? First, know that you will never again have to buy bread crumbs. A quick whirl in the food processor will turn those orphan slices into the most delicious bread crumbs imaginable! With not much more effort, you can create some delicious croutons that will make your salads sparkle. (See our recipes for croutons on page 239.) Bread pudding, stuffing, and French toast made with many of the breads in this cookbook will leave the realm of ordinary and achieve memorable status. If you're overworked, stressed out, and too busy to create something with those stray slices, dump them into a bag, visit your own backyard or the nearest park, and take a few quiet moments to feed your neighborhood birds, ducks, or squirrels. Your day will be brighter for it.

· Last and most important, have fun with this fabulous appliance! Experiment with new shapes and taste sensations. You can turn a plain dough into a masterpiece by braiding it, brushing it with egg white, and sprinkling poppyseeds or sesame seeds on top. How about sculpting a bread basket simply by twining ropes of bread dough around the outside of an inverted, greased bowl? After baking, remove the bowl and you have a lovely basket for your homemade rolls. You can do something similar by creating a cornucopia shape from wadded-up aluminum foil. It's the perfect centerpiece for Thanksgiving when filled with fresh homemade rolls or dried flowers and other seasonal decor. If you're not feeling quite that inspired, have fun just shaping small, individual bread bowls the next time you serve chili or stew to family or friends. One large, round loaf hollowed out and toasted in a 350°F oven is a tasty container for your favorite dip or fondue. Experiment with various cooking containers such as coffee cans and clay flowerpots. See how much fun you can have when you unleash your creative instincts! Who knows, you might come up with a bake-off winner or a blue ribbon at a state fair. Happy baking!

ABOUT OUR RECIPES

Our recipes are listed as "small, medium, large." The small is the 1-pound loaf that contains approximately 2 cups flour. The medium is the 1½-pound loaf that uses about 3 cups of flour. The large is the 2-pound loaf that calls for approximately 4 cups flour.

When trying a recipe for the first time, we suggest starting with the medium size first. Not all 2-pound loaf pans are created equal and you want to avoid over-flows whenever possible. If it didn't quite fill up the pan, you know you're safe to try the larger loaf.

In some of our recipes, we list vital wheat gluten as an optional ingredient. We include it because results sometimes varied greatly from one machine to the next. If some machines produced loaves that just needed a little more "oomph" than others, the gluten helped. We recommend trying the recipe first without the gluten. If it doesn't rise high enough or needs more body, cross out the word "optional," so you'll know next time to add the gluten.

You may notice that some recipes require all-purpose flour for one size loaf and bread flour for the other sizes or vice versa. We had to switch to all-purpose flour in some instances because the bread rose too high using bread flour.

All eggs used in these recipes are the large-size eggs.

When a recipe lists beer as an ingredient, either use flat beer or pour off the foamy head before measuring.

We list liquid amounts with a 2-tablespoon range in quantity to allow for the variances among machines. You'll soon learn whether your machine produces better loaves using the lower or higher amount of liquid. Again, and we can't stress it enough, it pays to check the dough as it mixes.

We used Red Star brand active dry yeast when testing all the recipes in this book. If you choose to use other brands, we suggest you experiment a little first because not all yeasts are created equal. With some you may need to use ½ to 1 teaspoon more than called for in the recipe; for others you might be able to use a little less.

Don't overlook the "blurbs" at the beginning of each recipe. We often used them to note or emphasize an important step or ingredient.

We have included nutritional analysis at the end of each recipe to be used as a general guideline. The information was calculated on an average medium loaf containing fourteen ½-inch-thick slices of bread.

All of our recipes can be baked in the oven instead of in the bread machine. For those who want to work the dough with their hands and bake a more traditional loaf, we suggest you place the ingredients in the bread pan and set the machine on Dough. When it beeps that it's done, turn the dough out onto a floured countertop and knead it for 1 or 2 minutes. Place the large loaf in two greased 8½ × 4½ × 2½-inch loaf pans. Place the medium loaf in a greased 9 × 5 × 3-inch loaf pan. Place the small loaf in a greased 8½ × 4½ × 2½-inch loaf pan. (Or in the case of a free-form bread, shape the dough as desired and place on a greased baking sheet.) Cover dough with a dish towel and let rise in a warm place until doubled, about 30 to 45 minutes.

You can bake most loaves at 375°F for 35 to 45 minutes until golden brown. Breads with a thin, crisp crust, such as French and sourdough, should be baked at a higher temperature, 400 to 450°F, for approximately 25 minutes.

And one final suggestion: If your machine doesn't have a Preheat cycle, warm all cold liquids prior to mixing.

White Breads

Basic White Bread

This is a very basic recipe for white bread and probably similar to the one that comes with your machine. It's a good place to start—the ingredients are readily available and it makes a nicely shaped loaf of bread.

	SMALL RECIPE	MEDIUM RECIPE	LARGE RECIPE
WATER	½ to ⅝ cup	½ to ⅝ cup	⅞ to 1 cup
MILK	⅜ cup	⅝ cup	¾ cup
BUTTER OR MARGARINE	1 tablespoon	1½ tablespoons	2 tablespoons
SUGAR	2 tablespoons	3 tablespoons	¼ cup
SALT	1 teaspoon	1½ teaspoons	2 teaspoons
BREAD FLOUR	2 cups	3 cups	4 cups
RED STAR BRAND ACTIVE DRY YEAST	1½ teaspoons	1½ teaspoons	2 teaspoons

1. Place all ingredients in bread pan, using the least amount of liquid listed in the recipe. Select Medium Crust setting and press Start.

2. Observe the dough as it kneads. After 5 to 10 minutes, if it appears dry and stiff, or if your machine sounds as if it's straining to knead it, add more liquid 1 tablespoon at a time until dough forms a smooth, soft, pliable ball that is slightly tacky to the touch.

3. After the baking cycle ends, remove bread from pan, place on cake rack, and allow to cool 1 hour before slicing.

CRUST: Medium
BAKE CYCLE: Standard
OPTIONAL BAKE CYCLES: Rapid Bake

NUTRITIONAL INFORMATION PER SLICE
Calories 121 / Fat 1.3 grams / Carbohydrates 23.6 grams / Protein 3.2 grams / Fiber .8 gram / Sodium 250 milligrams / Cholesterol .5 milligram

---

Brown Bagger's White Bread

For sandwiches, we often use this hearty white bread because it holds up well in a lunch box or picnic basket.

	SMALL RECIPE	MEDIUM RECIPE	LARGE RECIPE
WATER	⅜ to ½ cup	½ to ⅝ cup	¾ to ⅞ cup
MILK	⅜ cup	½ cup	⅝ cup
EGG	1	1	2
OIL	1 tablespoon	1½ tablespoons	2 tablespoons
SUGAR	2 tablespoons	3 tablespoons	¼ cup
SALT	1 teaspoon	1½ teaspoons	2 teaspoons
BREAD FLOUR	2 cups	3 cups	4 cups
WHEAT GERM	2 tablespoons	3 tablespoons	¼ cup
INSTANT POTATO FLAKES	1 tablespoon	2 tablespoons	2 tablespoons
RED STAR BRAND ACTIVE DRY YEAST	1½ teaspoons	1½ teaspoons	2 teaspoons

I. Place all ingredients in bread pan, using the least amount of liquid listed in the recipe. Select Medium Crust setting and press Start.

2. Observe the dough as it kneads. After 5 to 10 minutes, if it appears dry and stiff, or if your machine sounds as if it's straining to knead it, add more liquid 1 tablespoon at a time until dough forms a smooth, soft, pliable ball that is slightly tacky to the touch.

3. After the baking cycle ends, remove bread from pan, place on cake rack, and allow to cool 1 hour before slicing.

CRUST: Medium
BAKE CYCLE: Standard
OPTIONAL BAKE CYCLES: Rapid Bake

NUTRITIONAL INFORMATION PER SLICE
Calories 138 / Fat 2.3 grams / Carbohydrates 24.7 grams / Protein 4.1 grams / Fiber 1 gram / Sodium 238 milligrams / Cholesterol 15.6 milligrams

DeDe's Buttermilk Bread

*L*inda's sister DeDe picked this moist, rich, and tender loaf as her favorite. *Almost everyone we've heard from agrees. Plain, white sandwich bread doesn't get much better than this!*

	SMALL RECIPE	MEDIUM RECIPE	LARGE RECIPE
BUTTERMILK	⅞ to 1 cup	1⅛ to 1¼ cups	1½ to 1⅝ cups
HONEY	2 tablespoons	3 tablespoons	¼ cup
SALT	1 teaspoon	1½ teaspoons	2 teaspoons
BUTTER OR MARGARINE	1 tablespoon	1 tablespoon	2 tablespoons
BREAD FLOUR	2 cups	3 cups	4 cups
RED STAR BRAND ACTIVE DRY YEAST	1½ teaspoons	2 teaspoons	2½ teaspoons

1.   Place all ingredients in bread pan, using the least amount of liquid listed in the recipe. Select Light Crust setting and press Start.

2.   Observe the dough as it kneads. After 5 to 10 minutes, if it appears dry and stiff, or if your machine sounds as if it's straining to knead it, add more liquid 1 tablespoon at a time until dough forms a smooth, soft, pliable ball that is slightly tacky to the touch.

3.   After the baking cycle ends, remove bread from pan, place on cake rack, and allow to cool 1 hour before slicing.

CRUST: Light
BAKE CYCLE: Standard
OPTIONAL BAKE CYCLES: Sweet Bread

NUTRITIONAL INFORMATION PER SLICE
Calories 125 / Fat 1.1 grams / Carbohydrates 25.1 grams / Protein 3.5 grams / Fiber .8 gram / Sodium 260 milligrams / Cholesterol .7 milligram

Egg Bread

Need a bread for sandwiches? Here's the perfect companion for anything from tuna to cheese. The eggs give it a rich, velvety taste and texture. We like to keep a loaf in the freezer for Sunday morning's French toast.

	SMALL RECIPE	MEDIUM RECIPE	LARGE RECIPE
MILK	½ to ⅝ cup	¾ to ⅞ cup	1 to 1⅛ cups
EGG	1	2	3
SALT	1 teaspoon	1½ teaspoons	2 teaspoons
BUTTER OR MARGARINE	2 tablespoons	3 tablespoons	4 tablespoons
SUGAR	3 tablespoons	¼ cup	¼ cup
BREAD FLOUR	2 cups	3 cups	4 cups
RED STAR BRAND ACTIVE DRY YEAST	1½ teaspoons	2 teaspoons	2½ teaspoons

1. Place all ingredients in bread pan, using the least amount of liquid listed in the recipe. Select Light Crust setting and press Start.

2. Observe the dough as it kneads. After 5 to 10 minutes, if it appears dry and stiff, or if your machine sounds as if it's straining to knead it, add more liquid 1 tablespoon at a time until dough forms a smooth, soft, pliable ball that is slightly tacky to the touch.

3. After the baking cycle ends, remove bread from pan, place on cake rack, and allow to cool 1 hour before slicing.

CRUST: Light
BAKE CYCLE: Standard
OPTIONAL BAKE CYCLES: Sweet Bread; Rapid Bake

NUTRITIONAL INFORMATION PER SLICE
Calories 145 / Fat 3 grams / Carbohydrates 24.7 grams / Protein 4.2 grams / Fiber .8 gram / Sodium 275 milligrams / Cholesterol 31 milligrams

---

Irish Potato Bread

We tested several potato breads and this one was by far the best. It is soft and spongy and has a wonderful flavor. You'll find that the amount of liquid you need to use depends on the moisture content of your potatoes. On some machines, this baked up best on the Rapid Bake cycle.

	SMALL RECIPE	MEDIUM RECIPE	LARGE RECIPE
MILK	⅜ cup	⅝ cup	⅞ cup
POTATO WATER*	¼ to ⅜ cup	¼ to ⅜ cup	¼ to ⅜ cup
BUTTER OR MARGARINE	1 tablespoon	1½ tablespoons	2 tablespoons
SUGAR	1 tablespoon	1½ tablespoons	2 tablespoons
SALT	1 teaspoon	1½ teaspoons	2 teaspoons
ALL-PURPOSE FLOUR	2 cups	3 cups	4 cups
PLAIN MASHED POTATO, ROOM TEMPERATURE	¼ cup	⅓ cup	½ cup
RED STAR BRAND ACTIVE DRY YEAST	1½ teaspoons	1½ teaspoons	2 teaspoons

1. Place all ingredients in bread pan, using the least amount of liquid listed in the recipe. Select Medium Crust setting and press Start.

2. Observe the dough as it kneads. After 5 to 10 minutes, if it appears dry and stiff or if your machine sounds as if it's straining to knead it, add more liquid 1 tablespoon at a time until dough forms a smooth, soft, pliable ball that is slightly tacky to the touch.

3. After the baking cycle ends, remove bread from pan, place on cake rack, and allow to cool 1 hour before slicing.

CRUST: Medium
BAKE CYCLE: Standard
OPTIONAL BAKE CYCLES: Rapid Bake

NUTRITIONAL INFORMATION PER SLICE
Calories 119 / Fat 1.3 grams / Carbohydrates 22.9 grams / Protein 3.3 grams / Fiber .9 gram / Sodium 250 milligrams / Cholesterol .5 milligram

*The water in which you cooked the potato

Linda's Easy Potato Bread

This bread is moist and fluffy and a family favorite for sandwiches. (Note: The 1-pound loaf must be baked on the Rapid Bake setting to prevent it from overflowing the pan.)

	SMALL RECIPE	MEDIUM RECIPE	LARGE RECIPE
INSTANT POTATO FLAKES	3 tablespoons	¼ cup	6 tablespoons
MILK	½ cup	¾ cup	1 cup
WATER	⅜ to ½ cup	⅜ to ½ cup	½ to ⅝ cup
BUTTER OR MARGARINE	1 tablespoon	1½ tablespoons	2 tablespoons
SUGAR	1 tablespoon	1½ tablespoons	2 tablespoons
SALT	1 teaspoon	1½ teaspoons	2 teaspoons
BREAD FLOUR	2 cups	3 cups	4 cups
RED STAR BRAND ACTIVE DRY YEAST	1½ teaspoons	2 teaspoons	2 teaspoons

For the Small Recipe

1. Place all ingredients in bread pan, using the least amount of liquid listed in the recipe. Select Medium Crust setting then the Rapid Bake cycle and press Start.

2. Observe the dough as it kneads. After 5 to 10 minutes, if it appears dry and stiff, or if your machine sounds as if it's straining to knead it, add more liquid 1 tablespoon at a time until dough forms a smooth, soft, pliable ball that is slightly tacky to the touch.

3. After the baking cycle ends, remove bread from pan, place on cake rack, and allow to cool 1 hour before slicing.

CRUST: Medium
BAKE CYCLE: Rapid Bake

For the Medium and Large Recipes

1. Place all ingredients in bread pan, using the least amount of liquid listed in the recipe. Select Medium Crust setting and press Start.

2. Observe the dough as it kneads. After 5 to 10 minutes, if it appears dry and stiff, or if your machine sounds as if it's straining to knead it, add more liquid 1 tablespoon at a time until dough forms a smooth, soft, pliable ball that is slightly tacky to the touch.

3. After the baking cycle ends, remove bread from pan, place on cake rack, and allow to cool 1 hour before slicing.

CRUST: Medium
BAKE CYCLE: Standard
OPTIONAL BAKE CYCLES: Rapid Bake

NUTRITIONAL INFORMATION PER SLICE
Calories 120 / Fat 1.3 grams / Carbohydrates 23.1 grams / Protein 3.4 grams / Fiber .9 gram / Sodium 252 milligrams / Cholesterol .5 milligram

---

Midnight-Sun Bread

This is an outstanding bread! It has a delicate, cakelike texture and combines the orange and caraway flavors that are popular in so many Scandinavian breads. It's also good toasted.

	SMALL RECIPE	MEDIUM RECIPE	LARGE RECIPE
BUTTERMILK	¾ to ⅞ cup	1⅛ to 1¼ cups	1½ to 1⅝ cups
BUTTER OR MARGARINE	1½ tablespoons	2 tablespoons	3 tablespoons
HONEY	1½ tablespoons	2 tablespoons	3 tablespoons
SALT	1 teaspoon	1½ teaspoons	2 teaspoons
BREAD FLOUR	2 cups	3 cups	4 cups
GRATED ORANGE RIND	2 teaspoons	1 tablespoon	1½ tablespoons
CARAWAY SEEDS	1 teaspoon	1½ teaspoons	2 teaspoons
RAISINS	⅓ cup	½ cup	⅔ cup
RED STAR BRAND ACTIVE DRY YEAST	1½ teaspoons	2 teaspoons	2½ teaspoons

1. Place all ingredients in bread pan, using the least amount of liquid listed in the recipe. Select Light Crust setting and press Start.

2. Observe the dough as it kneads. After 5 to 10 minutes, if it appears dry and stiff, or if your machine sounds as if it's straining to knead it, add more liquid 1 tablespoon at a time until dough forms a smooth, soft, pliable ball that is slightly tacky to the touch.

3. After the baking cycle ends, remove bread from pan, place on cake rack, and allow to cool 1 hour before slicing.

CRUST: Light
BAKE CYCLE: Standard
OPTIONAL BAKE CYCLES: Sweet Bread; Raisin/Nut

NUTRITIONAL INFORMATION PER SLICE
Calories 129 / Fat 1.7 grams / Carbohydrates 24.4 grams / Protein 3.6 grams / Fiber .9 gram / Sodium 270 milligrams / Cholesterol .7 milligram

English Toasting Bread

This is a special bread that's coated with cornmeal, so it needs to be baked in a loaf pan in the oven. It's heavenly with orange marmalade.

	SMALL RECIPE	MEDIUM RECIPE	LARGE RECIPE
MILK	⅝ cup	¾ cup	⅞ cup
WATER	¼ to ⅜ cup	⅜ to ½ cup	½ to ⅝ cup
SUGAR	1½ teaspoons	2 teaspoons	3 teaspoons
SALT	½ teaspoon	1 teaspoon	1 teaspoon
BREAD FLOUR	2 cups	3 cups	4 cups
BAKING SODA	¼ teaspoon	¼ teaspoon	½ teaspoon
RED STAR BRAND ACTIVE DRY YEAST	2 teaspoons	2 teaspoons	2½ teaspoons
CORNMEAL	as needed	as needed	as needed

1. Place all ingredients except cornmeal in bread pan, select Dough setting, and press Start.

2. When the dough has risen long enough, the machine will beep. Turn off bread machine, remove bread pan, and turn out dough onto a lightly floured countertop or cutting board.

For the Small and Medium Recipes
Grease an 8½ × 4½ × 2½-inch loaf pan; sprinkle all sides with cornmeal.

For the Large Recipe
Grease two 8½ × 4½ × 2½-inch loaf pans; sprinkle all sides with cornmeal. Cut dough in half.

3. Place dough into prepared loaf pan(s). With your hands, carefully press dough evenly into pan(s). Sprinkle top with cornmeal. Cover and let rise in a warm oven for 20 to 30 minutes or until dough almost reaches the top of the pan. (Hint: To warm oven slightly, turn oven on Warm setting for 1 minute, then turn it off and place covered dough in oven to rise. Remove pan from oven before preheating.)

4. Preheat oven to 400°F. Bake for 25 minutes.

5. Remove from oven, then remove loaf (or loaves) from pan and cool on cake rack. To serve, cut into thick slices and toast.

BAKE CYCLE: Dough

Small recipe yields 1 loaf
Medium recipe yields 1 loaf
Large recipe yields 2 loaves

NTRITIONAL INFORMATION PER SLICE

Calories 106 / Fat .4 gram / Carbohydrates 21.7 grams / Protein 3.3 grams / Fiber .8 gram / Sodium 174 milligrams / Cholesterol .5 milligram

Authentic French Bread

This fine-tasting bread is a fixture at our dinner parties. Since it contains no fat, it starts to go stale in just a matter of hours. Plan to serve this bread shortly after it comes out of the oven. Set a tub of sweet creamery butter next to it and watch the loaf disappear!

	SMALL RECIPE	MEDIUM RECIPE	LARGE RECIPE
WATER	¾ to ⅞ cup	1 to 1⅛ cups	1¼ to 1⅜ cups
SALT	1 teaspoon	1½ teaspoons	2 teaspoons
BREAD FLOUR	2 cups	3 cups	4 cups
RED STAR BRAND ACTIVE DRY YEAST	2 teaspoons	2 teaspoons	2½ teaspoons
CORNMEAL	as needed	as needed	as needed

1. Place all ingredients except cornmeal in bread pan, select Dough setting, and press Start.

2. When the dough has risen long enough, the machine will beep. Turn off bread machine, remove bread pan, and turn out dough onto a lightly floured countertop or cutting board.

For the Small Recipe
Shape dough into one 10-inch oblong loaf or 1 large round loaf or one thin 24-inch-long baguette or 6 French rolls.

For the Medium Recipe
Shape dough into one 12-inch oblong loaf or 1 large round loaf or two thin 18-inch-long baguettes or 8 French rolls.

For the Large Recipe
Cut dough in half. Shape dough into two 10-inch oblong loaves or 2 large round loaves or two thin 24-inch-long baguettes or 10 French rolls.

3. Dust the top(s) with a little flour; rub it in. Place the loaves on a cookie sheet dusted with cornmeal. With a very sharp knife or razor blade, slash the tops of the rolls or baguettes straight down the center to make a cut about ½ inch deep. On the oblong loaf, make 3 diagonal slashes. On the round loaf, slash an *X* or # on top.

4. Cover and let rise in a warm oven 30 to 45 minutes until doubled in size. (Hint: To warm oven slightly, turn oven on Warm setting for 1 minute, then turn it off and place covered dough in oven to rise. Remove pan from oven before preheating.)

5. Place a pan of hot water on the bottom rack of the oven. (This will create steam, which is necessary to produce an authentic, crisp crust.) Preheat oven to 450°F. Bake the round or oblong loaves about 20 minutes, the baguettes about 15 minutes, and the rolls 10 to 12 minutes.

6. Remove from oven; cool on cake rack. This is best served within hours of baking. To preserve the crisp crust, do not store in plastic wrap or bags.

BAKE CYCLE: Dough

Small recipe yields 1 oblong or round loaf, 1 baguette, or 6 rolls
Medium recipe yields 1 oblong or round loaf, 2 baguettes, or 8 rolls
Large recipe yields 2 oblong or round loaves, 2 baguettes, or 10 rolls

NUTRITIONAL INFORMATION PER SLICE
Calories 98 / Fat .3 gram / Carbohydrates 20.5 grams / Protein 2.9 grams / Fiber .8 gram / Sodium 229 milligrams / Cholesterol 0 milligrams

Anadama Bread

There's a story that goes along with this classic bread, which dates back to Colonial times. A cantankerous New England backwoodsman had a very lazy wife named Anna, who fed him nothing but cornmeal mush for supper. Night after night he ate cornmeal mush, until one evening, he couldn't take it anymore. He grabbed some flour, molasses, and yeast off the shelf, stirred it into his mush, and put it in the fire to bake. As the loaf baked, he muttered over and over, "Anna, damn her!" That's the origin of the word "Anadama."

	SMALL RECIPE	MEDIUM RECIPE	LARGE RECIPE
WATER	¾ to ⅞ cup	1⅛ to 1¼ cups	1½ to 1⅝ cups
MOLASSES	2 tablespoons	3 tablespoons	¼ cup
SALT	1 teaspoon	1½ teaspoons	2 teaspoons
BUTTER OR MARGARINE	1 tablespoon	1½ tablespoons	2 tablespoons
BREAD FLOUR	2 cups	3 cups	4 cups
CORNMEAL	¼ cup	⅓ cup	½ cup
RED STAR BRAND ACTIVE DRY YEAST	1½ teaspoons	2 teaspoons	2½ teaspoons

1. Place all ingredients in bread pan, using the least amount of liquid listed in the recipe. Select Medium Crust setting and press Start.

2. Observe the dough as it kneads. After 5 to 10 minutes, if it appears dry and stiff, or if your machine sounds as if it's straining to knead it, add more liquid 1 tablespoon at a time until dough forms a smooth, soft, pliable ball that is slightly tacky to the touch.

3. After the baking cycle ends, remove bread from pan, place on cake rack, and allow to cool 1 hour before slicing.

CRUST: Medium
BAKE CYCLE: Standard
OPTIONAL BAKE CYCLES: Sweet Bread; Delayed Timer

NUTRITIONAL INFORMATION PER SLICE
Calories 130 / Fat 1.5 grams / Carbohydrates 25.4 grams / Protein 3.2 grams / Fiber 1 gram / Sodium 244 milligrams / Cholesterol 0 milligrams

Tangy Buttermilk Cheese Bread

*T*his is a tangy, tender bread. Use extra-sharp cheese for the best flavor.

	SMALL RECIPE	MEDIUM RECIPE	LARGE RECIPE
BUTTERMILK	⅞ to 1 cup	1⅛ to 1¼ cups	1¾ to 1⅞ cups
SUGAR	1 tablespoon	1½ tablespoons	2 tablespoons
SALT	1 teaspoon	1½ teaspoons	2 teaspoons
BREAD FLOUR	2 cups	3 cups	4 cups
GRATED EXTRA-SHARP CHEDDAR CHEESE	½ cup (2 ounces)	¾ cup (3 ounces)	1 cup (4 ounces)
RED STAR BRAND ACTIVE DRY YEAST	1½ teaspoons	1½ teaspoons	2 teaspoons

1. Place all ingredients in bread pan, using the least amount of liquid listed in the recipe. Select Light Crust setting and press Start.

2. Observe the dough as it kneads. After 5 to 10 minutes, if it appears dry and stiff, or if your machine sounds as if it's straining to knead it, add more liquid 1 tablespoon at a time until dough forms a smooth, soft, pliable ball that is slightly tacky to the touch.

3. After the baking cycle ends, remove bread from pan, place on cake rack, and allow to cool 1 hour before slicing.

CRUST: Light
BAKE CYCLE: Standard
OPTIONAL BAKE CYCLES: Sweet Bread

NUTRITIONAL INFORMATION PER SLICE
Calories 136 / Fat 2.5 grams / Carbohydrates 22.8 grams / Protein 5 grams / Fiber .8 gram / Sodium 287 milligrams / Cholesterol 7.1 milligrams

Herb Bread

*P*lan to be around while this one bakes because the aroma is absolutely out of this world! As for the taste, it's hard to limit yourself to just one slice of this zesty bread. We recommend it for croutons, also. (Note: When making the small loaf, use the Rapid Bake setting for a better-shaped bread.)

	SMALL RECIPE	MEDIUM RECIPE	LARGE RECIPE
MILK	¾ to ⅞ cup	⅞ to 1 cup	1¼ to 1⅜ cups
SUGAR	1 tablespoon	1½ tablespoons	2 tablespoons
SALT	1 teaspoon	1½ teaspoons	1½ teaspoons
BUTTER OR MARGARINE	2 tablespoons	3 tablespoons	¼ cup
CHOPPED ONION	⅓ cup	½ cup	⅔ cup
BREAD FLOUR	2 cups	3 cups	4 cups
DRIED DILL	½ teaspoon	½ teaspoon	1 teaspoon
DRIED BASIL	½ teaspoon	½ teaspoon	1 teaspoon
DRIED ROSEMARY	½ teaspoon	½ teaspoon	1 teaspoon
RED STAR BRAND ACTIVE DRY YEAST	1½ teaspoons	2 teaspoons	2½ teaspoons

For the Small Recipe

1. Place all ingredients in bread pan, using the least amount of liquid listed in the recipe. Select Medium Crust setting then the Rapid Bake cycle and press Start.

2. Observe the dough as it kneads. After 5 to 10 minutes, if it appears dry and stiff, or if your machine sounds as if it's straining to knead it, add more liquid 1 tablespoon at a time until dough forms a smooth, soft, pliable ball that is slightly tacky to the touch.

3. After the baking cycle ends, remove bread from pan, place on cake rack, and allow to cool 1 hour before slicing.

CRUST: Medium
BAKE CYCLE: Rapid Bake

For the Medium and Large Recipes

I. Place all ingredients in bread pan, using the least amount of liquid listed in the recipe. Select Medium Crust setting and press Start.

2. Observe the dough as it kneads. After 5 to 10 minutes, if it appears dry and stiff, or if your machine sounds as if it's straining to knead it, add more liquid 1 tablespoon at a time until dough forms a smooth, soft, pliable ball that is slightly tacky to the touch.

3. After the baking cycle ends, remove bread from pan, place on cake rack, and allow to cool 1 hour before slicing.

CRUST: Medium

BAKE CYCLE: Standard

OPTIONAL BAKE CYCLES: Rapid Bake

NUTRITIONAL INFORMATION PER SLICE
Calories 138 / Fat 3.3 grams / Carbohydrates 23.2 grams / Protein 3.5 grams / Fiber .9 gram / Sodium 259 milligrams / Cholesterol 9 milligrams

---

L & L Bakers' Dill Bread

Among the many virtues of this bread are its pungent herb-and-onion flavor and its very light texture. In addition, it holds a special significance for us: It was such a big hit as a gift that it inspired us to write this cookbook, now in its second edition. We urge you to give this bread as a gift and see what good fortune awaits you, too.

	SMALL RECIPE	MEDIUM RECIPE	LARGE RECIPE
MILK	3 tablespoons	¼ cup	6 tablespoons
WATER	3 to 4 tablespoons	¼ to ⅜ cup	6 to 8 tablespoons
EGG	1	1	2
SALT	1 teaspoon	1½ teaspoons	2 teaspoons
BUTTER OR MARGARINE	1 tablespoon	1½ tablespoons	2 tablespoons
SUGAR	2 tablespoons	3 tablespoons	¼ cup
LOW-FAT COTTAGE CHEESE	⅓ cup	⅔ cup	⅔ cup
BREAD FLOUR	2 cups	3 cups	4 cups
DRIED MINCED ONION	1 tablespoon	2 tablespoons	2 tablespoons
DRIED DILL	2 teaspoons	1 tablespoon	4 teaspoons
DRIED PARSLEY	2 teaspoons	1 tablespoon	4 teaspoons
RED STAR BRAND ACTIVE DRY YEAST	1½ teaspoons	2 teaspoons	2½ teaspoons

1. Place all ingredients in bread pan, using the least amount of liquid listed in the recipe. Select Light Crust setting and press Start.

2. Observe the dough as it kneads. After 5 to 10 minutes, if it appears dry and stiff, or if your machine sounds as if it's straining to knead it, add more liquid 1 tablespoon at a time until dough forms a smooth, soft, pliable ball that is slightly tacky to the touch.

3. After the baking cycle ends, remove bread from pan, place on cake rack, and allow to cool 1 hour before slicing.

CRUST: Light

BAKE CYCLE: Standard

OPTIONAL BAKE CYCLES: Sweet Bread; Rapid Bake

NUTRITIONAL INFORMATION PER SLICE
Calories 137 / Fat 2 grams / Carbohydrates 24.2 grams / Protein 4.9 grams / Fiber .9 gram / Sodium 294 milligrams / Cholesterol 15.9 milligrams

---

Anita's Italian Herb Bread

For the best breads, use the finest and freshest ingredients available. That is especially true for this particular recipe. Lois's sister Anita, who loves Italian food, will tell you that creating this fabulous bread is well worth the trip to your nearest Italian market or deli to purchase a chunk of imported Parmesan. Once you've tried it, you'll be disappointed with anything less.

	SMALL RECIPE	MEDIUM RECIPE	LARGE RECIPE
BUTTERMILK	⅞ to 1 cup	1⅛ to 1¼ cups	1½ to 1⅝ cups
OLIVE OIL	1 tablespoon	1½ tablespoons	2 tablespoons
SUGAR	2 teaspoons	1 tablespoon	4 teaspoons
SALT	1 teaspoon	1½ teaspoons	2 teaspoons
BREAD FLOUR	2 cups	3 cups	4 cups
FRESHLY GRATED PARMESAN CHEESE	⅓ cup (1½ ounces)	½ cup (2 ounces)	⅔ cup (3 ounces)
DRIED BASIL	¼ teaspoon	¼ teaspoon	½ teaspoon
DRIED OREGANO	¼ teaspoon	¼ teaspoon	½ teaspoon
RED STAR BRAND ACTIVE DRY YEAST	1½ teaspoons	1½ teaspoons	2 teaspoons

1. Place all ingredients in bread pan, using the least amount of liquid listed in the recipe. Select Medium Crust setting and press Start.

2. Observe the dough as it kneads. After 5 to 10 minutes, if it appears dry and stiff, or if your machine sounds as if it's straining to knead it, add more liquid 1 tablespoon at a time until dough forms a smooth, soft, pliable ball that is slightly tacky to the touch.

3. After the baking cycle ends, remove bread from pan, place on cake rack, and allow to cool 1 hour before slicing.

CRUST: Medium
BAKE CYCLE: Standard
OPTIONAL BAKE CYCLES: Sweet Bread; Rapid Bake

NUTRITIONAL INFORMATION PER SLICE
Calories 135 / Fat 2.8 grams / Carbohydrates 22.4 grams / Protein 4.7 grams / Fiber .8 gram / Sodium 303 milligrams / Cholesterol 3 milligrams

Sourdough Made Easy

W e condensed the many pages of sourdough data we had compiled into this brief instruction and fact sheet. If you follow this easy and nearly foolproof recipe, you can produce your first loaf of delicious sourdough bread within a week. Use only *fresh, good-quality yogurt with live, active cultures. (We recommend Dannon, Mountain High, or Altadena brands.)*

SOURDOUGH STARTER

1 cup skim (nonfat) milk

3 tablespoons plain, fresh, good-quality yogurt

1 cup bread flour

1.   In a small saucepan over medium heat, heat milk to 90° to 100°F (it should be very warm but not hot to the touch).

2.   Stir in yogurt.

3.   Pour mixture into a clean 1½-quart glass or ceramic crock, jar, or bowl. Cover with a nonmetallic lid; set in a warm place (70 to 90°F) for 24 hours. (Note: On warm days, you can place the starter in a sunny window or on a countertop in a warm kitchen. On cooler days, place it in a gas oven with a pilot light, an electric oven with the light left on, on top of the water heater, or on a heating pad set on low.)

4.   After 24 hours, the milk mixture will thicken and form curds. At this point, gradually stir in bread flour until well blended. Cover with lid and set in a warm place again until mixture ferments and bubbles and a clear liquid forms on top, 2 to 5 days. Stir daily.

5.   Starter is now ready to use. Stir again, cover loosely with plastic wrap, and refrigerate.

NOTE: IF AT ANY POINT IN THE PROCESS THE STARTER TURNS PINK, ORANGE, BLACK, OR FUZZY, THROW IT OUT AND START OVER.

Maintaining Your Starter

1.   Every time you use some of the starter, you must replace it with equal amounts of milk and flour. For instance, if you use 1 cup of starter, return 1 cup milk and 1 cup

of bread flour to the jar. Allow starter to stand in a warm place for 3 to 12 hours until it bubbles again. Stir, cover loosely with plastic wrap, and refrigerate. (Note: We prefer a thick starter and quite often use ⅔ cup milk for every 1 cup bread flour.)

2. Starters maintain their vitality and sourness best if used at least weekly. If you neglect your starter for several weeks, you can perk it up by feeding it equal amounts of milk and flour (1 cup each) and leaving it in a warm spot until it starts bubbling again. (As long as you're giving it some TLC, take a moment to freshen up its container as well. Pour the starter into a clean glass or ceramic bowl, feed it, and wash out its container, rinsing well if you're using soap. Once it shows signs of life again, pour it back into its original container, cover loosely with plastic wrap, and refrigerate.)

Sourdough Facts

· Use only wooden utensils and glass or ceramic containers when working with sourdough starter. The acid in the starter will corrode metal.

· Do not keep sourdough starters in tightly sealed containers. Instead, cover the container loosely with plastic wrap or cheesecloth. Gases that form must be allowed to escape. If they can't escape, expect a real explosion!

· The yellowish or grayish-beige liquid that rises to the top is the hooch. This liquid is about 14% alcohol and helps give sourdough bread its unique tangy flavor. Simply stir the hooch back into the starter before use. For a milder flavor, you can pour off some of the hooch before stirring the starter.

· Fluorides and chlorine in tap water can impair or kill sourdough's effectiveness. Use bottled spring water in your recipes instead.

· For the sourest tasting sourdough bread, mix the room-temperature starter with the liquid and half the flour called for in the recipe. Cover and allow to stand in a warm place until bubbly and very sour smelling, from 18 to 24 hours. At that point, combine the mixture in the bread machine with the rest of the ingredients in the recipe.

· Your starter can be frozen for up to 3 months. Before using it again, let it thaw completely at room temperature for 24 hours until bubbly. You may need to feed it once to bring it back to the bubbly stage before using. (Put starter in a warm place for 3 to 12 hours until it bubbles again.)

We have included a recipe for a San Francisco–type sourdough French bread. However, you could create some unique breads by using your starter in other recipes, such as Tangy Buttermilk Cheese Bread, Basic Whole Wheat Bread, Lois's

Rye Bread, and Russian Black Bread, just to name a few. Or try it in Apple Oatmeal Bread with Raisins, Dinner Rolls, Squaw Bread, Hamburger Buns, or English Muffins. Simply add ½ to 1 cup starter to the recipe (depending on how sour you want your bread) and decrease the liquid by approximately half the amount of starter used. (Example: If you use ½ cup starter, decrease the liquid by ¼ cup.)

"San Francisco" Sourdough French Bread

*M*ost people love the tangy, tart taste of sourdough. If you can't get to San Francisco for the real thing, this will do in a pinch. (Note: Starters vary in their consistency. If yours is thin, use the lesser amount of water listed in the recipe.)

	SMALL RECIPE	MEDIUM RECIPE	LARGE RECIPE
WATER	¼ to ⅜ cup	½ to ⅝ cup	¾ to ⅞ cup
SOURDOUGH STARTER	¾ cup	1 cup	1½ cups
SALT	1 teaspoon	1 teaspoon	2 teaspoons
SUGAR	1 teaspoon	1 teaspoon	2 teaspoons
BREAD FLOUR	2 cups	3 cups	4 cups
RED STAR BRAND ACTIVE DRY YEAST	2 teaspoons	2 teaspoons	2½ teaspoons

For a Mild Sourdough
I. Place all ingredients in bread pan, select Dough setting, and press Start.

For the Sourest Sourdough
I. In a medium bowl, combine the water, starter, and half the flour. Cover and let stand in a warm place up to 24 hours until very sour and bubbly. Then combine the mixture with the remaining ingredients in the bread pan, select Dough setting, and press Start.

2. When the dough has risen long enough, the machine will beep. Turn off bread machine, remove bread pan, and turn out dough onto a lightly floured countertop or cutting board.

For the Small Recipe

Shape dough into one 10-inch oblong loaf or 1 round loaf or one thin 24-inch-long baguette or 6 French rolls.

For the Medium Recipe

Shape dough into one 12-inch oblong loaf or 1 large round loaf or two thin 18-inch-long baguettes or 8 French rolls.

For the Large Recipe

Shape dough into two 10-inch oblong loaves or 2 round loaves or two thin 24-inch-long baguettes or 12 French rolls.

3. Place loaf (or loaves) on a baking sheet that is well greased or sprinkled with cornmeal. With a sharp knife or razor blade, slash the rolls or the baguettes straight down the center to make a cut about ½ inch deep. On the oblong loaf, make 3 diagonal slashes. On the round loaf, slash an X or # on top. Let rise in a warm oven 30 to 45 minutes until doubled in size. (Hint: To warm oven slightly, turn oven on Warm setting for 1 minute, then turn it off and place covered dough in oven to rise. Remove pan from oven before preheating.)

4. Preheat oven to 400°F. Fill a plant mister with water and mist each loaf (or lightly brush each loaf with water). Bake for 25 to 30 minutes until golden brown, misting with water twice more at 5-minute intervals. Remove from oven and cool on cake racks. To preserve the crisp crust, do not store in plastic wrap or bags. Bread can be loosely covered or left out for up to 2 days before it dries out completely.

BAKE CYCLE: Dough

Small recipe yields 1 loaf or 6 rolls
Medium recipe yields 1 loaf, 2 baguettes, or 8 rolls
Large recipe yields 2 loaves or 12 rolls

NUTRITIONAL INFORMATION PER SLICE
Calories 119 / Fat .3 gram / Carbohydrates 25.3 grams / Protein 3.7 grams / Fiber 1 gram / Sodium 155 milligrams / Cholesterol .1 milligram

---

Whole-Grain Breads

Basic Whole Wheat Bread

*L*ike the Basic White Bread recipe, this is a simple, easy-to-make whole wheat bread. Keep a sliced loaf in your freezer and you'll always have a healthy bread on hand for sandwiches.

	SMALL RECIPE	MEDIUM RECIPE	LARGE RECIPE
WATER	¼ to ⅜ cup	½ to ⅝ cup	½ to ⅝ cup
MILK	⅜ cup	⅜ cup	⅝ cup
EGG	1	1	1
OIL	1 tablespoon	1½ tablespoons	2 tablespoons
HONEY	1 tablespoon	1½ tablespoons	2 tablespoons
SALT	1 teaspoon	1½ teaspoons	2 teaspoons
WHOLE WHEAT FLOUR	1 cup	1½ cups	2 cups
BREAD FLOUR	1 cup	1½ cups	2 cups
RED STAR BRAND ACTIVE DRY YEAST	2 teaspoons	2 teaspoons	2½ teaspoons

1. Place all ingredients in bread pan, using the least amount of liquid listed in the recipe. Select Medium Crust setting then the Whole Wheat cycle and press Start.

2. Observe the dough as it kneads. After 5 to 10 minutes, if it appears dry and stiff or if your machine sounds as if it's straining to knead it, add more liquid 1 tablespoon at a time until dough forms a smooth, soft, pliable ball that is slightly tacky to the touch.

3. After the baking cycle ends, remove bread from pan, place on cake rack, and allow to cool 1 hour before slicing.

CRUST: Medium
BAKE CYCLE: Whole Wheat
OPTIONAL BAKE CYCLES: Standard

NUTRITIONAL INFORMATION PER SLICE
Calories 117 / Fat 2.3 grams / Carbohydrates 21 grams / Protein 3.8 grams / Fiber 2.1 grams / Sodium 237 milligrams / Cholesterol 15.5 milligrams

Heavenly Whole Wheat Bread

W*e think this is the best of our whole wheat breads. It's moist, has a good crust, and has a flavor that's out of this world.*

	SMALL RECIPE	MEDIUM RECIPE	LARGE RECIPE
WATER	¾ to ⅞ cup	1⅛ to 1¼ cups	1½ to 1⅝ cups
SALT	1 teaspoon	1½ teaspoons	2 teaspoons
BUTTER OR MARGARINE	3 tablespoons	4 tablespoons	6 tablespoons
SUGAR	1 tablespoon	2 tablespoons	2 tablespoons
WHOLE WHEAT FLOUR	1⅓ cups	2 cups	2⅔ cups
BREAD FLOUR	⅔ cups	1 cup	1⅓ cups
INSTANT POTATO FLAKES	3 tablespoons	¼ cup	6 tablespoons
VITAL WHEAT GLUTEN (OPTIONAL)	2 tablespoons	3 tablespoons	4 tablespoons
RED STAR BRAND ACTIVE DRY YEAST	1½ teaspoons	2 teaspoons	2 teaspoons

I.   Place all ingredients in bread pan, using the least amount of liquid listed in the recipe. Select Medium Crust setting then the Whole Wheat cycle and press Start.

2.   Observe the dough as it kneads. After 5 to 10 minutes, if it appears dry and stiff, or if your machine sounds as if it's straining to knead it, add more liquid 1 tablespoon at a time until dough forms a smooth, soft, pliable ball that is slightly tacky to the touch.

3.   After the baking cycle ends, remove bread from pan, place on cake rack, and allow to cool 1 hour before slicing.

CRUST: Medium
BAKE CYCLE: Whole Wheat
OPTIONAL BAKE CYCLES: Standard; Sweet Bread; Delayed Timer; Rapid Bake

---

NUTRITIONAL INFORMATION PER SLICE
Calories 130 / Fat 3.7 grams / Carbohydrates 21.7 grams / Protein 3.5 grams / Fiber 2.5 grams / Sodium 269 milligrams / Cholesterol 0 milligrams

Debbie's Honey Whole Wheat Bread

*T**his recipe took some doing to perfect, but it was well worth the effort. It makes a beautiful loaf with an exceptional texture and a sweet taste. Linda's sister Debbie loves serving this one to company. She says it's too sweet as a sandwich bread, but it is marvelous plain or toasted and buttered.*

	SMALL RECIPE	MEDIUM RECIPE	LARGE RECIPE
MILK	¾ to ⅞ cup	1⅛ to 1¼ cups	1½ to 1⅝ cups
BUTTER OR MARGARINE	2 teaspoons	1 tablespoon	4 teaspoons
HONEY	3 tablespoons	¼ cup	6 tablespoons
SALT	½ teaspoon	½ teaspoon	1 teaspoon
WHOLE WHEAT FLOUR	2 cups	2½ cups	4 cups
BREAD FLOUR	¼ cup	½ cup	½ cup
RED STAR BRAND ACTIVE DRY YEAST	2 teaspoons	2 teaspoons	2½ teaspoons

1. Place all ingredients in bread pan, using the least amount of liquid listed in the recipe. Select Medium Crust setting then the Whole Wheat cycle and press Start.

2. Observe the dough as it kneads. After 5 to 10 minutes, if it appears dry and stiff, or if your machine sounds as if it's straining to knead it, add more liquid 1 tablespoon at a time until dough forms a smooth, soft, pliable ball that is slightly tacky to the touch.

3. After the baking cycle ends, remove bread from pan, place on cake rack, and allow to cool 1 hour before slicing.

CRUST: Medium
BAKE CYCLE: Whole Wheat
OPTIONAL BAKE CYCLES: Standard; Sweet Bread

NUTRITIONAL INFORMATION PER SLICE
Calories 120 / Fat 1.3 grams / Carbohydrates 24.6 grams / Protein 4.1 grams / Fiber 2.9 grams / Sodium 97.5 milligrams / Cholesterol .8 milligram

Madeleine's Neighborly Bread

O *ur friend Madeleine loves this nicely shaped whole wheat potato bread. It's moist and wheaty, makes a lovely sandwich, and is a favorite of all the neighbors.*

	SMALL RECIPE	MEDIUM RECIPE	LARGE RECIPE
MILK	⅜ cup	⅝ cup	⅝ cup
POTATO WATER*	¼ to ⅜ cup	⅜ to ½ cup	½ to ¾ cup
BUTTER OR MARGARINE	1 tablespoon	1½ tablespoons	2 tablespoons
HONEY	1 tablespoon	1½ tablespoons	2 tablespoons
SALT	1 teaspoon	1½ teaspoons	2 teaspoons
WHOLE WHEAT FLOUR	1⅓ cups	2 cups	2⅔ cups
BREAD FLOUR	⅔ cup	1 cup	1⅓ cups
PLAIN MASHED POTATO, AT ROOM TEMPERATURE	¼ cup	⅓ cup	½ cup
RED STAR BRAND ACTIVE DRY YEAST	2 teaspoons	2 teaspoons	2 teaspoons

1. Place all ingredients in bread pan, using the least amount of liquid listed in the recipe. Select Medium Crust setting and press Start.

2. Observe the dough as it kneads. After 5 to 10 minutes, if it appears dry and stiff, or if your machine sounds as if it's straining to knead it, add more liquid 1 tablespoon at a time until dough forms a smooth, soft, pliable ball that is slightly tacky to the touch.

3. After the baking cycle ends, remove bread from pan, place on cake rack, and allow to cool 1 hour before slicing.

CRUST: Medium
BAKE CYCLE: Standard
OPTIONAL BAKE CYCLES: Whole Wheat; Sweet Bread; Rapid Bake

NUTRITIONAL INFORMATION PER SLICE
Calories 111 / Fat 1.4 grams / Carbohydrates 21.7 grams / Protein 3.7 grams / Fiber 2.5 grams / Sodium 250 milligrams / Cholesterol .5 milligram

*The water in which you cooked the potato

San Diego Sunshine

*J*ust *like our hometown, this bread will delight your senses! It's a sweet whole wheat loaf with a delicate hint of orange. Pack a picnic basket with a thermos of hot coffee or tea, a loaf of this bread, and some honey butter. Locate a city park or a sunny terrace and you'll have the makings for a romantic, leisurely breakfast.*

	SMALL RECIPE	MEDIUM RECIPE	LARGE RECIPE
WATER	¾ to ⅞ cup	1 to 1⅛ cups	1⅜ to 1½ cups
HONEY	1 tablespoon	2 tablespoons	2 tablespoons
SALT	1 teaspoon	1 teaspoon	2 teaspoons
BUTTER OR MARGARINE	1½ tablespoons	2 tablespoons	3 tablespoons
DARK BROWN SUGAR	1 tablespoon	2 tablespoons	2 tablespoons
BREAD FLOUR	1⅓ cups	2 cups	2⅔ cups
WHOLE WHEAT FLOUR	⅔ cup	1 cup	1⅓ cups
GRATED ORANGE RIND	1 tablespoon	1½ tablespoons	2 tablespoons
RED STAR BRAND ACTIVE DRY YEAST	1½ teaspoons	2 teaspoons	2½ teaspoons

1. Place all ingredients in bread pan, using the least amount of liquid listed in the recipe. Select Light Crust setting and press Start.

2. Observe the dough as it kneads. After 5 to 10 minutes, if it appears dry and stiff, or if your machine sounds as if it's straining to knead it, add more liquid 1 table-spoon at a time until dough forms a smooth, soft, pliable ball that is slightly tacky to the touch.

3. After the baking cycle ends, remove bread from pan, place on cake rack, and allow to cool 1 hour before slicing.

CRUST: Light
BAKE CYCLE: Standard
OPTIONAL BAKE CYCLES: Sweet Bread; Delayed Timer

NUTRITIONAL INFORMATION PER SLICE
Calories 127 / Fat 1.9 grams / Carbohydrates 24.6 grams / Protein 3.2 grams / Fiber 1.7 grams / Sodium 169 milligrams / Cholesterol 4.4 milligrams

Apple Butter Wheat Bread

H*ere's a good, mild, apple- and wheat-flavored breakfast toast. This is a very soft bread when it first comes out of the pan, so it's best to wait several hours before slicing it.*

	SMALL RECIPE	MEDIUM RECIPE	LARGE RECIPE
WATER	⅝ to ¾ cup	1 to 1⅛ cups	1¼ to 1⅜ cups
BUTTER OR MARGARINE	1 tablespoon	2 tablespoons	2 tablespoons
APPLE BUTTER	3 tablespoons	¼ cup	6 tablespoons
SALT	1 teaspoon	1½ teaspoons	2 teaspoons
WHOLE WHEAT FLOUR	1 cup	1½ cups	2 cups
ALL-PURPOSE FLOUR	1 cup	1½ cups	2 cups
RED STAR BRAND ACTIVE DRY YEAST	1½ teaspoons	1½ teaspoons	2 teaspoons

1. Place all ingredients in bread pan, using the least amount of liquid listed in the recipe. Select Medium Crust setting and press Start.

2. Observe the dough as it kneads. After 5 to 10 minutes, if it appears dry and stiff, or if your machine sounds as if it's straining to knead it, add more liquid 1 tablespoon at a time until dough forms a smooth, soft, pliable ball that is slightly tacky to the touch.

3. After the baking cycle ends, remove bread from pan, place on cake rack, and allow to cool 1 hour before slicing.

CRUST: Medium
BAKE CYCLE: Standard
OPTIONAL BAKE CYCLES: Whole Wheat; Sweet Bread; Delayed Timer; Rapid Bake

NUTRITIONAL INFORMATION PER SLICE
Calories 110 / Fat 1.6 grams / Carbohydrates 21.1 grams / Protein 3.2 grams / Fiber 2.1 grams / Sodium 250 milligrams / Cholesterol 0 milligrams

Daily Bread

Want wholesome, high-fiber bread for an afternoon snack? Try this excellent, hearty loaf. It's a very tightly crumbed bread because it contains no white flour and it doesn't rise as high as most loaves.

	SMALL RECIPE	MEDIUM RECIPE	LARGE RECIPE
MILLER'S BRAN	3 tablespoons	¼ cup	6 tablespoons
MILK	¼ cup	⅜ cup	½ cup
WATER	⅜ to ½ cup	½ to ⅝ cup	⅝ to ¾ cup
EGG	1	1	2
BUTTER OR MARGARINE	1 tablespoon	1½ tablespoons	2 tablespoons
HONEY	3 tablespoons	¼ cup	6 tablespoons
SALT	1 teaspoon	1½ teaspoons	2 teaspoons
WHOLE WHEAT FLOUR	2 cups	3 cups	4 cups
RAW UNSALTED SUNFLOWER SEEDS	¼ cup	⅓ cup	½ cup
RED STAR BRAND ACTIVE DRY YEAST	2 teaspoons	2 teaspoons	2½ teaspoons

1. Place all ingredients in bread pan, using the least amount of liquid listed in the recipe. Select Medium Crust setting then the Whole Wheat cycle and press Start.

2. Observe the dough as it kneads. After 5 to 10 minutes, if it appears dry and stiff, or if your machine sounds as if it's straining to knead it, add more liquid 1 tablespoon at a time until dough forms a smooth, soft, pliable ball that is slightly tacky to the touch.

3. After the baking cycle ends, remove bread from pan, place on cake rack, and allow to cool 1 hour before slicing.

CRUST: Medium
BAKE CYCLE: Whole Wheat
OPTIONAL BAKE CYCLES: Standard; Raisin/Nut

NUTRITIONAL INFORMATION PER SLICE
Calories 142 / Fat 3.4 grams / Carbohydrates 25 grams / Protein 5.1 grams / Fiber 3.8 grams / Sodium 253 milligrams / Cholesterol 15.5 milligrams

Whole Wheat Sunflower Bread

*T*his bread is simply bursting with good things to eat—like oats, whole wheat flour, wheat germ, and sunflower seeds. The refreshing hint of orange blends beautifully with all that goodness. Use it for toast, sandwiches, or just plain snacking.

	SMALL RECIPE	MEDIUM RECIPE	LARGE RECIPE
OLD-FASHIONED ROLLED OATS	⅓ cup	½ cup	⅔ cup
BUTTERMILK	⅝ to ¾ cup	1⅛ to 1¼ cups	1¼ to 1⅜ cups
EGG	1	1	2
BUTTER OR MARGARINE	1 tablespoon	1½ tablespoons	2 tablespoons
DARK BROWN SUGAR	1 tablespoon	2 tablespoons	2 tablespoons
SALT	1 teaspoon	1½ teaspoons	2 teaspoons
WHOLE WHEAT FLOUR	1 cup	1½ cups	2 cups
BREAD FLOUR	1 cup	1½ cups	2 cups
WHEAT GERM	2 teaspoons	1 tablespoon	4 teaspoons
RAW UNSALTED SUNFLOWER SEEDS	¼ cup	⅓ cup	½ cup
GRATED ORANGE RIND	1½ tablespoons	2 tablespoons	2½ tablespoons
RED STAR BRAND ACTIVE DRY YEAST	3 teaspoons	3 teaspoons	3 teaspoons

1. Place all ingredients in bread pan, using the least amount of liquid listed in the recipe. Select Medium Crust setting, then the Whole Wheat cycle and press Start.

2. Observe the dough as it kneads. After 5 to 10 minutes, if it appears dry and stiff, or if your machine sounds as if it's straining to knead it, add more liquid 1 tablespoon at a time until dough forms a smooth, soft, pliable ball that is slightly tacky to the touch.

3. After the baking cycle ends, remove bread from pan, place on cake rack, and allow to cool 1 hour before slicing.

CRUST: Medium
BAKE CYCLE: Whole Wheat
OPTIONAL BAKE CYCLES: Standard; Raisin/Nut

NUTRITIONAL INFORMATION PER SLICE
Calories 153 / Fat 3.6 grams / Carbohydrates 25.3 grams / Protein 5.7 grams / Fiber 2.8 grams / Sodium 285 milligrams / Cholesterol 16 milligrams

---

Shredded-Wheat Bread

*W*hen your mother told you to eat your shredded wheat, she never imagined it could be served up like this! This is a fine and flavorsome loaf of bread. (Note that the 1-pound loaf is baked on the Rapid Bake setting to prevent it from collapsing.)

	SMALL RECIPE	MEDIUM RECIPE	LARGE RECIPE
SHREDDED-WHEAT BISCUIT, CRUMBLED	1 large (½ cup)	2 large (1 cup)	3 large (1½ cups)
WATER	⅞ to 1 cup	1⅛ to 1¼ cups	2⅛ to 2¼ cups
BUTTER OR MARGARINE	1 tablespoon	1½ tablespoons	2 tablespoons
DARK BROWN SUGAR	1½ tablespoons	2 tablespoons	3 tablespoons
HONEY	1½ tablespoons	2 tablespoons	3 tablespoons
SALT	1 teaspoon	1½ teaspoons	2 teaspoons
WHOLE WHEAT FLOUR	2 cups	3 cups	4 cups
RED STAR BRAND ACTIVE DRY YEAST	2 teaspoons	2 teaspoons	2½ teaspoons

For the Small Recipe

1. Place all ingredients in bread pan, using the least amount of liquid listed in the recipe. Select Medium crust setting then the Rapid Bake cycle and press Start.

2. Observe the dough as it kneads. After 5 to 10 minutes, if it appears dry and stiff, or if your machine sounds as if it's straining to knead it, add more liquid 1 tablespoon at a time until dough forms a smooth, soft, pliable ball that is slightly tacky to the touch.

3. After the baking cycle ends, remove bread from pan, place on cake rack, and allow to cool 1 hour before slicing.

CRUST: Medium
BAKE CYCLE: Rapid Bake

For the Medium and Large Recipes

1. Place all ingredients in bread pan, using the least amount of liquid listed in the recipe. Select Medium Crust setting, then the Whole Wheat cycle and press Start.

2. Observe the dough as it kneads. After 5 to 10 minutes, if it appears dry and stiff, or if your machine sounds as if it's straining to knead it, add more liquid 1 tablespoon at a time until dough forms a smooth, soft, pliable ball that is slightly tacky to the touch.

3. After the baking cycle ends, remove bread from pan, place on cake rack, and allow to cool 1 hour before slicing.

CRUST: Medium
BAKE CYCLE: Whole Wheat
OPTIONAL BAKE CYCLES: Standard; Sweet Bread; Delayed Timer

NUTRITIONAL INFORMATION PER SLICE
Calories 122 / Fat 1.5 grams / Carbohydrates 24.6 grams / Protein 4 grams / Fiber 3.6 grams / Sodium 246 milligrams / Cholesterol 0 milligrams

Lou's Beer Bread

T his one was contributed by a good friend who knows just about everything there is to know about beer. It's a moist, evenly textured bread that's good enough to eat plain. Cheers!

	SMALL RECIPE	MEDIUM RECIPE	LARGE RECIPE
MILK	¼ cup	½ cup	⅜ cup
FLAT BOCK OR ANY OTHER DARK BEER	⅝ to ¾ cup	1 to 1⅛ cups	1⅛ to 1¼ cups
BUTTER OR MARGARINE	3 tablespoons	4 tablespoons	6 tablespoons
MOLASSES	1 tablespoon	1½ tablespoons	2 tablespoons
HONEY	1 tablespoon	1½ tablespoons	2 tablespoons
SALT	½ teaspoon	1 teaspoon	1 teaspoon
WHOLE WHEAT FLOUR	2 cups	3 cups	3 cups
BREAD FLOUR	None	None	1 cup
WHEAT GERM	2 tablespoons	3 tablespoons	¼ cup
RED STAR BRAND ACTIVE DRY YEAST	2 teaspoons	2 teaspoons	2½ teaspoons

I. Place all ingredients in bread pan, using the least amount of liquid listed in the recipe. Select Medium Crust setting then the Whole Wheat cycle and press Start.

2. Observe the dough as it kneads. After 5 to 10 minutes, if it appears dry and stiff, or if your machine sounds as if it's straining to knead it, add more liquid 1 tablespoon at a time until dough forms a smooth, soft, pliable ball that is slightly tacky to the touch.

3. After the baking cycle ends, remove bread from pan, place on cake rack, and allow to cool 1 hour before slicing.

CRUST: Medium
BAKE CYCLE: Whole Wheat
OPTIONAL BAKE CYCLES: Standard; Sweet Bread

NUTRITIONAL INFORMATION PER SLICE
Calories 137 / Fat 3.2 grams / Carbohydrates 23.5 grams / Protein 4.3 grams / Fiber 3.6 grams / Sodium 200 milligrams / Cholesterol .4 milligram

Miller's Bran Bread

If you're looking for a good sandwich bread, try this soft, light bran bread. It's a nice change from the stronger whole wheat taste, yet it is still nutritious.

	SMALL RECIPE	MEDIUM RECIPE	LARGE RECIPE
MILLER'S BRAN	⅓ cup	½ cup	⅔ cup
WATER	⅝ to ¾ cup	¾ to ⅞ cup	1 to 1⅛ cups
EGG	1	1	2
OIL	1 tablespoon	1½ tablespoons	2 tablespoons
HONEY	1 tablespoon	1½ tablespoons	2 tablespoons
SALT	1 teaspoon	1½ teaspoons	2 teaspoons
BREAD FLOUR	1⅔ cups	2½ cups	3⅓ cups
RED STAR BRAND ACTIVE DRY YEAST	1½ teaspoons	1½ teaspoons	2 teaspoons

1. Place all ingredients in bread pan, using the least amount of liquid listed in the recipe. Select Medium Crust setting and press Start.

2. Observe the dough as it kneads. After 5 to 10 minutes, if it appears dry and stiff, or if your machine sounds as if it's straining to knead it, add more liquid 1 tablespoon at a time until dough forms a smooth, soft, pliable ball that is slightly tacky to the touch.

3. After the baking cycle ends, remove bread from pan, place on cake rack, and allow to cool 1 hour before slicing.

CRUST: Medium
BAKE CYCLE: Standard
OPTIONAL BAKE CYCLES: Whole Wheat; Rapid Bake

NUTRITIONAL INFORMATION PER SLICE
Calories 110 / Fat 2.1 grams / Carbohydrates 19.8 grams / Protein 3.1 grams / Fiber 1.3 grams / Sodium 234 milligrams / Cholesterol 15.2 milligrams

---

Cracked Wheat Bread

Don't overlook the first step in this recipe: You must cook the cracked wheat to soften it. Although this requires a few extra minutes of preparation time, you'll be pleased with the results.

	SMALL RECIPE	MEDIUM RECIPE	LARGE RECIPE
WATER	½ cup	¾ cup	1 cup
CRACKED WHEAT	¼ cup	⅓ cup	½ cup
MILK	½ to ⅝ cup	¾ to ⅞ cup	1 to 1⅛ cups
BUTTER OR MARGARINE	1½ tablespoons	2 tablespoons	3 tablespoons
HONEY	1 tablespoon	1½ tablespoons	2 tablespoons
MOLASSES	1 tablespoon	1½ tablespoons	2 tablespoons
SALT	1 teaspoon	1½ teaspoons	2 teaspoons
BREAD FLOUR	1½ cups	2¼ cups	3 cups
WHOLE WHEAT FLOUR	½ cup	¾ cup	1 cup
VITAL WHEAT GLUTEN (OPTIONAL)	1 tablespoon	2 tablespoons	3 tablespoons
RED STAR BRAND ACTIVE DRY YEAST	2 teaspoons	2 teaspoons	2½ teaspoons

1.   In a small saucepan, bring the water to a boil, then add the cracked wheat. Cook on medium-high heat for approximately 6 minutes until all the water is absorbed; stir occasionally with a wooden spoon. Remove pan from heat and allow cracked wheat to cool to room temperature.

2.   Place all ingredients, including cooled cracked wheat, in bread pan, using the least amount of liquid listed in the recipe. Select Medium Crust setting and press Start.

3.   Observe the dough as it kneads. After 5 to 10 minutes, if it appears dry and stiff, or if your machine sounds as if it's straining to knead it, add more liquid 1 tablespoon at a time until dough forms a smooth, soft, pliable ball that is slightly tacky to the touch.

4. After the baking cycle ends, remove bread from pan, place on cake rack, and allow to cool 1 hour before slicing.

CRUST: Medium
BAKE CYCLE: Standard
OPTIONAL BAKE CYCLES: Whole Wheat

NUTRITIONAL INFORMATION PER SLICE
Calories 134 / Fat 1.7 grams / Carbohydrates 26 grams / Protein 3.9 grams / Fiber 2.1 grams / Sodium 257 milligrams / Cholesterol .5 milligram

Buttermilk Cracked-Wheat Bread

Raw cracked wheat adds a crunchy texture to this noteworthy whole wheat bread. It's not as tall as some loaves, but it's just as delicious. Serve it proudly with dinner or use it for sandwiches.

	SMALL RECIPE	MEDIUM RECIPE	LARGE RECIPE
CRACKED WHEAT	⅓ cup	½ cup	⅔ cup
BUTTERMILK	⅞ to 1 cup	1⅜ to 1½ cups	2 to 2⅛ cups
HONEY	1½ tablespoons	2 tablespoons	3 tablespoons
SALT	1 teaspoon	1½ teaspoons	2 teaspoons
SHORTENING	1 tablespoon	1 tablespoon	2 tablespoons
WHOLE WHEAT FLOUR	1⅓ cups	2 cups	2⅔ cups
BREAD FLOUR	⅔ cup	1 cup	1⅓ cups
VITAL WHEAT GLUTEN (OPTIONAL)	2 tablespoons	3 tablespoons	4 tablespoons
RED STAR BRAND ACTIVE DRY YEAST	1½ teaspoons	2 teaspoons	2½ teaspoons

1. Place all ingredients in bread pan, using the least amount of liquid listed in the recipe. Select Medium Crust setting then the Whole Wheat cycle and press Start.

2. Observe the dough as it kneads. After 5 to 10 minutes, if it appears dry and stiff, or if your machine sounds as if it's straining to knead it, add more liquid 1 tablespoon at a time until dough forms a smooth, soft, pliable ball that is slightly tacky to the touch.

3. After the baking cycle ends, remove bread from pan, place on cake rack, and allow to cool 1 hour before slicing.

CRUST: Medium
BAKE CYCLE: Whole Wheat
OPTIONAL BAKE CYCLES: Standard; Sweet Bread

NUTRITIONAL INFORMATION PER SLICE
Calories 136 / Fat 1.6 grams / Carbohydrates 26.7 grams / Protein 4.8 grams / Fiber 3.6 grams / Sodium 256 milligrams / Cholesterol .9 milligram

Bulgur Wheat Bread

*H*ealthy never tasted so good! Try this superb bread while it's slightly warm for the most intense whole-grain flavor. Hold off adding extra liquid to this one until it has kneaded for at least 5 minutes. The dough can appear deceptively dry at first. Don't overlook the first step on this bread. The bulgur must be cooked to soften it.

	SMALL RECIPE	MEDIUM RECIPE	LARGE RECIPE
WATER	½ cup	½ cup	1 cup
BULGUR WHEAT	¼ cup	⅓ cup	½ cup
OLD-FASHIONED ROLLED OATS	¼ cup	½ cup	½ cup
WATER	⅞ to 1 cup	1⅛ to 1¼ cups	1⅜ to 1½ cups
BUTTER OR MARGARINE	1 tablespoon	2 tablespoons	2 tablespoons
MOLASSES	2 teaspoons	1 tablespoon	4 teaspoons
HONEY	2 teaspoons	1 tablespoon	4 teaspoons
SALT	1 teaspoon	1½ teaspoons	2 teaspoons
BREAD FLOUR	1 cup	1½ cups	2 cups
WHOLE WHEAT FLOUR	1 cup	1½ cups	2 cups
CORNMEAL	1 tablespoon	2 tablespoons	2 tablespoons
RED STAR BRAND ACTIVE DRY YEAST	2 teaspoons	2 teaspoons	2½ teaspoons

1.   In a small saucepan, bring the water to a boil, then add the bulgur. Cook on medium-high heat for 5 to 6 minutes until all the water is absorbed; stir occasionally with a wooden spoon. Remove pan from heat and allow bulgur to cool to room temperature.

2.   Place all ingredients in bread pan, using the least amount of liquid listed in the recipe. Select Medium Crust setting then the Whole Wheat cycle and press Start.

3.   Observe the dough as it kneads. After 5 to 10 minutes, if it appears dry and stiff, or if your machine sounds as if it's straining to knead it, add more liquid 1 tablespoon at a time until dough forms a smooth, soft, pliable ball that is slightly tacky to the touch.

4. After the baking cycle ends, remove bread from pan, place on cake rack, and allow to cool 1 hour before slicing.

CRUST: Medium

BAKE CYCLE: Whole Wheat

OPTIONAL BAKE CYCLES: Standard; Delayed Timer

NUTRITIONAL INFORMATION PER SLICE

Calories 138 / Fat 1.9 grams / Carbohydrates 26.8 grams / Protein 4.2 grams / Fiber 3.2 grams / Sodium 251 milligrams / Cholesterol 0 milligrams

---

Lois's Rye Bread

*L*ois's favorite bread is this densely textured basic rye bread. It has a great crust and is reminiscent of a good Jewish rye. Toasted or used for a sandwich, it's delicious.

	SMALL RECIPE	MEDIUM RECIPE	LARGE RECIPE
MILK	½ cup	⅝ cup	1 cup milk
WATER	⅜ to ½ cup	¾ to ⅞ cup	¾ to ⅞ cup
BUTTER OR MARGARINE	1 tablespoon	1½ tablespoons	2 tablespoons
MOLASSES	2 tablespoons	3 tablespoons	¼ cup
SALT	1 teaspoon	1½ teaspoons	2 teaspoons
WHOLE WHEAT FLOUR	1 cup	1½ cups	2 cups
BREAD FLOUR	1 cup	1½ cups	2 cups
RYE FLOUR	½ cup	1 cup	1 cup
VITAL WHEAT GLUTEN (OPTIONAL)	1 tablespoon	1½ tablespoons	2 tablespoons
CARAWAY SEEDS	2 teaspoons	1 tablespoon	4 teaspoons
RED STAR BRAND ACTIVE DRY YEAST	2 teaspoons	2 teaspoons	2½ teaspoons

1. Place all ingredients in bread pan, using the least amount of liquid listed in the recipe. Select Medium Crust setting and press Start.

2. Observe the dough as it kneads. After 5 to 10 minutes, if it appears dry and stiff, or if your machine sounds as if it's straining to knead it, add more liquid 1 tablespoon at a time until dough forms a smooth, soft, pliable ball that is slightly tacky to the touch.

3. After the baking cycle ends, remove bread from pan, place on cake rack, and allow to cool 1 hour before slicing.

CRUST: Medium
BAKE CYCLE: Standard
OPTIONAL BAKE CYCLES: Whole Wheat

NUTRITIONAL INFORMATION PER SLICE
Calories 144 / Fat 1.6 grams / Carbohydrates 28.3 grams / Protein 4.4 grams / Fiber 3.25 grams / Sodium 251 milligrams / Cholesterol .5 milligram

Lorraine's Buttermilk Rye Bread

A *good friend and our favorite critic, Lorraine, loved every loaf she sampled. She selected this as one of her favorites and we agree. With its creamy texture and rich flavor, it's perfect for sandwiches.*

	SMALL RECIPE	MEDIUM RECIPE	LARGE RECIPE
BUTTERMILK	⅞ to 1 cup	1⅜ to 1½ cups	1¾ to 1⅞ cups
SALT	1 teaspoon	1½ teaspoons	2 teaspoons
BUTTER OR MARGARINE	1 tablespoon	1½ tablespoons	2 tablespoons
DARK BROWN SUGAR	1½ tablespoons	2 tablespoons	3 tablespoons
BREAD FLOUR	2 cups	3 cups	3⅓ cups
RYE FLOUR	⅓ cup	⅔ cup	1⅓ cups
CARAWAY SEEDS	1 teaspoon	1 teaspoon	2 teaspoons
RED STAR BRAND ACTIVE DRY YEAST	2 teaspoons	3 teaspoons	3 teaspoons

1. Place all ingredients in bread pan, using the least amount of liquid listed in the recipe. Select Medium Crust setting and press Start.

2. Observe the dough as it kneads. After 5 to 10 minutes, if it appears dry and stiff, or if your machine sounds as if it's straining to knead it, add more liquid 1 tablespoon at a time until dough forms a smooth, soft, pliable ball that is slightly tacky to the touch.

3. After the baking cycle ends, remove bread from pan, place on cake rack, and allow to cool 1 hour before slicing.

CRUST: Medium
BAKE CYCLE: Standard
OPTIONAL BAKE CYCLES: Whole Wheat; Sweet Bread

NUTRITIONAL INFORMATION PER SLICE
Calories 154 / Fat 1.9 grams / Carbohydrates 29.2 grams / Protein 4.5 grams / Fiber 2 grams / Sodium 270 milligrams / Cholesterol .9 milligram

Cheddar Rye Bread

*B*ecause this loaf doesn't rise very high, it has a very dense texture. For exceptional hors d'oeuvres, slice it thin and spread chopped liver or a pâté on top. We've found that this bread doesn't keep well; after a day or two, the crust hardens. Use it for hors d'oeuvres the first day or as a doorstop the third day.

	SMALL RECIPE	MEDIUM RECIPE	LARGE RECIPE
BUTTERMILK	⅜ cup	⅝ cup	⅞ cup
WATER	⅜ to ½ cup	½ to ⅝ cup	⅝ to ¾ cup
OIL	1 teaspoon	1½ teaspoons	2 teaspoons
LIGHT BROWN SUGAR	1 tablespoon	1½ tablespoons	2 tablespoons
SALT	¾ teaspoon	1 teaspoon	1½ teaspoons
BREAD FLOUR	1⅔ cups	2½ cups	3⅓ cups
RYE FLOUR	⅔ cup	1 cup	1⅓ cups
VITAL WHEAT GLUTEN (OPTIONAL)	1 tablespoon	2 tablespoons	3 tablespoons
GRATED SHARP CHEDDAR CHEESE	½ cup (2 ounces)	1 cup (4 ounces)	1 cup (4 ounces)
CARAWAY SEEDS	2 teaspoons	1 tablespoon	4 teaspoons
RED STAR BRAND ACTIVE DRY YEAST	2 teaspoons	3 teaspoons	3 teaspoons

1.   Place all ingredients in bread pan, using the least amount of liquid listed in the recipe. Select Light Crust setting and press Start.

2.   Observe the dough as it kneads. After 5 to 10 minutes, if it appears dry and stiff, or if your machine sounds as if it's straining to knead it, add more liquid 1 tablespoon at a time until dough forms a smooth, soft, pliable ball that is slightly tacky to the touch.

3.   After the baking cycle ends, remove bread from pan, place on cake rack, and allow to cool 1 hour before slicing.

CRUST: Light
BAKE CYCLE: Standard
OPTIONAL BAKE CYCLES: Whole Wheat; Sweet Bread

NUTRITIONAL INFORMATION PER SLICE
Calories 158 / Fat 3.7 grams / Carbohydrates 25 grams / Protein 5.6 grams / Fiber 1.9 grams / Sodium 215 milligrams / Cholesterol 8.9 milligrams

His Favorite Rye

*T*his is a small, well-shaped loaf with a robust, yeasty, and slightly sweet taste. Half a bottle of beer goes into this loaf; the other half goes to the nearest man. So if you ask, he'll probably tell you this is his favorite rye bread.

	SMALL RECIPE	MEDIUM RECIPE	LARGE RECIPE
FLAT BEER	⅝ cup	¾ cup	1 cup
WATER	¼ to ⅜ cup	⅜ to ½ cup	⅝ to ¾ cup
SHORTENING	1 tablespoon	1½ tablespoons	2 tablespoons
DARK BROWN SUGAR	1½ tablespoons	2 tablespoons	3 tablespoons
MOLASSES	1½ tablespoons	2 tablespoons	3 tablespoons
SALT	½ teaspoon	½ teaspoon	1 teaspoon
BREAD FLOUR	1½ cups	2½ cups	3 cups
RYE FLOUR	¾ cup	1 cup	1½ cups
VITAL WHEAT GLUTEN (OPTIONAL)	1 tablespoon	1½ tablespoons	2 tablespoons
GRATED ORANGE RIND (OPTIONAL)	1 tablespoon	1½ tablespoons	2 tablespoons
CARAWAY SEEDS	1 teaspoon	1½ teaspoons	2 teaspoons
RED STAR BRAND ACTIVE DRY YEAST	2 teaspoons	3 teaspoons	3 teaspoons

1. Place all ingredients in bread pan, using the least amount of liquid listed in the recipe. Select Medium Crust setting and press Start.

2. Observe the dough as it kneads. After 5 to 10 minutes, if it appears dry and stiff, or if your machine sounds as if it's straining to knead it, add more liquid 1 tablespoon at a time until dough forms a smooth, soft, pliable ball that is slightly tacky to the touch.

3. After the baking cycle ends, remove bread from pan, place on cake rack, and allow to cool 1 hour before slicing.

CRUST: Medium
BAKE CYCLE: Standard
OPTIONAL BAKE CYCLES: Whole Wheat; Sweet Bread

NUTRITIONAL INFORMATION PER SLICE
Calories 140 / Fat 1.8 grams / Carbohydrates 26.6 grams / Protein 3.3 grams / Fiber 2 grams / Sodium 78.8 milligrams / Cholesterol 0 milligrams

Michael's Onion Rye Bread

When Lois's son Michael comes to visit, she bakes this bread, which has a very welcoming aroma. Serve this tasty rye slightly warm to enjoy it at its best.

	SMALL RECIPE	MEDIUM RECIPE	LARGE RECIPE
WATER	¾ to ⅞ cup	1⅛ to 1¼ cups	1⅝ to 1¾ cups
OIL	2 teaspoons	1 tablespoon	4 teaspoons
MOLASSES	2 teaspoons	1 tablespoon	4 teaspoons
MINCED FRESH ONION	¼ cup	⅓ cup	½ cup
SALT	1 teaspoon	1½ teaspoons	2 teaspoons
WHOLE WHEAT FLOUR	1 cup	1½ cups	2 cups
BREAD FLOUR	1 cup	1½ cups	2 cups
RYE FLOUR	½ cup	¾ cup	1 cup
VITAL WHEAT GLUTEN (OPTIONAL)	1 tablespoon	1½ tablespoons	2 tablespoons
CARAWAY SEEDS	1 teaspoon	1 teaspoon	2 teaspoons
RED STAR BRAND ACTIVE DRY YEAST	1½ teaspoons	2 teaspoons	2½ teaspoons

1. Place all ingredients in bread pan, using the least amount of liquid listed in the recipe. Select Medium Crust setting then the Whole Wheat cycle and press Start.

2. Observe the dough as it kneads. After 5 to 10 minutes, if it appears dry and stiff, or if your machine sounds as if it's straining to knead it, add more liquid 1 tablespoon at a time until dough forms a smooth, soft, pliable ball that is slightly tacky to the touch.

3. After the baking cycle ends, remove bread from pan, place on cake rack, and allow to cool 1 hour before slicing.

CRUST: Medium
BAKE CYCLE: Whole Wheat
OPTIONAL BAKE CYCLES: Standard; Delayed Timer; Rapid Bake

NUTRITIONAL INFORMATION PER SLICE
Calories 127 / Fat 1.5 grams / Carbohydrates 25 grams / Protein 3.9 grams / Fiber 3 grams / Sodium 230 milligrams / Cholesterol 0 milligrams

Citrus Rye

T his aromatic rye bread has a delicate citrus flavor. It makes superb croutons for a Caesar salad.

	SMALL RECIPE	MEDIUM RECIPE	LARGE RECIPE
MILK	½ cup	⅝ cup	⅞ cup
WATER	⅜ to ½ cup	½ to ⅝ cup	⅝ to ¾ cup
SHORTENING	1½ tablespoons	2 tablespoons	3 tablespoons
MOLASSES	1 tablespoon	2 tablespoons	2 tablespoons
DARK BROWN SUGAR	1 tablespoon	2 tablespoons	2 tablespoons
SALT	1 teaspoon	1½ teaspoons	2 teaspoons
BREAD FLOUR	2 cups	2½ cups	3 cups
RYE FLOUR	½ cup	1 cup	1 cup
GRATED ORANGE RIND	2 tablespoons	3 tablespoons	4 tablespoons
GRATED LEMON RIND	1½ tablespoons	2 tablespoons	3 tablespoons
CARAWAY SEEDS	2 teaspoons	1 tablespoon	4 teaspoons
VITAL WHEAT GLUTEN (OPTIONAL)	1 tablespoon	1½ tablespoons	2 tablespoons
RED STAR BRAND ACTIVE DRY YEAST	2 teaspoons	2 teaspoons	2½ teaspoons

1. Place all ingredients in bread pan, using the least amount of liquid listed in the recipe. Select Medium Crust setting and press Start.

2. Observe the dough as it kneads. After 5 to 10 minutes, if it appears dry and stiff, or if your machine sounds as if it's straining to knead it, add more liquid 1 tablespoon at a time until dough forms a smooth, soft, pliable ball that is slightly tacky to the touch.

3. After the baking cycle ends, remove bread from pan, place on cake rack, and allow to cool 1 hour before slicing.

CRUST: Medium
BAKE CYCLE: Standard
OPTIONAL BAKE CYCLES: Whole Wheat; Sweet Bread

NUTRITIONAL INFORMATION PER SLICE
Calories 145 / Fat 2.4 grams / Carbohydrates 27 grams / Protein 3.6 grams / Fiber 1.9 grams / Sodium 236 milligrams / Cholesterol .5 milligram

---

Swedish Limpa Rye Bread

*T*he fennel seeds add an unusual licorice flavor to this bread. Thinly sliced, it's good enough for any smorgasbord.

	SMALL RECIPE	MEDIUM RECIPE	LARGE RECIPE
WATER	¾ to ⅞ cup	1⅛ to 1¼ cups	1¾ to 1⅞ cups
OIL	2 teaspoons	1 tablespoon	4 teaspoons
HONEY	2 teaspoons	1 tablespoon	4 teaspoons
SALT	½ teaspoon	1 teaspoon	1 teaspoon
BREAD FLOUR	1⅓ cups	2½ cups	2⅔ cups
RYE FLOUR	⅔ cup	1 cup	1⅓ cups
CARAWAY SEEDS	½ teaspoon	1 teaspoon	1 teaspoon
FENNEL SEEDS	¼ teaspoon	½ teaspoon	½ teaspoon
GRATED ORANGE RIND	1½ tablespoons	2 tablespoons	2½ tablespoons
VITAL WHEAT GLUTEN (OPTIONAL)	1½ tablespoons	2 tablespoons	3 tablespoons
RED STAR BRAND ACTIVE DRY YEAST	1½ teaspoons	1½ teaspoons	2½ teaspoons

1. Place all ingredients in bread pan, using the least amount of liquid listed in the recipe. Select Medium Crust setting and press Start.

2. Observe the dough as it kneads. After 5 to 10 minutes, if it appears dry and stiff, or if your machine sounds as if it's straining to knead it, add more liquid 1 tablespoon at a time until dough forms a smooth, soft, pliable ball that is slightly tacky to the touch.

3. After the baking cycle ends, remove bread from pan, place on cake rack, and allow to cool 1 hour before slicing.

CRUST: Medium
BAKE CYCLE: Standard
OPTIONAL BAKE CYCLES: Whole Wheat; Delayed Timer

NUTRITIONAL INFORMATION PER SLICE
Calories 123 / Fat 1.4 grams / Carbohydrates 24.3 grams / Protein 3.2 grams / Fiber 1.9 grams / Sodium 153 milligrams / Cholesterol 0 milligrams

Sauerkraut Rye Bread

*T*alk about a hearty bread... here's one that's almost a meal in itself! It's moist, soft, and has the unmistakable flavor of sauerkraut. A slice of this bread would be a great accompaniment to steaming hot vegetable soup on a chilly winter night. It would also taste wonderful with thin slices of corned beef, Swiss cheese, and a sweet, hot mustard.

	SMALL RECIPE	MEDIUM RECIPE	LARGE RECIPE
WATER	½ to ⅝ cup	¾ to ⅞ cup	1⅛ to 1¼ cups
SAUERKRAUT, SQUEEZED, WELL DRAINED, AND CHOPPED	½ cup	1 cup	1 cup
BUTTER OR MARGARINE	1 tablespoon	1½ tablespoons	2 tablespoons
MOLASSES	1 tablespoon	1½ tablespoons	2 tablespoons
DARK BROWN SUGAR	1 tablespoon	1½ tablespoons	2 tablespoons
SALT	1 teaspoon	1½ teaspoons	2 teaspoons
BREAD FLOUR	1⅓ cups	2 cups	2⅔ cups
RYE FLOUR	⅔ cups	1 cup	1⅓ cups
CARAWAY SEEDS	2 teaspoons	1 tablespoon	4 teaspoons
VITAL WHEAT GLUTEN (OPTIONAL)	1½ tablespoon	2 tablespoons	3 tablespoons
RED STAR BRAND ACTIVE DRY YEAST	2 teaspoons	2 teaspoons	2½ teaspoons

1. Place all ingredients in bread pan, using the least amount of liquid listed in the recipe. Select Medium Crust setting and press Start.

2. Observe the dough as it kneads. After 5 to 10 minutes, if it appears dry and stiff, or if your machine sounds as if it's straining to knead it, add more liquid 1 tablespoon at a time until dough forms a smooth, soft, pliable ball that is slightly tacky to the touch.

3. After the baking cycle ends, remove bread from pan, place on cake rack, and allow to cool 1 hour before slicing.

CRUST: Medium

BAKE CYCLE: Standard

OPTIONAL BAKE CYCLES: Whole Wheat; Sweet Bread; Delayed Timer

---

NUTRITIONAL INFORMATION PER SLICE

Calories 115 / Fat 1.3 grams / Carbohydrates 22.8 grams/ Protein 2.9 grams / Fiber 2 grams / Sodium 357 milligrams / Cholesterol 0 milligrams

---

Dilly Deli Rye

his will be a taste sensation at dinner. Your guests will rave! It's a rye bread with the unmistakable flavor of pickles.

	SMALL RECIPE	MEDIUM RECIPE	LARGE RECIPE
WATER	⅜ to ½ cup	⅝ to ¾ cup	⅝ to ¾ cup
BRINE FROM DILL PICKLES	¼ cup	⅜ cup	½ cup
EGG	1	1	2
OIL	1 tablespoon	1½ tablespoons	2 tablespoons
SUGAR	1½ tablespoons	2 tablespoons	3 tablespoons
SALT	¾ teaspoon	1 teaspoon	1½ teaspoons
BREAD FLOUR	1⅓ cups	2 cups	2⅔ cups
RYE FLOUR	⅔ cup	1 cup	1⅓ cups
VITAL WHEAT GLUTEN (OPTIONAL)	1 tablespoon	1½ tablespoons	2 tablespoons
DRIED DILL	1 teaspoon	1½ teaspoons	2 teaspoons
RED STAR BRAND ACTIVE DRY YEAST	2 teaspoons	2 teaspoons	2½ teaspoons

1. Place all ingredients in bread pan, using the least amount of liquid listed in the recipe. Select Medium Crust setting and press Start.

2. Observe the dough as it kneads. After 5 to 10 minutes, if it appears dry and stiff, or if your machine sounds as if it's straining to knead it, add more liquid 1 tablespoon at a time until dough forms a smooth, soft, pliable ball that is slightly tacky to the touch.

3. After the baking cycle ends, remove bread from pan, place on cake rack, and allow to cool 1 hour before slicing.

CRUST: Medium
BAKE CYCLE: Standard
OPTIONAL BAKE CYCLES: Whole Wheat

NUTRITIONAL INFORMATION PER SLICE
Calories 118 / Fat 2.1 grams / Carbohydrates 21.2 grams / Protein 3.1 grams / Fiber 1.6 grams / Sodium 158 milligrams / Cholesterol 15.2 milligrams

Vollkornbrot

We almost tossed this recipe out, because it consistently resulted in oddly shaped loaves. But the flavor of this stouthearted bread so closely resembled some of the wonderful breads we'd eaten in Germany it would have been a crime to omit it. Just be forewarned—it's a funny-looking bread with a flavor and personality all its own. You haven't lived until you've tried this one with a hunk of cheese. Wunderbar! (*Note: This is a very heavy dough. If your bread machine stalls or sounds like it is straining to knead the dough, add water 1 tablespoon at a time to soften it.*)

	SMALL RECIPE	MEDIUM RECIPE	LARGE RECIPE
BUTTERMILK	⅞ to 1 cup	1¼ to 1⅜ cups	1½ to 1⅝ cups
WATER	3 tablespoons	¼ cup	½ cup
BUTTER OR MARGARINE	1 tablespoon	1½ tablespoons	2 tablespoons
MOLASSES	2 tablespoons	¼ cup	5 tablespoons
SALT	½ teaspoon	1 teaspoon	1½ teaspoons
WHOLE WHEAT FLOUR	1 cup	2½ cups	3 cups
BREAD FLOUR	1 cup	½ cup	¾ cup
RYE FLOUR	2 tablespoons	½ cup	¾ cup
BUCKWHEAT FLOUR	2 tablespoons	¼ cup	⅓ cup
WHEAT GERM	2 tablespoons	¼ cup	⅓ cup
RED STAR BRAND ACTIVE DRY YEAST	3 teaspoons	3 teaspoons	3 teaspoons

I. Place all ingredients in bread pan, using the least amount of liquid listed in the recipe. Select Light Crust setting then the Whole Wheat cycle and press Start.

2. Observe the dough as it kneads. After 5 to 10 minutes, if it appears dry and stiff, or if your machine sounds as if it's straining to knead it, add more liquid 1 tablespoon at a time until dough forms a smooth, soft, pliable ball that is slightly tacky to the touch.

3. After the baking cycle ends, remove bread from pan, place on cake rack, and allow to cool 1 hour before slicing.

CRUST: Light
BAKE CYCLE: Whole Wheat
OPTIONAL BAKE CYCLES: Standard; Sweet Bread

NUTRITIONAL INFORMATION PER SLICE
Calories 147 / Fat 1.9 grams / Carbohydrates 28.8 grams / Protein 5.5 grams / Fiber 3.9 grams / Sodium 193 milligrams / Cholesterol .8 milligram

---

Black Forest Pumpernickel

*T*his makes a dark loaf with that fabulous, distinctive rye flavor. Pair this soul-satisfying bread with thin slices of ham and cheese or a mug of homemade potato soup.

	SMALL RECIPE	MEDIUM RECIPE	LARGE RECIPE
WATER	¾ to ⅞ cup	1⅛ to 1¼ cups	1½ to 1⅝ cups
OIL	1 tablespoon	1½ tablespoons	2 tablespoons
MOLASSES	3 tablespoons	⅓ cup	6 tablespoons
SALT	1 teaspoon	1½ teaspoons	2 teaspoons
BREAD FLOUR	⅔ cup	1½ cups	1⅓ cups
RYE FLOUR	⅔ cup	1 cup	1⅓ cups
WHOLE WHEAT FLOUR	⅔ cup	1 cup	1⅓ cups
VITAL WHEAT GLUTEN (OPTIONAL)	2 tablespoons	3 tablespoons	¼ cup
COCOA POWDER	2 tablespoons	3 tablespoons	¼ cup
CARAWAY SEEDS	2 teaspoons	1 tablespoon	4 teaspoons
RED STAR BRAND ACTIVE DRY YEAST	1½ teaspoons	2 teaspoons	2½ teaspoons

I.   Place all ingredients in bread pan, using the least amount of liquid listed in the recipe. Select Medium Crust setting then the Whole Wheat cycle and press Start.

2.   Observe the dough as it kneads. After 5 to 10 minutes, if it appears dry and stiff, or if your machine sounds as if it's straining to knead it, add more liquid 1 tablespoon at a time until dough forms a smooth, soft, pliable ball that is slightly tacky to the touch.

3.   After the baking cycle ends, remove bread from pan, place on cake rack, and allow to cool 1 hour before slicing.

CRUST: Medium

BAKE CYCLE: Whole Wheat

OPTIONAL BAKE CYCLES: Standard; Sweet Bread; Delayed Timer

NUTRITIONAL INFORMATION PER SLICE

Calories 139 / Fat 2.2 grams / Carbohydrates 27.1 grams / Protein 3.7 grams / Fiber 3.1 grams / Sodium 231 milligrams / Cholesterol 0 milligrams

Morris and Evelyn's
Old World Pumpernickel

Because it has a bumpy top, this pumpernickel may not be the best looking of breads, but its flavor can't be beat! Its pleasant, tangy taste is enhanced by the moist texture of potato. This bread is named for Lois's parents who adored Old World breads such as this one.

	SMALL RECIPE	MEDIUM RECIPE	LARGE RECIPE
MILLER'S BRAN	1 tablespoon	2 tablespoons	2 tablespoons
POTATO WATER, COOLED*	¾ to ⅞ cup	1 to 1⅛ cups	1½ to 1⅝ cups
PLAIN MASHED POTATO, ROOM TEMPERATURE	¼ cup	½ cup	½ cup
BUTTER OR MARGARINE	1 tablespoon	1½ tablespoons	2 tablespoons
MOLASSES	1 tablespoon	1½ tablespoons	2 tablespoons
SALT	1 teaspoon	1½ teaspoons	2 teaspoons
WHOLE WHEAT FLOUR	2 cups	3 cups	4 cups
RYE FLOUR	⅓ cup	½ cup	⅔ cup
CORNMEAL	1 tablespoon	2 tablespoons	2 tablespoons
CARAWAY SEEDS	½ teaspoon	1 teaspoon	1 teaspoon
VITAL WHEAT GLUTEN (OPTIONAL)	2 tablespoons	3 tablespoons	¼ cup
RED STAR BRAND ACTIVE DRY YEAST	2 teaspoons	3 teaspoons	3 teaspoons

1.   Place all ingredients in bread pan, using the least amount of liquid listed in the recipe. Select Medium Crust setting then the Whole Wheat cycle and press Start.

2.   Observe the dough as it kneads. After 5 to 10 minutes, if it appears dry and stiff, or if your machine sounds as if it's straining to knead it, add more liquid 1 tablespoon at a time until dough forms a smooth, soft, pliable ball that is slightly tacky to the touch.

*The water in which you cooked the potato

3. After the baking cycle ends, remove bread from pan, place on cake rack, and allow to cool 1 hour before slicing.

CRUST: Medium

BAKE CYCLE: Whole Wheat

OPTIONAL BAKE CYCLES: Standard; Delayed Timer

NUTRITIONAL INFORMATION PER SLICE

Calories 125 / Fat 1.5 grams / Carbohydrates 25 grams / Protein 4.4 grams / Fiber 4.3 grams / Sodium 246 milligrams / Cholesterol 0 milligrams

Russian Black Bread

*T*he vinegar in this lush, dark pumpernickel adds a bite to it. For a glorious combination of international flavors, try a slice of this unusually tall loaf of Slavic bread with an icy mug of German beer and some good Danish cheese.

	SMALL RECIPE	MEDIUM RECIPE	LARGE RECIPE
WATER	7/8 to 1 cup	1 1/8 to 1 1/4 cups	1 5/8 to 1 3/4 cups
CIDER VINEGAR	1 1/2 tablespoons	2 tablespoons	3 tablespoons
DARK CORN SYRUP	1 1/2 tablespoons	2 tablespoons	3 tablespoons
BUTTER OR MARGARINE	1 1/2 tablespoons	2 tablespoons	3 tablespoons
DARK BROWN SUGAR	2 teaspoons	1 tablespoon	4 teaspoons
SALT	1 teaspoon	1 teaspoon	2 teaspoons
BREAD FLOUR	2 cups	2 1/2 cups	4 cups
RYE FLOUR	1/2 cup	1 cup	1 cup
COCOA POWDER	2 tablespoons	3 tablespoons	4 tablespoons
INSTANT COFFEE POWDER	3/4 teaspoon	1 teaspoon	1 1/2 teaspoons
CARAWAY SEEDS	2 teaspoons	1 tablespoon	4 teaspoons
FENNEL SEEDS (OPTIONAL)	1 pinch	1/4 teaspoon	1/2 teaspoon
RED STAR BRAND ACTIVE DRY YEAST	2 teaspoons	2 teaspoons	2 1/2 teaspoons

1. Place all ingredients in bread pan, using the least amount of liquid listed in the recipe. Select Medium Crust setting and press Start.

2. Observe the dough as it kneads. After 5 to 10 minutes, if it appears dry and stiff, or if your machine sounds as if it's straining to knead it, add more liquid 1 tablespoon at a time until dough forms a smooth, soft, pliable ball that is slightly tacky to the touch.

3. After the baking cycle ends, remove bread from pan, place on cake rack, and allow to cool 1 hour before slicing.

CRUST: Medium

BAKE CYCLE: Standard

OPTIONAL BAKE CYCLES: Whole Wheat; Sweet Bread; Delayed Timer

---

NUTRITIONAL INFORMATION PER SLICE

Calories 137 / Fat 1.8 grams / Carbohydrates 26.8 grams / Protein 3.4 grams / Fiber 2.2 grams / Sodium 176 milligrams / Cholesterol 0 milligrams

Rick's Seven-Grain Bread

Seven-grain cereal can usually be found in health-food stores, if not at your local market. This bread smells lovely baking, rises beautifully, and has a slightly crunchy texture. It's great for munching on in the wee hours of the morning when only computer wizards, like Linda's brother-in-law Rick, are still awake.

	SMALL RECIPE	MEDIUM RECIPE	LARGE RECIPE
WATER	⅝ to ¾ cup	⅞ to 1 cup	1 to 1⅛ cups
EGG	1	1	2
OIL	1½ tablespoons	2 tablespoons	3 tablespoons
HONEY	1½ tablespoons	2 tablespoons	3 tablespoons
SALT	1 teaspoon	1½ teaspoons	2 teaspoons
WHOLE WHEAT FLOUR	1⅔ cups	2½ cups	3⅓ cups
SEVEN-GRAIN CEREAL	⅓ cup	½ cup	⅔ cup
VITAL WHEAT GLUTEN (OPTIONAL)	1 tablespoon	1½ tablespoons	2 tablespoons
RED STAR BRAND ACTIVE DRY YEAST	2 teaspoons	2 teaspoons	2½ teaspoons

1. Place all ingredients in bread pan, using the least amount of liquid listed in the recipe. Select Medium Crust setting then the Whole Wheat cycle and press Start.

2. Observe the dough as it kneads. After 5 to 10 minutes, if it appears dry and stiff, or if your machine sounds as if it's straining to knead it, add more liquid 1 tablespoon at a time until dough forms a smooth, soft, pliable ball that is slightly tacky to the touch.

3. After the baking cycle ends, remove bread from pan, place on cake rack, and allow to cool 1 hour before slicing.

CRUST: Medium
BAKE CYCLE: Whole Wheat
OPTIONAL BAKE CYCLES: Standard

NUTRITIONAL INFORMATION PER SLICE
Calories 111 / Fat 2.7 grams / Carbohydrates 19.3 grams / Protein 3.7 grams / Fiber 3 grams / Sodium 234 milligrams / Cholesterol 15.2 milligrams

Multigrain Buttermilk Bread

A*n earthy, wholesome-tasting bread, this makes sublime sandwiches.*

	SMALL RECIPE	MEDIUM RECIPE	LARGE RECIPE
CRACKED WHEAT	¼ cup	⅓ cup	½ cup
BUTTERMILK	⅞ to 1 cup	1¼ to 1⅜ cups	1¾ to 1⅞ cups
BUTTER OR MARGARINE	1 tablespoon	1½ tablespoons	2 tablespoons
HONEY	1½ tablespoons	2 tablespoons	3 tablespoons
SALT	1 teaspoon	1½ teaspoons	2 teaspoons
BREAD FLOUR	1 cup	1½ cups	2 cups
WHOLE WHEAT FLOUR	1 cup	1½ cups	2 cups
WHEAT GERM	1½ tablespoons	2 tablespoons	3 tablespoons
CORNMEAL	3 tablespoons	¼ cup	6 tablespoons
RED STAR BRAND ACTIVE DRY YEAST	2 teaspoons	3 teaspoons	3 teaspoons

1. Place all ingredients in bread pan, using the least amount of liquid listed in the recipe. Select Medium Crust setting and press Start.

2. Observe the dough as it kneads. After 5 to 10 minutes, if it appears dry and stiff, or if your machine sounds as if it's straining to knead it, add more liquid 1 tablespoon at a time until dough forms a smooth, soft, pliable ball that is slightly tacky to the touch.

3. After the baking cycle ends, remove bread from pan, place on cake rack, and allow to cool 1 hour before slicing.

CRUST: Medium
BAKE CYCLE: Standard
OPTIONAL BAKE CYCLES: Whole Wheat

NUTRITIONAL INFORMATION PER SLICE
Calories 143 / Fat 1.7 grams / Carbohydrates 27.8 grams / Protein 4.9 grams / Fiber 3.1 grams / Sodium 268 milligrams / Cholesterol .8 milligram

---

Marilyn's Everday Health Bread

A create-your-own recipe from our friend Marilyn, this is a good one for using up those odds and ends of various grains you may have on hand. Marilyn owns a bread machine, too, and this is the only bread she makes!

	SMALL RECIPE	MEDIUM RECIPE	LARGE RECIPE
WATER	⅞ to 1 cup	1¼ to 1⅜ cups	1¾ to 1⅞ cups
BUTTER OR MARGARINE	1 tablespoon	1½ tablespoons	2 tablespoons
SUGAR	2 tablespoons	3 tablespoons	¼ cup
SALT	1 teaspoon	1½ teaspoons	2 teaspoons
WHOLE WHEAT FLOUR	1 cup	1½ cups	2 cups
BREAD FLOUR	1 cup	1½ cups	2 cups
WHOLE GRAINS*	½ cup	½ cup	1 cup
NONFAT DRY MILK POWDER	1 tablespoon	1½ tablespoons	2 tablespoons
VITAL WHEAT GLUTEN (OPTIONAL)	1½ tablespoons	2 tablespoons	3 tablespoons
RED STAR BRAND ACTIVE DRY YEAST	2 teaspoons	2 teaspoons	2½ teaspoons

1. Place all ingredients in bread pan, using the least amount of liquid listed in the recipe. Select Medium Crust setting and press Start.

2. Observe the dough as it kneads. After 5 to 10 minutes, if it appears dry and stiff, or if your machine sounds as if it's straining to knead it, add more liquid 1 tablespoon at a time until dough forms a smooth, soft, pliable ball that is slightly tacky to the touch.

*The whole grains could be oats, miller's bran, cracked wheat, oat bran, or any combination of these grains to equal the ½ cup or 1 cup called for in the recipe.

3. After the baking cycle ends, remove bread from pan, place on cake rack, and allow to cool 1 hour before slicing.

CRUST: Medium

BAKE CYCLE: Standard

OPTIONAL BAKE CYCLES: Whole Wheat; Delayed Timer

NUTRITIONAL INFORMATION PER SLICE
Calories 131 / Fat 1.4 grams / Carbohydrates 26.3 grams / Protein 415 grams / Fiber 3.2 grams / Sodium 248 milligrams / Cholesterol .1 milligram

---

Zuni Indian Bread

*T*his is one of the first whole-grain breads we made in a bread machine. We've baked this nourishing bread many times since; it's definitely one of our favorites. We've also found it to be one of our most appreciated gift breads.

	SMALL RECIPE	MEDIUM RECIPE	LARGE RECIPE
BUTTERMILK	⅝ to ¾ cup	⅞ to 1 cup	1⅛ to 1¼ cups
EGG	1	1	2
BUTTER OR MARGARINE	1 tablespoon	1½ tablespoons	2 tablespoons
MOLASSES	2 tablespoons	3 tablespoons	¼ cup
SALT	1 teaspoon	1½ teaspoons	2 teaspoons
WHOLE WHEAT FLOUR	1 cup	1⅔ cups	2 cups
BREAD FLOUR	¾ cup	1 cup	1½ cups
CORNMEAL	¼ cup	⅓ cup	½ cup
RAW UNSALTED SUNFLOWER SEEDS	¼ cup	⅓ cup	½ cup
VITAL WHEAT GLUTEN (OPTIONAL)	1 tablespoons	1½ tablespoons	2 tablespoons
RED STAR BRAND ACTIVE DRY YEAST	3 teaspoons	3 teaspoons	3½ teaspoons

1. Place all ingredients in bread pan, using the least amount of liquid listed in the recipe. Select Medium Crust setting then the Whole Wheat cycle and press Start.

2. Observe the dough as it kneads. After 5 to 10 minutes, if it appears dry and stiff, or if your machine sounds as if it's straining to knead it, add more liquid 1 tablespoon at a time until dough forms a smooth, soft, pliable ball that is slightly tacky to the touch.

3. After the baking cycle ends, remove bread from pan, place on cake rack, and allow to cool 1 hour before slicing.

CRUST: Medium
BAKE CYCLE: Whole Wheat
OPTIONAL BAKE CYCLES: Standard; Sweet Bread

NUTRITIONAL INFORMATION PER SLICE
Calories 138 / Fat 3.4 grams / Carbohydrates 22.8 grams / Protein 4.9 grams / Fiber 2.6 grams / Sodium 266 milligrams / Cholesterol 15.8 milligrams

Briscoe's Irish Brown Bread

*T*he combination of caraway and raisins gives this healthy bread an unusual taste. We hope you like it as much as Briscoe (our favorite terrier) did.

	SMALL RECIPE	MEDIUM RECIPE	LARGE RECIPE
OLD-FASHIONED ROLLED OATS	¼ cup	⅓ cup	½ cup
BUTTERMILK	1 to 1⅛ cups	1¼ to 1⅜ cups	1⅞ to 2 cups
BUTTER OR MARGARINE	1 tablespoon	1½ tablespoons	2 tablespoons
DARK BROWN SUGAR	2 tablespoons	3 tablespoons	¼ cup
SALT	1 teaspoon	1 teaspoon	1½ teaspoons
WHOLE WHEAT FLOUR	1⅓ cups	2 cups	2⅔ cups
BREAD FLOUR	⅔ cup	1 cup	1⅓ cups
OAT BRAN	1 tablespoon	2 tablespoons	2 tablespoons
RAISINS	2 tablespoons	3 tablespoons	¼ cup
CARAWAY SEEDS	2 teaspoons	1 tablespoon	4 teaspoons
RED STAR BRAND ACTIVE DRY YEAST	2 teaspoons	2 teaspoons	2½ teaspoons

1.   Place all ingredients in bread pan, using the least amount of liquid listed in the recipe. Select Medium Crust setting then the Whole Wheat cycle and press Start.

2.   Observe the dough as it kneads. After 5 to 10 minutes, if it appears dry and stiff, or if your machine sounds as if it's straining to knead it, add more liquid 1 tablespoon at a time until dough forms a smooth, soft, pliable ball that is slightly tacky to the touch.

3.   After the baking cycle ends, remove bread from pan, place on cake rack, and allow to cool 1 hour before slicing.

CRUST: Medium
BAKE CYCLE: Whole Wheat
OPTIONAL BAKE CYCLES: Standard; Raisin/Nut

NUTRITIONAL INFORMATION PER SLICE
Calories 136 / Fat 1.8 grams / Carbohydrates 27 grams / Protein 4.7 grams / Fiber 3.1 grams / Sodium 193 milligrams / Cholesterol .8 milligram

Whole-Wheat Soda Bread

*C*hildren *love this rich-tasting soda bread. It's one that rises quite high in our bread machines.*

	SMALL RECIPE	MEDIUM RECIPE	LARGE RECIPE
BUTTERMILK	⅞ to 1 cup	1¼ to 1⅜ cups	2⅛ to 2¼ cups
BUTTER OR MARGARINE	1 tablespoon	1½ tablespoons	2 tablespoons
HONEY	1 tablespoon	1½ tablespoons	2 tablespoons
SALT	1 teaspoon	1½ teaspoons	2 teaspoons
WHOLE WHEAT FLOUR	1⅓ cups	2 cups	2½ cups
BREAD FLOUR	⅔ cup	1 cup	1½ cups
BAKING SODA	¼ teaspoon	½ teaspoon	¾ teaspoon
VITAL WHEAT GLUTEN (OPTIONAL)	2 tablespoons	3 tablespoons	4 tablespoons
RED STAR BRAND ACTIVE DRY YEAST	2 teaspoons	2 teaspoons	2½ teaspoons

1.   Place all ingredients in bread pan, using the least amount of liquid listed in the recipe. Select Medium Crust setting then the Whole Wheat cycle and press Start.

2.   Observe the dough as it kneads. After 5 to 10 minutes, if it appears dry and stiff, or if your machine sounds as if it's straining to knead it, add more liquid 1 tablespoon at a time until dough forms a smooth, soft, pliable ball that is slightly tacky to the touch.

3.   After the baking cycle ends, remove bread from pan, place on cake rack, and allow to cool 1 hour before slicing.

CRUST: Medium
BAKE CYCLE: Whole Wheat
OPTIONAL BAKE CYCLES: Standard

NUTRITIONAL INFORMATION PER SLICE
Calories 125 / Fat 1.8 grams / Carbohydrates 23.1 grams / Protein 4.9 grams / Fiber 2.5 grams / Sodium 296 milligrams / Cholesterol .8 milligram

---

Irish Soda Bread

*Y*our friends will love you if you give them a loaf of this bread! It has a scrumptious old-country flavor.

	SMALL RECIPE	MEDIUM RECIPE	LARGE RECIPE
OLD-FASHIONED ROLLED OATS	⅓ cup	½ cup	⅔ cup
BUTTERMILK	⅞ to 1 cup	1¼ to 1⅜ cups	1¾ to 1⅞ cups
BUTTER OR MARGARINE	1 tablespoon	1½ tablespoons	2 tablespoons
HONEY	2 tablespoons	3 tablespoons	¼ cup
SALT	1 teaspoon	1 teaspoon	2 teaspoons
WHOLE WHEAT FLOUR	2 cups	3 cups	4 cups
BAKING SODA	½ teaspoon	½ teaspoon	1 teaspoon
RAISINS (OPTIONAL)	¼ cup	⅓ cup	½ cup
RED STAR BRAND ACTIVE DRY YEAST	1½ teaspoons	3 teaspoons	3 teaspoons

1. Place all ingredients in bread pan, using the least amount of liquid listed in the recipe. Select Medium Crust setting then the Whole Wheat cycle and press Start.

2. Observe the dough as it kneads. After 5 to 10 minutes, if it appears dry and stiff, or if your machine sounds as if it's straining to knead it, add more liquid 1 tablespoon at a time until dough forms a smooth, soft, pliable ball that is slightly tacky to the touch.

3. After the baking cycle ends, remove bread from pan, place on cake rack, and allow to cool 1 hour before slicing.

CRUST: Medium
BAKE CYCLE: Whole Wheat
OPTIONAL BAKE CYCLES: Standard; Sweet Bread; Raisin/Nut

NUTRITIONAL INFORMATION PER SLICE
Calories 142 / Fat 1.9 grams / Carbohydrates 28.8 grams / Protein 5.1 grams / Fiber 4 grams / Sodium 222 milligrams / Cholesterol .8 milligram

---

Honey 'n Oats Bread

*T*he egg and oats lend a wonderful, rich, creamy flavor to this bread. Serve it with a crock of sweet butter and homemade preserves.

	SMALL RECIPE	MEDIUM RECIPE	LARGE RECIPE
OLD-FASHIONED ROLLED OATS	⅓ cup	½ cup	⅔ cup
BUTTERMILK	¾ to ⅞ cup	1 to 1⅛ cups	1⅜ to 1½ cups
EGG	1	1	2
HONEY	1 tablespoon	1½ tablespoons	2 tablespoons
SALT	1 teaspoon	1½ teaspoons	2 teaspoons
WHOLE WHEAT FLOUR	1 cup	1½ cups	2 cups
BREAD FLOUR	1 cup	1½ cups	2 cups
RED STAR BRAND ACTIVE DRY YEAST	1½ teaspoons	2 teaspoons	2 teaspoons

I. Place all ingredients in bread pan, using the least amount of liquid listed in the recipe. Select Medium Crust setting then the Whole Wheat cycle and press Start.

2. Observe the dough as it kneads. After 5 to 10 minutes, if it appears dry and stiff, or if your machine sounds as if it's straining to knead it, add more liquid 1 tablespoon at a time until dough forms a smooth, soft, pliable ball that is slightly tacky to the touch.

3. After the baking cycle ends, remove bread from pan, place on cake rack, and allow to cool 1 hour before slicing.

CRUST: Medium
BAKE CYCLE: Whole Wheat
OPTIONAL BAKE CYCLES: Standard; Sweet Bread; Rapid Bake

NUTRITIONAL INFORMATION PER SLICE
Calories 124 / Fat 1.1 grams / Carbohydrates 24.2 grams / Protein 4.8 grams / Fiber 2.4 grams / Sodium 252 milligrams / Cholesterol 15.9 milligrams

---

Sweet Oatmeal Bread

*W*hat a nicely shaped loaf this is! To enjoy this lush, fat-free bread at its best, cut a thick slice and toast it.

	SMALL RECIPE	MEDIUM RECIPE	LARGE RECIPE
OLD-FASHIONED ROLLED OATS	½ cup	¾ cup	1 cup
WATER	¾ to ⅞ cup	1¼ to 1⅜ cups	1⅝ to 1¾ cups
MOLASSES	2 tablespoons	3 tablespoons	¼ cup
SUGAR	1 tablespoon	1½ tablespoons	2 tablespoons
SALT	1 teaspoon	1½ teaspoons	2 teaspoons
BREAD FLOUR	2 cups	3 cups	4 cups
RED STAR BRAND ACTIVE DRY YEAST	1½ teaspoons	1½ teaspoons	2 teaspoons

1. Place all ingredients in bread pan, using the least amount of liquid listed in the recipe. Select Light Crust setting and press Start.

2. Observe the dough as it kneads. After 5 to 10 minutes, if it appears dry and stiff, or if your machine sounds as if it's straining to knead it, add more liquid 1 tablespoon at a time until dough forms a smooth, soft, pliable ball that is slightly tacky to the touch.

3. After the baking cycle ends, remove bread from pan, place on cake rack, and allow to cool 1 hour before slicing.

CRUST: Light
BAKE CYCLE: Standard
OPTIONAL BAKE CYCLES: Whole Wheat; Sweet Bread; Delayed Timer; Rapid Bake

---

NUTRITIONAL INFORMATION PER SLICE
Calories 129 / Fat .5 grams / Carbohydrates 27 grams / Protein 3.6 grams / Fiber 1.3 grams / Sodium 230 milligrams / Cholesterol 0 milligrams

---

Dennis's Blarney-Stone Bread

A husband pleaser, and a loaf to make any Irishman proud, this oat bread gives off a lovely aroma when you cut into it. It has a creamy white interior and a chewy texture.

	SMALL RECIPE	MEDIUM RECIPE	LARGE RECIPE
OLD-FASHIONED ROLLED OATS	½ cup	1 cup	1 cup
MILK	⅝ to ¾ cup	1¼ to 1⅜ cups	1¼ to 1⅜ cups
EGG	1	1	2
BUTTER OR MARGARINE	1 tablespoon	1½ tablespoons	2 tablespoons
HONEY	2 tablespoons	3 tablespoons	¼ cup
SALT	1 teaspoon	1½ teaspoons	2 teaspoons
BREAD FLOUR	2 cups	3 cups	4 cups
RED STAR BRAND ACTIVE DRY YEAST	1½ teaspoons	1½ teaspoons	2 teaspoons

1. Place all ingredients in bread pan, using the least amount of liquid listed in the recipe. Select Medium Crust setting and press Start.

2. Observe the dough as it kneads. After 5 to 10 minutes, if it appears dry and stiff, or if your machine sounds as if it's straining to knead it, add more liquid 1 tablespoon at a time until dough forms a smooth, soft, pliable ball that is slightly tacky to the touch.

3. After the baking cycle ends, remove bread from pan, place on cake rack, and allow to cool 1 hour before slicing.

CRUST: Medium
BAKE CYCLE: Standard
OPTIONAL BAKE CYCLES: Sweet Bread; Rapid Bake

NUTRITIONAL INFORMATION PER SLICE
Calories 148 / Fat 1.9 grams / Carbohydrates 28.1 grams / Protein 4.3 grams / Fiber 1.4 grams / Sodium 249 milligrams / Cholesterol 15.2 milligrams

---

Olde English Barley Bread

*T*he barley flour in this bread imparts a mild, sweet, nutty flavor. It's good toasted or used for sandwiches.

	SMALL RECIPE	MEDIUM RECIPE	LARGE RECIPE
WATER	⅜ to ½ cup	½ to ⅝ cup	⅝ to ¾ cup
MILK	¼ cup	½ cup	½ cup
EGG	1	1	2
OIL	1 tablespoon	1½ tablespoons	2 tablespoons
HONEY	1 tablespoon	1½ tablespoons	2 tablespoons
SALT	1 teaspoon	1½ teaspoons	2 teaspoons
BREAD FLOUR	2 cups	3 cups	4 cups
BARLEY FLOUR	⅓ cup	½ cup	⅔ cup
RED STAR BRAND ACTIVE DRY YEAST	2 teaspoons	2 teaspoons	2 teaspoons

1. Place all ingredients in bread pan, using the least amount of liquid listed in the recipe. Select Medium Crust setting and press Start.

2. Observe the dough as it kneads. After 5 to 10 minutes, if it appears dry and stiff, or if your machine sounds as if it's straining to knead it, add more liquid 1 tablespoon at a time until dough forms a smooth, soft, pliable ball that is slightly tacky to the touch.

3. After the baking cycle ends, remove bread from pan, place on cake rack, and allow to cool 1 hour before slicing.

CRUST: Medium

BAKE CYCLE: Standard

OPTIONAL BAKE CYCLES: Whole Wheat; Rapid Bake

NUTRITIONAL INFORMATION PER SLICE
Calories 142 / Fat 2.3 grams / Carbohydrates 26 grams / Protein 4.2 grams / Fiber 1.4 grams / Sodium 238 milligrams / Cholesterol 15.6 milligrams

---

Wheat and Barley Bread

Here's a bread that will appeal to health-minded bread lovers. It has a full-bodied flavor that harmonizes well with any sandwich filling.

	SMALL RECIPE	MEDIUM RECIPE	LARGE RECIPE
WATER	⅞ to 1 cup	1⅛ to 1¼ cups	1¾ to 1⅞ cups
BUTTER OR MARGARINE	1 tablespoon	1½ tablespoons	2 tablespoons
MOLASSES	1 tablespoon	1½ tablespoons	2 tablespoons
SALT	1 teaspoon	1½ teaspoons	2 teaspoons
BREAD FLOUR	1 cup	1½ cups	2 cups
WHOLE WHEAT FLOUR	1 cup	1½ cups	2 cups
BARLEY FLOUR	⅓ cup	½ cup	⅔ cup
NONFAT DRY MILK POWDER	1 tablespoon	1½ tablespoons	2 tablespoons
VITAL WHEAT GLUTEN (OPTIONAL)	1½ tablespoons	2 tablespoons	3 tablespoons
RED STAR BRAND ACTIVE DRY YEAST	2 teaspoons	2 teaspoons	2½ teaspoons

1. Place all ingredients in bread pan, using the least amount of liquid listed in the recipe. Select Medium Crust setting then the Whole Wheat cycle and press Start.

2. Observe the dough as it kneads. After 5 to 10 minutes, if it appears dry and stiff, or if your machine sounds as if it's straining to knead it, add more liquid 1 tablespoon at a time until dough forms a smooth, soft, pliable ball that is slightly tacky to the touch.

3. After the baking cycle ends, remove bread from pan, place on cake rack, and allow to cool 1 hour before slicing.

CRUST: Medium
BAKE CYCLE: Whole Wheat
OPTIONAL BAKE CYCLES: Standard; Delayed Timer

NUTRITIONAL INFORMATION PER SLICE
Calories 122 / Fat 1.4 grams / Carbohydrates 24.1 grams / Protein 4 grams / Fiber 2.6 grams / Sodium 248 milligrams / Cholesterol .1 milligram

---

Buckwheat Bread

T his bread should satisfy any buckwheat lover in the household. It has a mild buckwheat flavor, making it a good choice for a breakfast bread.

	SMALL RECIPE	MEDIUM RECIPE	LARGE RECIPE
INSTANT POTATO FLAKES	3 tablespoons	¼ cup	6 tablespoons
MILK	½ cup	⅝ cup	⅞ cup
WATER	⅜ to ½ cup	⅝ to ¾ cup	⅞ to 1 cup
BUTTER OR MARGARINE	1 tablespoon	1½ tablespoons	2 tablespoons
DARK CORN SYRUP	1 tablespoon	2 tablespoons	2 tablespoons
SALT	1 teaspoon	1½ teaspoons	2 teaspoons
BREAD FLOUR	1½ cups	2 cups	3 cups
WHOLE WHEAT FLOUR	½ cup	1 cup	1 cup
BUCKWHEAT FLOUR	¼ cup	⅓ cup	½ cup
VITAL WHEAT GLUTEN (OPTIONAL)	1½ tablespoons	2 tablespoons	3 tablespoons
RED STAR BRAND ACTIVE DRY YEAST	2 teaspoons	2 teaspoons	2½ teaspoons

1. Place all ingredients in bread pan, using the least amount of liquid listed in the recipe. Select Medium Crust setting then the Whole Wheat cycle and press Start.

2. Observe the dough as it kneads. After 5 to 10 minutes, if it appears dry and stiff, or if your machine sounds as if it's straining to knead it, add more liquid 1 tablespoon at a time until dough forms a smooth, soft, pliable ball that is slightly tacky to the touch.

3. After the baking cycle ends, remove bread from pan, place on cake rack, and allow to cool 1 hour before slicing.

CRUST: Medium
BAKE CYCLE: Whole Wheat
OPTIONAL BAKE CYCLES: Standard; Sweet Bread

NUTRITIONAL INFORMATION PER SLICE
Calories 126 / Fat 1.4 grams / Carbohydrates 24.7 grams / Protein 3.8 grams / Fiber 1.9 grams / Sodium 253 milligrams / Cholesterol .5 milligram

Shayna's Millet Bread

*L*inda's daughter requests this bread whenever she comes home from college. She's a vegetarian and this bread satisfies her need for nutrition and a hearty taste.

	SMALL RECIPE	MEDIUM RECIPE	LARGE RECIPE
BUTTERMILK	¾ cup	1⅛ cups	1½ cups
WATER	¼ to ⅜ cup	⅜ to ½ cup	½ to ⅝ cup
OIL	1 tablespoon	1½ tablespoons	2 tablespoons
HONEY	1 tablespoon	1½ tablespoons	2 tablespoons
SALT	1 teaspoon	1 teaspoon	1½ teaspoons
WHOLE WHEAT FLOUR	1⅓ cups	2 cups	2⅔ cups
BREAD FLOUR	⅔ cup	1 cup	1⅓ cups
MILLET FLOUR	½ cup	¾ cup	1 cup
VITAL WHEAT GLUTEN (OPTIONAL)	1½ tablespoon	2 tablespoons	3 tablespoons
RED STAR BRAND ACTIVE DRY YEAST	2 teaspoons	2 teaspoons	2½ teaspoons

1. Place all ingredients in bread pan, using the least amount of liquid listed in the recipe. Select Medium Crust setting then the Whole Wheat cycle and press Start.

2. Observe the dough as it kneads. After 5 to 10 minutes, if it appears dry and stiff, or if your machine sounds as if it's straining to knead it, add more liquid 1 tablespoon at a time until dough forms a smooth, soft, pliable ball that is slightly tacky to the touch.

3. After the baking cycle ends, remove bread from pan, place on cake rack, and allow to cool 1 hour before slicing.

CRUST: Medium
BAKE CYCLE: Whole Wheat
OPTIONAL BAKE CYCLES: Standard; Delayed Timer

NUTRITIONAL INFORMATION PER SLICE
Calories 138 / Fat 2.1 grams / Carbohydrates 26.3 grams / Protein 4.4 grams / Fiber 2.8 grams / Sodium 174 milligrams / Cholesterol .7 milligram

---

Cheri's Orange Millet Bread

*C*heri was our chief bread baker and friend in need during the writing of the first edition of this book. She baked and tested most of the featured breads. Of them all, this bread was her favorite. It's a wholesome loaf bursting with different flavors and textures.

	SMALL RECIPE	MEDIUM RECIPE	LARGE RECIPE
WATER	⅜ to ½ cup	⅝ to ¾ cup	⅞ to 1 cup
ORANGE JUICE	⅜ cup	½ cup	¾ cup
BUTTER OR MARGARINE	1 tablespoon	1½ tablespoons	2 tablespoons
HONEY	1 tablespoon	1½ tablespoons	3 tablespoons
SALT	1 teaspoon	1½ teaspoons	2 teaspoons
BREAD FLOUR	1 cup	2 cups	2½ cups
WHOLE WHEAT FLOUR	1 cup	1 cup	1½ cups
WHOLE MILLET	2 tablespoons	3 tablespoons	¼ cup
RAW UNSALTED SUNFLOWER SEEDS	2 tablespoons	3 tablespoons	¼ cup
RAISINS	2 tablespoons	3 tablespoons	¼ cup
GRATED ORANGE RIND	2 teaspoons	1 tablespoon	4 teaspoons
VITAL WHEAT GLUTEN (OPTIONAL)	1 tablespoon	2 tablespoons	3 tablespoons
RED STAR BRAND ACTIVE DRY YEAST	1½ teaspoons	3 teaspoons	3 teaspoons

1. Place all ingredients in bread pan, using the least amount of liquid listed in the recipe. Select Medium Crust setting then the Whole Wheat cycle and press Start.

2. Observe the dough as it kneads. After 5 to 10 minutes, if it appears dry and stiff, or if your machine sounds as if it's straining to knead it, add more liquid 1 tablespoon at a time until dough forms a smooth, soft, pliable ball that is slightly tacky to the touch.

3. After the baking cycle ends, remove bread from pan, place on cake rack, and allow to cool 1 hour before slicing.

CRUST: Medium
BAKE CYCLE: Whole Wheat
OPTIONAL BAKE CYCLES: Standard; Raisin/Nut; Delayed Timer

NUTRITIONAL INFORMATION PER SLICE
Calories 137 / Fat 2.3 grams / Carbohydrates 25.7 grams / Protein 4 grams / Fiber 2.1 grams / Sodium 245 milligrams / Cholesterol 0 milligrams

Sunny California Bread

Y̴ou can almost taste the sunshine in this delightful whole wheat bread. This tall loaf is great for snacking or toasted for breakfast.

	SMALL RECIPE	MEDIUM RECIPE	LARGE RECIPE
ORANGE JUICE	⅜ to ½ cup	½ to ⅝ cup	¾ to ⅞ cup
MILK	¼ cup	⅜ cup	½ cup
EGG	1	1	2
BUTTER OR MARGARINE	1½ tablespoons	2 tablespoons	3 tablespoons
SUGAR	2 tablespoons	3 tablespoons	¼ cup
SALT	1 teaspoon	1 teaspoon	2 teaspoons
BREAD FLOUR	1⅓ cups	2 cups	2⅔ cups
WHOLE WHEAT FLOUR	⅔ cup	1 cup	1⅓ cups
VITAL WHEAT GLUTEN (OPTIONAL)	1 tablespoon	1½ tablespoons	2 tablespoons
GRATED ORANGE RIND	2 teaspoons	1 tablespoon	4 teaspoons
RAW UNSALTED SUNFLOWER SEEDS	⅓ cup	½ cup	⅔ cup
RED STAR BRAND ACTIVE DRY YEAST	2 teaspoons	2 teaspoons	2½ teaspoons

1. Place all ingredients in bread pan, using the least amount of liquid listed in the recipe. Select Medium Crust setting and press Start.

2. Observe the dough as it kneads. After 5 to 10 minutes, if it appears dry and stiff, or if your machine sounds as if it's straining to knead it, add more liquid 1 tablespoon at a time until dough forms a smooth, soft, pliable ball that is slightly tacky to the touch.

3. After the baking cycle ends, remove bread from pan, place on cake rack, and allow to cool 1 hour before slicing.

CRUST: Medium
BAKE CYCLE: Standard
OPTIONAL BAKE CYCLES: Whole Wheat; Sweet Bread; Raisin/Nut

NUTRITIONAL INFORMATION PER SLICE
Calories 158 / Fat 4.6 grams / Carbohydrates 25 grams / Protein 5 grams / Fiber 2.1 grams / Sodium 181 milligrams / Cholesterol 15.5 milligrams

Sunflower Bread

H*ere's another whole-grain bread with a distinctive, nutty flavor and texture. It's delicious on the dinner table as well as in the lunch box.*

	SMALL RECIPE	MEDIUM RECIPE	LARGE RECIPE
OLD-FASHIONED ROLLED OATS	⅓ cup	½ cup	⅔ cup
BUTTERMILK	⅜ cup	½ cup	¾ cup
WATER	¼ to ⅜ cup	½ to ⅝ cup	½ to ⅝ cup
EGG	1	1	2
BUTTER OR MARGARINE	1 tablespoon	1½ tablespoons	2 tablespoons
HONEY	1 tablespoon	2 tablespoons	2 tablespoons
MOLASSES	2 teaspoons	1 tablespoon	4 teaspoons
SALT	1 teaspoon	1½ teaspoons	2 teaspoons
BREAD FLOUR	1⅔ cups	2½ cups	3⅓ cups
WHOLE WHEAT FLOUR	⅓ cup	½ cup	⅔ cup
RAW UNSALTED SUNFLOWER SEEDS	¼ cup	⅓ cup	½ cup
RED STAR BRAND ACTIVE DRY YEAST	1½ teaspoons	2 teaspoons	2 teaspoons

1. Place all ingredients in bread pan, using the least amount of liquid listed in the recipe. Select Medium Crust setting and press Start.

2. Observe the dough as it kneads. After 5 to 10 minutes, if it appears dry and stiff, or if your machine sounds as if it's straining to knead it, add more liquid 1 tablespoon at a time until dough forms a smooth, soft, pliable ball that is slightly tacky to the touch.

3. After the baking cycle ends, remove bread from pan, place on cake rack, and allow to cool 1 hour before slicing.

CRUST: Medium
BAKE CYCLE: Standard
OPTIONAL BAKE CYCLES: Whole Wheat; Sweet Bread; Raisin/Nut

NUTRITIONAL INFORMATION PER SLICE
Calories 155 / Fat 3.4 grams / Carbohydrates 26.4 grams / Protein 4.9 grams / Fiber 1.8 grams / Sodium 258 milligrams / Cholesterol 15.5 milligrams

Vegetable
Breads

Carrot-Herb Bread

*G*et your vitamin A with this beautifully shaped loaf that has a mild carrot flavor. You can vary the amounts of herbs in this bread to suit your own taste. We like the dill so we always add a dash more. This is a superb sandwich bread. (Note: In the large recipe, ⅔ cup water worked fine in all the machines we tested. But if your carrots aren't very moist, you can always add 1 or 2 more tablespoons water, if needed.)

	SMALL RECIPE	MEDIUM RECIPE	LARGE RECIPE
WATER	⅓ to ½ cup	½ to ⅝ cup	⅔ cup
MILK	⅓ cup	⅜ cup	⅔ cup
BUTTER OR MARGARINE	1½ tablespoons	2 tablespoons	3 tablespoons
HONEY	1 tablespoon	1½ tablespoons	2 tablespoons
SALT	1 teaspoon	1½ teaspoons	2 teaspoons
WHOLE WHEAT FLOUR	1⅓ cups	2 cups	2⅔ cups
BREAD FLOUR	⅔ cup	1 cup	1⅓ cups
FINELY GRATED CARROT	½ cup	⅔ cup	1 cup
DRIED DILL	½ teaspoon	¾ teaspoon	1 teaspoon
DRIED THYME	½ teaspoon	¾ teaspoon	1 teaspoon
DRIED PARSLEY	½ teaspoon	¾ teaspoon	1 teaspoon
VITAL WHEAT GLUTEN (OPTIONAL)	1 tablespoon	2 tablespoons	3 tablespoons
RED STAR BRAND ACTIVE DRY YEAST	1½ teaspoons	1½ teaspoons	2 teaspoons

1. Place all ingredients in bread pan, using the least amount of liquid listed in the recipe. Select Medium Crust setting then the Whole Wheat cycle and press Start.

2. Observe the dough as it kneads. After 5 to 10 minutes, if it appears dry and stiff, or if your machine sounds as if it's straining to knead it, add more liquid 1 tablespoon at a time until dough forms a smooth, soft, pliable ball that is slightly tacky to the touch.

3. After the baking cycle ends, remove bread from pan, place on cake rack, and allow to cool 1 hour before slicing.

CRUST: Medium

BAKE CYCLE: Whole Wheat

OPTIONAL BAKE CYCLES: Standard; Sweet Bread

NUTRITIONAL INFORMATION PER SLICE

Calories 114 / Fat 1.7 grams / Carbohydrates 22 grams / Protein 3.6 grams / Fiber 2.7 grams / Sodium 255 milligrams / Cholesterol .3 milligram

---

Crunchy Carrot Bread

*T*he kids will love this flavorful, crunchy whole wheat bread. Sliced, it's a great-looking loaf flecked with grated carrot and poppyseeds. The moisture content of carrots can vary, so keep an eye on the dough as it starts to mix. You may need to adjust the liquid or flour amounts if the dough appears too wet or dry.

	SMALL RECIPE	MEDIUM RECIPE	LARGE RECIPE
WATER	½ to ⅝ cup	⅞ to 1 cup	1 to 1⅛ cups
BUTTER OR MARGARINE	1½ tablespoons	2 tablespoons	3 tablespoons
HONEY	1 tablespoon	2 tablespoons	2 tablespoons
SALT	1 teaspoon	1½ teaspoons	2 teaspoons
WHOLE WHEAT FLOUR	1½ cups	2 cups	3 cups
BREAD FLOUR	½ cup	1 cup	1 cup
VITAL WHEAT GLUTEN (OPTIONAL)	1 tablespoon	2 tablespoons	3 tablespoons
FINELY GRATED CARROT	⅔ cup	1 cup	1⅓ cups
POPPYSEEDS	2 teaspoons	1 tablespoon	4 teaspoons
RED STAR BRAND ACTIVE DRY YEAST	2 teaspoons	2 teaspoons	2½ teaspoons

1.   Place all ingredients in bread pan, using the least amount of liquid listed in the recipe. Select Medium Crust setting then the Whole Wheat cycle and press Start.

2.   Observe the dough as it kneads. After 5 to 10 minutes, if it appears dry and stiff, or if your machine sounds as if it's straining to knead it, add more liquid 1 tablespoon at a time until dough forms a smooth, soft, pliable ball that is slightly tacky to the touch.

3.   After the baking cycle ends, remove bread from pan, place on cake rack, and allow to cool 1 hour before slicing.

CRUST: Medium
BAKE CYCLE: Whole Wheat
OPTIONAL BAKE CYCLES: Standard; Sweet Bread; Delayed Timer

NUTRITIONAL INFORMATION PER SLICE
Calories 119 / Fat 1.9 grams / Carbohydrates 22.7 grams / Protein 3.6 grams / Fiber 2.8 grams / Sodium 253 milligrams / Cholesterol 0 milligrams

Broccoli-Cheese Bread

*T*his bread will surprise your guests. What fun to have them guess what's in it! It not only tastes exotic but also has a tantalizing aroma as it bakes.

	SMALL RECIPE	MEDIUM RECIPE	LARGE RECIPE
10-OUNCE PACKAGE FROZEN BROCCOLI WITH CHEESE SAUCE	1	1	1
MILK	1 to 2 tablespoons	⅜ to ½ cup	⅜ to ½ cup
EGG	1	1	2
MINCED FRESH ONION	3 tablespoons	¼ cup	6 tablespoons
BUTTER OR MARGARINE	1 tablespoon	1½ tablespoons	2 tablespoons
SALT	1 teaspoon	1 teaspoon	1½ teaspoons
BREAD FLOUR	2 cups	3 cups	4 cups
RED STAR BRAND ACTIVE DRY YEAST	1½ teaspoons	1½ teaspoons	2 teaspoons

1. Place all ingredients in bread pan, using the least amount of liquid listed in the recipe. Select Medium Crust setting and press Start.

2. Observe the dough as it kneads. After 5 to 10 minutes, if it appears dry and stiff, or if your machine sounds as if it's straining to knead it, add more liquid 1 tablespoon at a time until dough forms a smooth, soft, pliable ball that is slightly tacky to the touch.

3. After the baking cycle ends, remove bread from pan, place on cake rack, and allow to cool 1 hour before slicing.

CRUST: Medium
BAKE CYCLE: Standard
OPTIONAL BAKE CYCLES: Whole Wheat

NUTRITIONAL INFORMATION PER SLICE
Calories 142 / Fat 3.2 grams / Carbohydrates 22.8 grams / Protein 4.2 grams / Fiber 1.2 grams / Sodium 276 milligrams / Cholesterol 16.1 milligrams

Tomato Bread

*T**here's** no mistaking this one: It's a bright pumpkin color with a very definite tomato flavor, and the aroma as it bakes is extraordinary! Leftovers make wonderful croutons.*

	SMALL RECIPE	MEDIUM RECIPE	LARGE RECIPE
MILK	¼ to ⅜ cup	⅝ to ¾ cup	¾ to ⅞ cup
TOMATO PASTE	6 tablespoons	one 6-ounce can	¾ cup
EGG	1	1	2
OLIVE OIL	2 teaspoons	1 tablespoon	4 teaspoons
SUGAR	2 teaspoons	1 tablespoon	2 tablespoons
SALT	½ teaspoon	½ teaspoon	1 teaspoon
BREAD FLOUR	2 cups	3¼ cups	4 cups
ITALIAN SEASONING	½ teaspoon	1 teaspoon	1½ teaspoons
DRIED MINCED ONION	1½ teaspoons	2 teaspoons	1 tablespoon
GARLIC POWDER	¼ teaspoon	¼ teaspoon	½ teaspoon
GRATED NUTMEG	¼ teaspoon	½ teaspoon	½ teaspoon
RED STAR BRAND ACTIVE DRY YEAST	1½ teaspoons	2 teaspoons	2½ teaspoons

1. Place all ingredients in bread pan, using the least amount of liquid listed in the recipe. Select Light Crust setting and press Start.

2. Observe the dough as it kneads. After 5 to 10 minutes, if it appears dry and stiff, or if your machine sounds as if it's straining to knead it, add more liquid 1 tablespoon at a time until dough forms a smooth, soft, pliable ball that is slightly tacky to the touch.

3. After the baking cycle ends, remove bread from pan, place on cake rack, and allow to cool 1 hour before slicing.

CRUST: Light
BAKE CYCLE: Standard
OPTIONAL BAKE CYCLES: Rapid Bake

NUTRITIONAL INFORMATION PER SLICE
Calories 140 / Fat 1.9 grams / Carbohydrates 26.2 grams / Protein 4.4 grams / Fiber 1.4 grams / Sodium 183 milligrams / Cholesterol 15.7 milligrams

---

Elliot and Sara's Red Pepper Bread

*T*his is probably the best of the vegetable breads. For gourmet cooks like Lois's son Elliot and his wife, this bread is good enough to serve to friends as an appetizer. Turn any leftovers into croutons to top a special soup or salad. (Note: Give this bread several extra minutes to knead before you check the texture of the dough and decide to add more liquid. It takes a while for the red peppers to give up their moisture.)

	SMALL RECIPE	MEDIUM RECIPE	LARGE RECIPE
WATER	½ to ⅝ cup	½ to ⅝ cup	⅞ to 1 cup
TOMATO JUICE	3 tablespoons	¼ cup	5 tablespoons
BUTTER OR MARGARINE	1 tablespoon	1½ tablespoons	2 tablespoons
MOLASSES	1 tablespoon	2 tablespoons	2 tablespoons
SALT	1 teaspoon	1½ teaspoons	2 teaspoons
BREAD FLOUR	1⅔ cups	2½ cups	3⅓ cups
WHOLE WHEAT FLOUR	⅓ cup	½ cup	⅔ cup
VITAL WHEAT GLUTEN (OPTIONAL)	1 tablespoon	1½ tablespoons	2 tablespoons
MINCED RED BELL PEPPER	⅓ cup	½ cup	⅔ cup
DRIED TARRAGON	1 teaspoon	1½ teaspoons	2 teaspoons
RED STAR BRAND ACTIVE DRY YEAST	1½ teaspoons	1½ teaspoons	2 teaspoons

1.   Place all ingredients in bread pan, using the least amount of liquid listed in the recipe. Select Medium Crust setting and press Start.

2.   Observe the dough as it kneads. After 10 minutes, if it appears dry and stiff, or if your machine sounds as if it's straining to knead it, add more liquid 1 tablespoon at a time until dough forms a smooth, soft, pliable ball that is slightly tacky to the touch.

3.   After the baking cycle ends, remove bread from pan, place on cake rack, and allow to cool 1 hour before slicing.

CRUST: Medium

BAKE CYCLE: Standard

OPTIONAL BAKE CYCLES: Whole Wheat; Delayed Timer

NUTRITIONAL INFORMATION PER SLICE
Calories 113 / Fat 1.25 grams / Carbohydrates 22.2 grams / Protein 3.1 grams / Fiber 1.33 grams / Sodium 261 milligrams / Cholesterol 0 milligrams

---

Onion Soup Bread

*T*his bread smells so terrific while baking that it's hard to let it cool before slicing into it! A glorious onion flavor makes it an excellent addition to your next barbecue meal.

	SMALL RECIPE	MEDIUM RECIPE	LARGE RECIPE
MILK	⅛ cup	¼ cup	¼ cup
WATER	⅛ to ¼ cup	¼ to ⅜ cup	¼ to ⅜ cup
EGG	1	1	2
SOUR CREAM	⅓ cup	½ cup	⅔ cup
BUTTER OR MARGARINE	2 teaspoons	1 tablespoon	4 teaspoons
SUGAR	2 teaspoons	1 tablespoon	4 teaspoons
BREAD FLOUR	2 cups	3 cups	4 cups
DRY ONION SOUP MIX	2 tablespoons	2½ tablespoons	4 tablespoons
RED STAR BRAND ACTIVE DRY YEAST	1½ teaspoons	1½ teaspoons	2 teaspoons

1. Place all ingredients in bread pan, using the least amount of liquid listed in the recipe. Select Medium Crust setting and press Start.

2. Observe the dough as it kneads. After 5 to 10 minutes, if it appears dry and stiff, or if your machine sounds as if it's straining to knead it, add more liquid 1 tablespoon at a time until dough forms a smooth, soft, pliable ball that is slightly tacky to the touch.

3. After the baking cycle ends, remove bread from pan, place on cake rack, and allow to cool 1 hour before slicing.

CRUST: Medium
BAKE CYCLE: Standard
OPTIONAL BAKE CYCLES: Rapid Bake

NUTRITIONAL INFORMATION PER SLICE
Calories 135 / Fat 3.1 grams / Carbohydrates 22.6 grams / Protein 3.9 grams / Fiber .8 gram / Sodium 130 milligrams / Cholesterol 19.1 milligrams

Jalapeño-Cheese Bread

*W*ow—*hot stuff! Serve this coarsely textured, very spicy bread at your next cocktail party and watch it disappear. It's great with a glass of wine or a cold beer, but its perfect partner is a frosty margarita!*

	SMALL RECIPE	MEDIUM RECIPE	LARGE RECIPE
SOUR CREAM	½ cup	¾ cup	¾ cup
WATER	⅛ to ¼ cup	⅛ to ¼ cup	⅝ to ¾ cup
EGG	1	1	2
SALT	1 teaspoon	1½ teaspoons	2 teaspoons
SUGAR	1½ tablespoons	2 tablespoons	3 tablespoons
BREAD FLOUR	2 cups	3 cups	4 cups
GRATED SHARP CHEDDAR CHEESE	¾ cup (3 ounces)	1 cup (4 ounces)	1 cup (4 ounces)
SEEDED AND CHOPPED, FRESH or CANNED JALAPEÑO PEPPERS	2 tablespoons (about 3 peppers)	3 tablespoons (about 4 peppers)	¼ cup (5 to 6 peppers)
RED STAR BRAND ACTIVE DRY YEAST	1½ teaspoons	2 teaspoons	2½ teaspoons

1. Place all ingredients in bread pan, using the least amount of liquid listed in the recipe. Select Light Crust setting and press Start.

2. Observe the dough as it kneads. After 5 to 10 minutes, if it appears dry and stiff, or if your machine sounds as if it's straining to knead it, add more liquid 1 tablespoon at a time until dough forms a smooth, soft, pliable ball that is slightly tacky to the touch.

3. After the baking cycle ends, remove bread from pan, place on cake rack, and allow to cool 1 hour before slicing.

CRUST: Light
BAKE CYCLE: Standard
OPTIONAL BAKE CYCLES: Whole Wheat; Sweet Bread; Raisin/Nut

NUTRITIONAL INFORMATION PER SLICE
Calories 169 / Fat 5.9 grams / Carbohydrates 23 grams / Protein 5.7 grams / Fiber .9 grams / Sodium 305 milligrams / Cholesterol 29.2 milligrams

Autumn Harvest Bread

*W*elcome in the fall season with this delightful bread—a perfect combination of autumn's colorful fruits and vegetables. This tender, slightly tangy bread is delectable served with an orange butter.

	SMALL RECIPE	MEDIUM RECIPE	LARGE RECIPE
DICED CARROTS, COOKED AND PUREED	⅓ cup	½ cup	⅔ cup
CANNED PUMPKIN OR DICED BANANA SQUASH, COOKED AND PUREED	⅓ cup	½ cup	⅔ cup
UNSWEETENED APPLESAUCE	⅓ cup	½ cup	⅔ cup
CARROT WATER*	None	¼ to ⅜ cup	6 to 7 tablespoons
BUTTER OR MARGARINE	1 tablespoon	1½ tablespoons	2 tablespoons
HONEY	1 tablespoon	2 tablespoons	2 tablespoons
SALT	1 teaspoon	1½ teaspoons	2 teaspoons
WHOLE WHEAT FLOUR	1 cup	1½ cups	2 cups
BREAD FLOUR	1 cup	1½ cups	2 cups
GROUND ALLSPICE	¼ teaspoon	¼ teaspoon	½ teaspoon
RED STAR BRAND ACTIVE DRY YEAST	2 teaspoons	2 teaspoons	2½ teaspoons

1.   Place all ingredients in bread pan, using the least amount of liquid listed in the recipe. Select Medium Crust setting then the Whole Wheat cycle and press Start.

2.   Observe the dough as it kneads. After 5 to 10 minutes, if it appears dry and stiff, or if your machine sounds as if it's straining to knead it, add more liquid 1 tablespoon at a time until dough forms a smooth, soft, pliable ball that is slightly tacky to the touch.

*The water in which you cooked the carrots

3. After the baking cycle ends, remove bread from pan, place on cake rack, and allow to cool 1 hour before slicing.

CRUST: Medium

BAKE CYCLE: Whole Wheat

OPTIONAL BAKE CYCLES: Standard; Sweet Bread; Delayed Timer

NUTRITIONAL INFORMATION PER SLICE

Calories 120 / Fat 1.3 grams / Carbohydrates 24.4 grams / Protein 3.5 grams / Fiber 2.6 grams / Sodium 249 milligrams / Cholesterol 0 milligrams

---

I Yam What I Yam Bread

*F*riends will ask, "What's in this bread?" It has a lovely golden color and a sweet, elusive taste. It would be an elegant addition to your Thanksgiving dinner, but don't wait until then to try it.

	SMALL RECIPE	MEDIUM RECIPE	LARGE RECIPE
MILK	⅜ to ½ cup	½ to ⅝ cup	¾ to ⅞ cup
EGG	1	1	2
DRAINED AND CHOPPED CANNED YAMS	¼ cup	½ cup	½ cup
BUTTER OR MARGARINE	1 tablespoon	1½ tablespoons	2 tablespoons
DARK BROWN SUGAR	1 tablespoon	2 tablespoons	2 tablespoons
SALT	1 teaspoon	1½ teaspoons	2 teaspoons
BREAD FLOUR	2 cups	3 cups	4 cups
MINI MARSHMALLOWS (OPTIONAL)	¼ cup	⅓ cup	½ cup
RED STAR BRAND ACTIVE DRY YEAST	1½ teaspoons	1½ teaspoons	2 teaspoons

1. Place all ingredients in bread pan, using the least amount of liquid listed in the recipe. Select Medium Crust setting and press Start.

2. Observe the dough as it kneads. After 5 to 10 minutes, if it appears dry and stiff, or if your machine sounds as if it's straining to knead it, add more liquid 1 tablespoon at a time until dough forms a smooth, soft, pliable ball that is slightly tacky to the touch.

3. After the baking cycle ends, remove bread from pan, place on cake rack, and allow to cool 1 hour before slicing.

CRUST: Medium
BAKE CYCLE: Standard
OPTIONAL BAKE CYCLES: Whole Wheat; Sweet Bread; Raisin/Nut

NUTRITIONAL INFORMATION PER SLICE
Calories 135 / Fat 1.7 grams / Carbohydrates 25.8 grams / Protein 3.7 grams / Fiber 1 gram / Sodium 256 milligrams / Cholesterol 15.6 milligrams

Zucchini-Carrot Bread

*T*he carrot, zucchini, and spices in this deceptive loaf of bread make it seem highly sweetened; it isn't. You can eat that second slice without guilt. (Note: You'll find that the amount of liquid you need depends greatly on the moisture level in your carrots and zucchini.)

	SMALL RECIPE	MEDIUM RECIPE	LARGE RECIPE
WATER	½ to ⅝ cup	¾ to ⅞ cup	1⅛ to 1¼ cups
GRATED ZUCCHINI	¼ cup	⅓ cup	½ cup
GRATED CARROT	¼ cup	⅓ cup	½ cup
BUTTER OR MARGARINE	1 tablespoon	1½ tablespoons	2 tablespoons
HONEY	1 tablespoon	1½ tablespoons	2 tablespoons
SALT	1 teaspoon	1½ teaspoons	2 teaspoons
BREAD FLOUR	2 cups	3 cups	4 cups
NONFAT DRY MILK POWDER	1 tablespoon	1½ tablespoons	2 tablespoons
GROUND CINNAMON	1 teaspoon	1½ teaspoons	2 teaspoons
GROUND CLOVES	½ teaspoon	¾ teaspoon	1 teaspoon
VITAL WHEAT GLUTEN (OPTIONAL)	1½ tablespoons	2 tablespoons	3 tablespoons
RED STAR BRAND ACTIVE DRY YEAST	1½ teaspoons	1½ teaspoons	2 teaspoons

1.   Place all ingredients in bread pan, using the least amount of liquid listed in the recipe. Select Medium Crust setting and press Start.

2.   Observe the dough as it kneads. After 5 to 10 minutes, if it appears dry and stiff, or if your machine sounds as if it's straining to knead it, add more liquid 1 tablespoon at a time until dough forms a smooth, soft, pliable ball that is slightly tacky to the touch.

3. After the baking cycle ends, remove bread from pan, place on cake rack, and allow to cool 1 hour before slicing.

CRUST: Medium

BAKE CYCLE: Standard

OPTIONAL BAKE CYCLES: Whole Wheat; Sweet Bread; Delayed Timer

---

NUTRITIONAL INFORMATION PER SLICE
Calories 117 / Fat 1.2 grams / Carbohydrates 23.1 grams / Protein 3.1 grams / Fiber 1 gram / Sodium 248 milligrams / Cholesterol .1 milligram

---

Zucchini Wheat Bread

*T*he zucchini adds moisture and a comforting flavor to this nutritious bread. (Note: Don't be too quick to add extra liquid… the zucchini take a while to give up their moisture.)

	SMALL RECIPE	MEDIUM RECIPE	LARGE RECIPE
MILK	3 to 5 tablespoons	¼ to ⅜ cup	⅜ to ½ cup
EGG	1	1	2
GRATED ZUCCHINI	1 cup	1½ cups	2 cups
BUTTER OR MARGARINE	1 tablespoon	1½ tablespoons	2 tablespoons
DARK BROWN SUGAR	1 tablespoon	1½ tablespoons	2 tablespoons
SALT	1 teaspoon	1½ teaspoons	2 teaspoons
BREAD FLOUR	1½ cups	2¼ cups	3 cups
WHOLE WHEAT FLOUR	½ cup	¾ cup	1 cup
WHEAT GERM	3 tablespoons	¼ cup	6 tablespoons
GROUND CORIANDER	1 teaspoon	1½ teaspoons	2 teaspoons
RED STAR BRAND ACTIVE DRY YEAST	1½ teaspoons	1½ teaspoons	2 teaspoons

1. Place all ingredients in bread pan, using the least amount of liquid listed in the recipe. Select Medium Crust setting and press Start.

2. Observe the dough as it kneads. After 10 minutes, if it appears dry and stiff, or if your machine sounds as if it's straining to knead it, add more liquid 1 tablespoon at a time until dough forms a smooth, soft, pliable ball that is slightly tacky to the touch.

3. After the baking cycle ends, remove bread from pan, place on cake rack, and allow to cool 1 hour before slicing.

CRUST: Medium
BAKE CYCLE: Standard
OPTIONAL BAKE CYCLES: Whole Wheat

NUTRITIONAL INFORMATION PER SLICE
Calories 127 / Fat 1.9 grams / Carbohydrates 23.1 grams / Protein 4.4 grams / Fiber 1.9 grams / Sodium 252 milligrams / Cholesterol 15.4 milligrams

---

Fruit
Breads

Aloha Bread

This is a delightful whole wheat bread with a surprising flavor of the tropics. It is wonderful in bread pudding or as French toast.

	SMALL RECIPE	MEDIUM RECIPE	LARGE RECIPE
BUTTERMILK	½ to ⅝ cup	¾ to ⅞ cup	¾ to ⅞ cup
8-OUNCE CAN CRUSHED PINEAPPLE, WELL DRAINED	1	1	2
BUTTER OR MARGARINE	1 tablespoon	1½ tablespoons	2 tablespoons
SUGAR	2 tablespoons	3 tablespoons	¼ cup
SALT	½ teaspoon	1 teaspoon	1 teaspoon
WHOLE WHEAT FLOUR	1⅓ cups	2 cups	2⅔ cups
BREAD FLOUR	⅔ cup	1 cup	1⅓ cups
FLAKED SWEETENED COCONUT	¼ cup	⅓ cup	½ cup
VITAL WHEAT GLUTEN (OPTIONAL)	1½ tablespoons	2 tablespoons	3 tablespoons
RED STAR BRAND ACTIVE DRY YEAST	1½ teaspoons	1½ teaspoons	2 teaspoons

1. Place all ingredients in bread pan, using the least amount of liquid listed in the recipe. Select Medium Crust setting then the Whole Wheat cycle and press Start.

2. Observe the dough as it kneads. After 5 to 10 minutes, if it appears dry and stiff, or if your machine sounds as if it's straining to knead it, add more liquid 1 tablespoon at a time until dough forms a smooth, soft, pliable ball that is slightly tacky to the touch.

3. After the baking cycle ends, remove bread from pan, place on cake rack, and allow to cool 1 hour before slicing.

CRUST: Medium
BAKE CYCLE: Whole Wheat
OPTIONAL BAKE CYCLES: Standard; Sweet Bread; Raisin/Nut

NUTRITIONAL INFORMATION PER SLICE
Calories 136 / Fat 2.5 grams / Carbohydrates 25.5 grams / Protein 4 grams / Fiber 2.9 grams / Sodium 183 milligrams / Cholesterol .5 milligram

Sunday Morning Apricot Bread

*T*his is a welcome addition to the breakfast table, but don't wait for Sunday morning; it's great every day. This bread is well received as a gift. Everyone seems to like the strong apricot flavor. (Hint: Use unsulphured apricots if you can find them.)

	SMALL RECIPE	MEDIUM RECIPE	LARGE RECIPE
OLD-FASHIONED ROLLED OATS	⅓ cup	½ cup	⅔ cup
BUTTERMILK	⅝ to ¾ cup	1 to 1⅛ cups	1¼ to 1⅜ cups
EGG	1	1	1
BUTTER OR MARGARINE	1½ tablespoons	2 tablespoons	3 tablespoons
APRICOT PRESERVES	3 tablespoons	¼ cup	6 tablespoons
SALT	1 teaspoon	1½ teaspoons	2 teaspoons
BREAD FLOUR	1⅓ cups	2 cups	2⅔ cups
WHOLE WHEAT FLOUR	⅔ cup	1 cup	1⅓ cups
VITAL WHEAT GLUTEN (OPTIONAL)	1 tablespoon	2 tablespoons	3 tablespoons
CHOPPED DRIED APRICOTS	⅓ cup	½ cup	⅔ cup
RED STAR BRAND ACTIVE DRY YEAST	1½ teaspoons	1½ teaspoons	2 teaspoons

1.   Place all ingredients in bread pan, using the least amount of liquid listed in the recipe. Select Medium Crust setting and press Start.

2.   Observe the dough as it kneads. After 5 to 10 minutes, if it appears dry and stiff, or if your machine sounds as if it's straining to knead it, add more liquid 1 table-spoon at a time until dough forms a smooth, soft, pliable ball that is slightly tacky to the touch.

3. After the baking cycle ends, remove bread from pan, place on cake rack, and allow to cool 1 hour before slicing.

CRUST: Medium

BAKE CYCLE: Standard

OPTIONAL BAKE CYCLES: Whole Wheat; Sweet Bread; Raisin/Nut

NUTRITIONAL INFORMATION PER SLICE
Calories 150 / Fat 2.3 grams / Carbohydrates 27.8 grams / Protein 4.8 grams / Fiber 2.2 grams / Sodium 197 milligrams / Cholesterol 15.9 milligrams

---

Crunchy-Munchy Bread

The peanut butter flavor in this bread is so yummy, there's no need to adorn it. It's perfect as an after-school snack. You can add the peanuts and apple when the Raisin/Nut cycle beeps, if you'd like. They'll hold up a little better.

	SMALL RECIPE	MEDIUM RECIPE	LARGE RECIPE
MILK	⅞ to 1 cup	1⅛ to 1¼ cups	1¾ to 1⅞ cups
CHUNKY PEANUT BUTTER	3 tablespoons	¼ cup	6 tablespoons
HONEY	1 tablespoon	2 tablespoons	2 tablespoons
SALT	½ teaspoon	1 teaspoon	1 teaspoon
WHOLE WHEAT FLOUR	1 cup	2 cups	2½ cups
BREAD FLOUR	1½ cups	1 cup	1½ cups
CORED, UNPEELED, CHOPPED GRANNY SMITH APPLE	½ cup	1 cup	1 cup
UNSALTED PEANUTS	2 tablespoons	¼ cup	¼ cup
RED STAR BRAND ACTIVE DRY YEAST	1½ teaspoons	2 teaspoons	2 teaspoons

1. Place all ingredients in bread pan, using the least amount of liquid listed in the recipe. Select Medium Crust setting then the Whole Wheat cycle and press Start.

2. Observe the dough as it kneads. After 5 to 10 minutes, if it appears dry and stiff, or if your machine sounds as if it's straining to knead it, add more liquid 1 tablespoon at a time until dough forms a smooth, soft, pliable ball that is slightly tacky to the touch.

3. After the baking cycle ends, remove bread from pan, place on cake rack, and allow to cool 1 hour before slicing.

CRUST: Medium
BAKE CYCLE: Whole Wheat
OPTIONAL BAKE CYCLES: Standard; Sweet Bread; Raisin/Nut

NUTRITIONAL INFORMATION PER SLICE
Calories 155 / Fat 4.2 grams / Carbohydrates 25.3 grams / Protein 5.9 grams / Fiber 3.2 grams / Sodium 186 milligrams / Cholesterol .8 milligram

Johnny Appleseed Bread

*T*his is a sweet, chewy bread with a strong, delicious taste of apples. Try it toasted some morning.

	SMALL RECIPE	MEDIUM RECIPE	LARGE RECIPE
APPLE JUICE	⅓ to ½ cup	½ to ⅝ cup	¾ to ⅞ cup
UNSWEETENED APPLESAUCE	⅓ cup	½ cup	⅔ cup
BUTTER OR MARGARINE	1 tablespoon	1½ tablespoons	2 tablespoons
DARK BROWN SUGAR	2 tablespoons	3 tablespoons	¼ cup
SALT	1 teaspoon	1½ teaspoons	2 teaspoons
BREAD FLOUR	2 cups	3 cups	4 cups
GROUND CINNAMON	½ teaspoon	½ teaspoon	1 teaspoon
GRATED NUTMEG	1 pinch	1 pinch	¼ teaspoon
CORED, PEELED, CHOPPED GRANNY SMITH APPLE	⅓ cup	½ cup	⅔ cup
RAISINS (OPTIONAL)	3 tablespoons	¼ cup	6 tablespoons
RED STAR BRAND ACTIVE DRY YEAST	1½ teaspoons	1½ teaspoons	2 teaspoons

1. Place all ingredients in bread pan, using the least amount of liquid listed in the recipe. Select Medium Crust setting and press Start.

2. Observe the dough as it kneads. After 5 to 10 minutes, if it appears dry and stiff, or if your machine sounds as if it's straining to knead it, add more liquid 1 tablespoon at a time until dough forms a smooth, soft, pliable ball that is slightly tacky to the touch.

3. After the baking cycle ends, remove bread from pan, place on cake rack, and allow to cool 1 hour before slicing.

CRUST: Medium
BAKE CYCLE: Standard
OPTIONAL BAKE CYCLES: Whole Wheat; Sweet Bread; Raisin/Nut; Delayed Timer

NUTRITIONAL INFORMATION PER SLICE
Calories 137 / Fat 1.24 grams / Carbohydrates 28.3 grams / Protein 3 grams / Fiber 1.2 grams / Sodium 246 milligrams / Cholesterol 0 milligrams

Banana Oatmeal Bread

Y*ou'll be proud of this bread because it's beautifully shaped and luscious tasting. Each slice is moist and bursting with banana flavor. (Note: Use very, very ripe bananas for the best results... you know, the ones that are about a day away from being tossed out.)*

	SMALL RECIPE	MEDIUM RECIPE	LARGE RECIPE
OLD-FASHIONED ROLLED OATS	½ cup	1 cup	1 cup
EGG	1	1	2
WATER	None	1 to 2 tablespoons	3 to 4 tablespoons
SOUR CREAM	3 tablespoons	¼ cup	½ cup
SLICED VERY RIPE BANANA	1 cup (about 1 large)	2 cups (about 3 medium)	2 cups (about 3 medium)
BUTTER OR MARGARINE	2 teaspoons	1 tablespoon	1 tablespoon
HONEY	1½ tablespoons	2 tablespoons	3 tablespoons
SALT	½ teaspoon	1 teaspoon	1 teaspoon
BREAD FLOUR	1⅓ cups	2 cups	3 cups
WHOLE WHEAT FLOUR	⅔ cup	1 cup	1 cup
GROUND CINNAMON	½ teaspoon	½ teaspoon	1 teaspoon
GRATED NUTMEG	¼ teaspoon	¼ teaspoon	½ teaspoon
NONFAT DRY MILK POWDER	2 teaspoons	1 tablespoon	4 teaspoons
RED STAR BRAND ACTIVE DRY YEAST	2 teaspoons	2 teaspoons	2½ teaspoons

1. Place all ingredients in bread pan, using the least amount of liquid listed in the recipe. Select Medium Crust setting and press Start.

2. Observe the dough as it kneads. After 5 to 10 minutes, if it appears dry and stiff, or if your machine sounds as if it's straining to knead it, add more liquid 1 tablespoon at a time until dough forms a smooth, soft, pliable ball that is slightly tacky to the touch.

3. After the baking cycle ends, remove bread from pan, place on cake rack, and allow to cool 1 hour before slicing.

CRUST: Medium
BAKE CYCLE: Standard
OPTIONAL BAKE CYCLES: Whole Wheat; Sweet Bread

NUTRITIONAL INFORMATION PER SLICE
Calories 167 / Fat 2.7 grams / Carbohydrates 31.7 grams / Protein 5 grams / Fiber 2.8 grams / Sodium 172 milligrams / Cholesterol 17.1 milligrams

---

Anne and Bill's Apple Oatmeal Bread
with Raisins

*O*atmeal and applesauce combine to make this a lush, rich-tasting loaf. It's a *good snack for children and great for breakfast toast.*

	SMALL RECIPE	MEDIUM RECIPE	LARGE RECIPE
OLD-FASHIONED ROLLED OATS	⅓ cup	½ cup	⅔ cup
WATER	½ to ⅝ cup	⅝ to ¾ cup	⅞ to 1 cup
UNSWEETENED APPLESAUCE	⅓ cup	½ cup	⅔ cup
SALT	1 teaspoon	1½ teaspoons	1½ teaspoons
BUTTER OR MARGARINE	1 tablespoon	1½ tablespoons	2 tablespoons
DARK BROWN SUGAR	1 tablespoon	2 tablespoons	2 tablespoons
BREAD FLOUR	1¾ cups	2¾ cups	3½ cups
NONFAT DRY MILK POWDER	1 tablespoon	1½ tablespoons	2 tablespoons
RAISINS	¼ cup	⅓ cup	½ cup
GROUND CINNAMON	1 teaspoon	1 teaspoon	2 teaspoons
RED STAR BRAND ACTIVE DRY YEAST	1½ teaspoons	2 teaspoons	2½ teaspoons

1.   Place all ingredients in bread pan, using the least amount of liquid listed in the recipe. Select Light Crust setting and press Start.

2.   Observe the dough as it kneads. After 5 to 10 minutes, if it appears dry and stiff, or if your machine sounds as if it's straining to knead it, add more liquid 1 tablespoon at a time until dough forms a smooth, soft, pliable ball that is slightly tacky to the touch.

3. After the baking cycle ends, remove bread from pan, place on cake rack, and allow to cool 1 hour before slicing.

CRUST: Light
BAKE CYCLE: Standard
OPTIONAL BAKE CYCLES: Whole Wheat; Sweet Bread; Raisin/Nut; Delayed Timer

NUTRITIONAL INFORMATION PER SLICE
Calories 114 / Fat .5 gram / Carbohydrates 23.8 grams / Protein 3.4 grams / Fiber 1.3 grams / Sodium 232 milligrams / Cholesterol .1 milligram

Granola Date Bread

We experimented with several different types of granola from our local health-food store. The plain granola made a very tasty loaf of bread but a raspberry apple granola turned this into an extraordinary breakfast bread!

	SMALL RECIPE	MEDIUM RECIPE	LARGE RECIPE
GRANOLA	⅓ cup	½ cup	⅔ cup
BUTTERMILK	½ cup	¾ cup	1 cup
WATER	⅜ to ½ cup	½ to ⅝ cup	¾ to ⅞ cup
BUTTER OR MARGARINE	1 tablespoon	1½ tablespoons	2 tablespoons
HONEY	1½ tablespoons	2 tablespoons	3 tablespoons
SALT	1 teaspoon	1½ teaspoons	2 teaspoons
BREAD FLOUR	1 cup	2 cups	2 cups
WHOLE WHEAT FLOUR	1 cup	1 cup	2 cups
CHOPPED DATES	¼ cup	⅓ cup	½ cup
RED STAR BRAND ACTIVE DRY YEAST	1½ teaspoons	2 teaspoons	2 teaspoons

1. Place all ingredients in bread pan, using the least amount of liquid listed in the recipe. Select Medium Crust setting and press Start.

2. Observe the dough as it kneads. After 5 to 10 minutes, if it appears dry and stiff or if your machine sounds as if it's straining to knead it, add more liquid 1 tablespoon at a time until dough forms a smooth, soft, pliable ball that is slightly tacky to the touch.

3. After the baking cycle ends, remove bread from pan, place on cake rack, and allow to cool 1 hour before slicing.

CRUST: Medium
BAKE CYCLE: Standard
OPTIONAL BAKE CYCLES: Whole Wheat; Sweet Bread; Raisin/Nut

NUTRITIONAL INFORMATION PER SLICE
Calories 146 / Fat 2.1 grams / Carbohydrates 28.5 grams / Protein 4.1 grams / Fiber 2.4 grams / Sodium 267 milligrams / Cholesterol .5 milligram

Mixed Fruit Bread

If your friends don't care for the traditional gift of holiday fruitcake, this bread is a nice alternative.

	SMALL RECIPE	MEDIUM RECIPE	LARGE RECIPE
100% BRAN CEREAL	⅓ cup	½ cup	⅔ cup
BUTTERMILK	⅝ to ¾ cup	1 to 1⅛ cups	1¼ to 1⅜ cups
EGG	1	1	2
BUTTER OR MARGARINE	1 tablespoon	1½ tablespoons	2 tablespoons
HONEY	1 tablespoon	2 tablespoons	2 tablespoons
SALT	½ teaspoon	1 teaspoon	1 teaspoon
BREAD FLOUR	2 cups	3 cups	4 cups
GROUND CINNAMON	¼ teaspoon	¼ teaspoon	½ teaspoon
MIXED DRIED FRUITS, FINELY CHOPPED	½ cup	⅔ cup	1 cup
RED STAR BRAND ACTIVE DRY YEAST	2 teaspoons	2 teaspoons	2½ teaspoons

1. Place all ingredients in bread pan, using the least amount of liquid listed in the recipe. Select Medium Crust setting and press Start.

2. Observe the dough as it kneads. After 5 to 10 minutes, if it appears dry and stiff, or if your machine sounds as if it's straining to knead it, add more liquid 1 tablespoon at a time until dough forms a smooth, soft, pliable ball that is slightly tacky to the touch.

3. After the baking cycle ends, remove bread from pan, place on cake rack, and allow to cool 1 hour before slicing.

CRUST: Medium
BAKE CYCLE: Standard
OPTIONAL BAKE CYCLES: Whole Wheat; Sweet Bread; Raisin/Nut

NUTRITIONAL INFORMATION PER SLICE
Calories 150 / Fat 1.9 grams / Carbohydrates 29.5 grams / Protein 4.4 grams / Fiber 1.8 grams / Sodium 208 milligrams / Cholesterol 15.9 milligrams

Orange Bread

After much trial and error, we finally came up with a winning orange bread. Try it with chicken salad or as a breakfast toast. (Note: When grating the orange peels, be sure to use the rind only and not the bitter white pith underneath.)

	SMALL RECIPE	MEDIUM RECIPE	LARGE RECIPE
PEELED AND CHOPPED NAVEL ORANGE	¾ cup	1 cup	1½ cups
ORANGE JUICE	1 to 2 tablespoons	3 to 4 tablespoons	4 to 6 tablespoons
EGG	1	1	1
BUTTER OR MARGARINE	1 tablespoon	1 tablespoon	2 tablespoons
ORANGE MARMALADE	3 tablespoons	¼ cup	6 tablespoons
SALT	1 teaspoon	1 teaspoon	2 teaspoons
BREAD FLOUR	2 cups	3 cups	4 cups
GRATED ORANGE RIND	2 tablespoons	3 tablespoons	¼ cup
SLIVERED ALMONDS	¼ cup	⅓ cup	½ cup
VITAL WHEAT GLUTEN (OPTIONAL)	1 tablespoon	1½ tablespoons	2 tablespoons
RED STAR BRAND ACTIVE DRY YEAST	2 teaspoons	2 teaspoons	2½ teaspoons

1. Place all ingredients in bread pan, using the least amount of liquid listed in the recipe. Select Medium Crust setting and press Start.

2. Observe the dough as it kneads. After 5 to 10 minutes, if it appears dry and stiff, or if your machine sounds as if it's straining to knead it, add more liquid 1 tablespoon at a time until dough forms a smooth, soft, pliable ball that is slightly tacky to the touch.

3. After the baking cycle ends, remove bread from pan, place on cake rack, and allow to cool 1 hour before slicing.

CRUST: Medium
BAKE CYCLE: Standard
OPTIONAL BAKE CYCLES: Sweet Bread; Raisin/Nut

> NUTRITIONAL INFORMATION PER SLICE
> Calories 151 / Fat 2.8 grams / Carbohydrates 27.5 grams / Protein 4.1 grams / Fiber 1.6 grams / Sodium 169 milligrams / Cholesterol 15.2 milligrams

Marmalade and Oats Bread

Here's another winner. It's a beautiful-looking loaf, and the combination of orange marmalade and oatmeal makes it very tender, moist, and rich tasting.

	SMALL RECIPE	MEDIUM RECIPE	LARGE RECIPE
OLD-FASHIONED ROLLED OATS	½ cup	⅔ cup	1 cup
MILK	⅞ to 1 cup	1⅛ to 1¼ cups	1⅜ to 1½ cups
ORANGE MARMALADE	⅓ cup	½ cup	⅔ cup
BUTTER OR MARGARINE	1 tablespoon	1½ tablespoons	2 tablespoons
SALT	1 teaspoon	1½ teaspoons	2 teaspoons
BREAD FLOUR	2 cups	3 cups	4 cups
RED STAR BRAND ACTIVE DRY YEAST	1½ teaspoons	2 teaspoons	2 teaspoons

1. Place all ingredients in bread pan, using the least amount of liquid listed in the recipe. Select Medium Crust setting and press Start.

2. Observe the dough as it kneads. After 5 to 10 minutes, if it appears dry and stiff, or if your machine sounds as if it's straining to knead it, add more liquid 1 tablespoon at a time until dough forms a smooth, soft, pliable ball that is slightly tacky to the touch.

3. After the baking cycle ends, remove bread from pan, place on cake rack, and allow to cool 1 hour before slicing.

CRUST: Medium
BAKE CYCLE: Standard
OPTIONAL BAKE CYCLES: Whole Wheat; Sweet Bread

NUTRITIONAL INFORMATION PER SLICE
Calories 162 / Fat 1.9 grams / Carbohydrates 31.9 grams / Protein 4.2 grams / Fiber 1.3 grams / Sodium 256 milligrams / Cholesterol .8 milligram

Eric and Janey's Poppyseed Peach Bread

*D*uring *their recent visit, Lois's son and daughter-in-law sampled this fruit bread fresh from the machine and loved it. But this bread has us baffled: It has a lovely peach flavor the first few days, but if kept longer than that in the freezer, the peach flavor disappears. So, eat it right away! You'll also find that the amount of liquid you need to use depends greatly on the juiciness of your peaches.*

	SMALL RECIPE	MEDIUM RECIPE	LARGE RECIPE
BUTTERMILK	3 to 4 tablespoons	¼ to ⅜ cup	5 to 7 tablespoons
PEELED, PITTED, CHOPPED PEACHES (FRESH, FROZEN, OR CANNED, WELL DRAINED)	1 cup	1½ cups	2 cups
BUTTER OR MARGARINE	1 tablespoon	1½ tablespoons	2 tablespoons
SUGAR	2 tablespoons	3 tablespoons	¼ cup
DARK BROWN SUGAR	2 tablespoons	3 tablespoons	¼ cup
SALT	1 teaspoon	1½ teaspoons	2 teaspoons
BREAD FLOUR	1½ cups	2¼ cups	3 cups
WHOLE WHEAT FLOUR	⅔ cup	1 cup	1⅓ cups
POPPYSEEDS	2 teaspoons	1 tablespoon	4 teaspoons
RED STAR BRAND ACTIVE DRY YEAST	1½ teaspoons	1½ teaspoons	2 teaspoons

I.   Place all ingredients in bread pan, using the least amount of liquid listed in the recipe. Select Medium Crust setting and press Start.

2.   Observe the dough as it kneads. After 5 to 10 minutes, if it appears dry and stiff, or if your machine sounds as if it's straining to knead it, add more liquid 1 tablespoon at a time until dough forms a smooth, soft, pliable ball that is slightly tacky to the touch.

3. After the baking cycle ends, remove bread from pan, place on cake rack, and allow to cool 1 hour before slicing.

CRUST: Medium

BAKE CYCLE: Standard

OPTIONAL BAKE CYCLES: Whole Wheat; Sweet Bread

NUTRITIONAL INFORMATION PER SLICE

Calories 145 / Fat 1.6 grams / Carbohydrates 29.5 grams / Protein 3.7 grams / Fiber 2.1 grams / Sodium 251 milligrams / Cholesterol .2 milligram

---

Peaches and Spice Bread

What a sensational taste this peach bread has! It's a tall and beautifully shaped gift bread. If you don't give it away, toast it or try it in a bread pudding.

	SMALL RECIPE	MEDIUM RECIPE	LARGE RECIPE
OLD-FASHIONED ROLLED OATS	½ cup	1 cup	1 cup
MILLER'S BRAN	3 tablespoons	¼ cup	6 tablespoons
APPLE JUICE	2 to 3 tablespoons	4 to 5 tablespoons	4 to 6 tablespoons
EGG	1	1	2
PEELED, PITTED, CHOPPED PEACHES (FRESH, FROZEN, OR CANNED, WELL DRAINED)	1 cup	1½ cups	2 cups
BUTTER OR MARGARINE	1 tablespoon	1½ tablespoons	2 tablespoons
HONEY	1 tablespoon	2 tablespoons	2 tablespoons
SALT	1 teaspoon	1½ teaspoons	2 teaspoons
WHOLE WHEAT FLOUR	1 cup	1½ cups	2 cups
BREAD FLOUR	1 cup	1½ cups	2 cups
GROUND CINNAMON	¾ teaspoon	1 teaspoon	1½ teaspoons
GROUND GINGER	¾ teaspoon	1 teaspoon	1½ teaspoons
GRATED NUTMEG	¾ teaspoon	1 teaspoon	1½ teaspoons
CHOPPED WALNUTS	¼ cup	⅓ cup	½ cup
RED STAR BRAND ACTIVE DRY YEAST	2 teaspoons	2 teaspoons	2½ teaspoons

1. Place all ingredients in bread pan, using the least amount of liquid listed in the recipe. Select Medium Crust setting then the Whole Wheat cycle and press Start.

2. Observe the dough as it kneads. After 5 to 10 minutes, if it appears dry and stiff, or if your machine sounds as if it's straining to knead it, add more liquid 1 tablespoon at a time until dough forms a smooth, soft, pliable ball that is slightly tacky to the touch.

3. After the baking cycle ends, remove bread from pan, place on cake rack, and allow to cool 1 hour before slicing.

CRUST: Medium
BAKE CYCLE: Whole Wheat
OPTIONAL BAKE CYCLES: Standard; Sweet Bread; Raisin/Nut

NUTRITIONAL INFORMATION PER SLICE
Calories 163 / Fat 3.4 grams / Carbohydrates 30 grams / Protein 4.9 grams / Fiber 3.5 grams / Sodium 246 milligrams / Cholesterol 0 milligrams

Sweet Leilani Bread

*T*his Hawaiian-style bread is a spectacular addition to any luncheon buffet. It's moist, light, and elegant. Don't let the long list of ingredients prevent you from trying this bread. It's definitely one of the best in the book. Keep an eye on it the first time you make it; it's a high riser in some machines.

	SMALL RECIPE	MEDIUM RECIPE	LARGE RECIPE
CANNED PINEAPPLE CHUNKS, CUT UP AND WELL DRAINED (RESERVE JUICE)	⅓ cup	½ cup	⅔ cup
BUTTERMILK	3 to 4 tablespoons	¼ to ⅜ cup	⅜ to ½ cup
RESERVED PINEAPPLE JUICE	2 tablespoons	¼ cup	¼ cup
EGG	1	1	2
SLICED VERY RIPE BANANA	⅓ cup	½ cup	⅔ cup
SALT	1 teaspoon	1 teaspoon	2 teaspoons
BUTTER OR MARGARINE	2 tablespoons	3 tablespoons	¼ cup
SUGAR	1 tablespoon	1½ tablespoons	2 tablespoons
BREAD FLOUR	2 cups	3 cups	4 cups
WHOLE WHEAT FLOUR	3 tablespoons	¼ cup	6 tablespoons
FLAKED SWEETENED COCONUT	⅓ cup	½ cup	⅔ cup
CHOPPED MACADAMIA NUTS	¼ cup	⅓ cup	½ cup
RED STAR BRAND ACTIVE DRY YEAST	1½ teaspoons	2 teaspoons	2½ teaspoons

1.   Place all ingredients in bread pan, using the least amount of liquid listed in the recipe. Select Light Crust setting and press Start.

2.   Observe the dough as it kneads. After 5 to 10 minutes, if it appears dry and stiff, or if your machine sounds as if it's straining to knead it, add more liquid 1 tablespoon at a time until dough forms a smooth, soft, pliable ball that is slightly tacky to the touch.

3. After the baking cycle ends, remove bread from pan, place on cake rack, and allow to cool 1 hour before slicing.

CRUST: Light

BAKE CYCLE: Standard

OPTIONAL BAKE CYCLES: Whole Wheat; Sweet Bread; Raisin/Nut

NUTRITIONAL INFORMATION PER SLICE
Calories 191 / Fat 6.8 grams / Carbohydrates 28.7 grams / Protein 4.2 grams / Fiber 1.8 grams / Sodium 215 milligrams / Cholesterol 22 milligrams

Dinner Rolls

Pan Rolls

Grease a 9 × 13 × 2-inch pan or a 9-inch round or square cake pan. Gently roll and stretch dough into a log shape. With a sharp knife, divide dough into the desired number of rolls. Roll each piece into a ball and place close together in pan. Cover and let rise in a warm oven 30 to 45 minutes until doubled. Bake as directed in recipe.

Cloverleaf Rolls

Grease a 12-cup muffin tin. Gently roll and stretch dough into a log shape. With a sharp knife, divide dough into the desired number of rolls. Cut each roll into thirds. Roll each piece of dough into a small ball; place 3 in each greased muffin cup. Cover and let rise in a warm oven 30 to 45 minutes until doubled. Bake as directed in recipe.

For easy cloverleaf rolls, don't cut rolls into thirds. Instead, roll each piece of dough into a ball and place each in a greased muffin cup. With clean scissors dipped in flour, cut the top of each roll in half, then in quarters. Cover and let rise as above.

SNAILS

Grease a large baking sheet. Stretch dough into a log shape and, with a sharp knife, divide dough into the desired number of rolls. Roll each piece into a 12-inch-long rope. Hold one end of the rope (the center of the snail) in place on the baking sheet. Coil the rest of the rope around the center; tuck the end underneath. Cover and let rise in a warm oven 30 to 45 minutes until doubled. Bake as directed in recipe. (Optional: Before baking, brush rolls with beaten egg, then sprinkle with sesame or poppyseeds.)

BUTTERHORNS AND CRESCENT ROLLS

Grease a large baking sheet. With a sharp knife, divide large dough into quarters; divide medium dough into thirds; or divide small dough in half. Roll each piece into an 8- or 9-inch circle. With a knife or pizza cutter, divide each circle into 8 wedges, as if cutting a pizza. Separate the wedges.

Starting at the wide end, roll up each wedge toward the point. Place on baking sheet with points underneath. For crescent rolls, curve each roll on the baking sheet into a crescent shape by bringing the points slightly toward each other. Cover and let rise in a warm oven 30 to 45 minutes until doubled. Bake as directed in recipe.

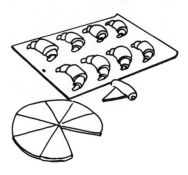

PARKER HOUSE ROLLS

Grease a large baking sheet. With a rolling pin, roll out dough to a ¼-inch thickness. With a 2- to 2½-inch biscuit cutter, cut out rolls. Brush each with melted butter. Holding both ends of a clean pen or pencil, press it into each roll slightly off center to make a crease. Fold the larger side over the smaller side; press the edges together lightly. Place on baking sheet. Cover and let rise in a warm oven 30 to 45 minutes until doubled. Bake as directed in the recipe.

FAN TANS

Butter a 12-cup muffin tin. With a rolling pin, roll dough into a 9 × 12-inch or 9 × 16-inch rectangle. Brush with melted butter. With a sharp knife, cut 6 lengthwise strips about 1½ inches wide. Stack strips on top of each other, then cut crosswise into twelve 1-inch pieces. Place them cut side down in buttered muffin cups. Cover and let rise in a warm oven 20 to 30 minutes until almost doubled. Bake as directed in recipe.

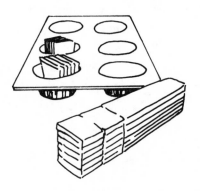

Basic Dinner Rolls

hese tasty 4-star rolls will disappear from the table before they're even cool.

	SMALL	MEDIUM	LARGE
WATER	½ cup	¾ cup	¾ cup
EGG	1	1	2
BUTTER OR MARGARINE	2 tablespoons	3 tablespoons	¼ cup
SUGAR	2 tablespoons	3 tablespoons	¼ cup
SALT	1 teaspoon	1½ teaspoons	2 teaspoons
ALL-PURPOSE FLOUR	2 cups	3 cups	4 cups
NONFAT DRY MILK POWDER	2 tablespoons	3 tablespoons	¼ cup
RED STAR BRAND ACTIVE DRY YEAST	1½ teaspoons	1½ teaspoons	2 teaspoons
MELTED BUTTER OR MARGARINE	2 tablespoons	2 tablespoons	¼ cup

1. Place all ingredients except melted butter in bread pan, select Dough setting, and press Start.

2. Grease a large baking sheet.

3. When the dough has risen long enough, the machine will beep. Turn off bread machine, remove bread pan, and turn out dough onto a lightly floured countertop or cutting board. Gently roll and stretch dough into an 18-inch rope.

For the Small Recipe
  With a sharp knife, divide dough into 10 pieces.

For the Medium Recipe
  With a sharp knife, divide dough into 15 pieces.

For the Large Recipe
  With a sharp knife, divide dough into 20 pieces.

4. Form dough into desired roll shapes (see page 132). Place rolls on baking sheet; cover and let rise in a warm oven 30 to 45 minutes until doubled in size. (Hint: To warm oven slightly, turn oven on Warm setting for 1 minute, then turn it off and place covered dough in oven to rise. Remove pan from oven before preheating.)

5. Preheat oven to 400°F. Brush rolls with melted butter; bake for 12 to 15 minutes until brown.

6. Remove from oven and serve warm.

BAKE CYCLE: Dough

Small recipe yields 1 0 rolls
Medium recipe yields 1 5 rolls
Large recipe yields 2 0 rolls

NUTRITIONAL INFORMATION PER ROLL
Calories 135 / Fat 3.5 grams / Carbohydrates 22.1 grams / Protein 3.4 grams / Fiber .8 gram / Sodium 270 milligrams / Cholesterol 14.4 milligrams

---

Potato Rolls

These home-style rolls are crusty on the outside, tender and flavorful inside.

	SMALL	MEDIUM	LARGE
WATER	½ cup	¾ cup	¾ cup
EGG	1	1	2
SHORTENING	3 tablespoons	¼ cup	6 tablespoons
SUGAR	3 tablespoons	¼ cup	6 tablespoons
SALT	1 teaspoon	1 teaspoon	2 teaspoons
ALL-PURPOSE FLOUR	2 cups	3 cups	4 cups
PLAIN MASHED POTATOES	⅓ cup	½ cup	⅔ cup
RED STAR BRAND ACTIVE DRY YEAST	1½ teaspoons	1½ teaspoons	2 teaspoons

1. Place dough ingredients in bread pan, select Dough setting, and press Start.

2. When the dough has risen long enough, the machine will beep. Turn off bread machine, remove bread pan, and turn out dough onto a heavily floured countertop or cutting board.

For the Small Recipe

Grease two 12-cup muffin tins. Gently roll and stretch dough into an 18-inch rope. With a sharp knife, divide dough into 54 pieces. (Hint: First cut dough into 9 equal pieces, then cut each of those into 6 tiny pieces.) Roll each piece into a ball and place 3 balls in each greased muffin cup.

For the Medium Recipe

Grease two 12-cup muffin tins. Gently roll and stretch dough into a 24-inch rope. With a sharp knife, divide dough into 72 pieces. (Hint: First cut dough into 12 equal pieces, then cut each of those into 6 tiny pieces.) Roll each piece into a ball and place 3 balls in each greased muffin cup.

For the Large Recipe

Grease three 12-cup muffin tins. Divide dough in half. Gently roll and stretch each half into an 18-inch rope. With a sharp knife, divide each rope into 54 pieces.

(Hint: First cut each rope into 9 equal pieces, then cut each of those into 6 tiny pieces.) Roll each piece into a ball and place 3 balls in each greased muffin cup.

3.   Cover and let rise in a warm oven 30 to 45 minutes until doubled in size. (Hint: To warm oven slightly, turn oven on Warm setting for 1 minute, then turn it off, and place covered dough in oven to rise. Remove pan from oven before preheating.)

4.   Preheat oven to 400°F. Bake for 12 minutes until golden.

5.   Remove from oven and serve warm.

BAKE CYCLE: Dough

Small recipe yields 18 rolls
Medium recipe yields 24 rolls
Large recipe yields 36 rolls

NUTRITIONAL INFORMATION PER ROLL
Calories 89.7 / Fat 2.5 grams / Carbohydrates 14.6 grams / Protein 2 grams / Fiber .5 gram / Sodium 92 milligrams / Cholesterol 8.9 milligrams

---

VARIATION

For large, pillowlike potato rolls, use either the small or large recipes. For the small recipe: Grease one 9 × 13 × 2-inch pan. Divide the dough into 12 pieces, roll into balls, and place in pan. Cover and let rise in a warm oven for at least 1 hour until the rolls almost fill the pan and have more than doubled in size. Just before baking as above, dust tops lightly with flour.

For the large recipe: Grease two 9 × 13 × 2-inch pans. Divide the dough into 24 pieces, roll into balls, and place in pans. Cover and let rise in a warm oven for at least 1 hour until the rolls almost fill the pans and have more than doubled in size. Just before baking as above, dust tops lightly with flour.

BAKE CYCLE: Dough

Small recipe yields 12 rolls
Large recipe yields 24 rolls

NUTRITIONAL INFORMATION PER ROLL
Calories 128 / Fat 3.8 grams / Carbohydrates 20.2 grams / Protein 2.9 grams / Fiber .8 gram / Sodium 184 milligrams / Cholesterol 17.7 milligrams

---

Honey Wheat Rolls

*T*hese dinner rolls are far superior to any packaged rolls you can buy. They're lovely on the Thanksgiving table and also very popular as a snack fresh out of the oven, split in half, and filled with thinly sliced ham and a dab of mustard. Either way, they disappear in a hurry!

	SMALL RECIPE	MEDIUM RECIPE	LARGE RECIPE
WATER	½ cup	¾ cup	⅞ cup
EGG	1	1	2
HONEY	1½ tablespoons	2 tablespoons	3 tablespoons
SALT	½ teaspoon	1 teaspoon	1½ teaspoons
BUTTER OR MARGARINE	1½ tablespoons	2 tablespoons	3 tablespoons
ALL-PURPOSE FLOUR	1⅓ cups	2 cups	2⅔ cups
WHOLE WHEAT FLOUR	⅔ cup	1 cup	1⅓ cups
RED STAR BRAND ACTIVE DRY YEAST	1½ teaspoons	1½ teaspoons	2 teaspoons

1. Place dough ingredients in bread pan, select Dough setting, and press Start.

2. When the dough has risen long enough, the machine will beep. Turn off bread machine, remove bread pan, and turn out dough onto a lightly floured countertop or cutting board. Gently roll and stretch dough into an 18-inch rope.

For the Small Recipe
Grease one 12-cup muffin tin. With a sharp knife, divide dough into 12 pieces.

For the Medium Recipe
Grease two 12-cup muffin tins. With a sharp knife, divide dough into 18 pieces. (Hint: First cut dough into 6 equal pieces, then cut each of those into 3 pieces.)

For the Large Recipe
Grease two 12-cup muffin tins. With a sharp knife, divide dough into 24 pieces. (Hint: First cut dough into 12 equal pieces, then cut each of those in half.)

3. Place rolls in muffin tin(s). Cover and let rise in a warm oven 20 to 30 minutes until doubled in size. (Hint: To warm oven slightly, turn oven on Warm setting for 1

minute, then turn it off and place covered dough in oven to rise. Remove pan from oven before preheating.)

4. Preheat oven to 400°F. Bake for 12 minutes until brown.

5. Remove from oven and serve warm.

BAKE CYCLE: Dough

Small recipe yields 12 rolls
Medium recipe yields 18 rolls
Large recipe yields 24 rolls

NUTRITIONAL INFORMATION PER ROLL
Calories 96 / Fat 1.8 grams / Carbohydrates 17.4 grams / Protein 2.8 grams / Fiber 1.3 grams / Sodium 138 milligrams / Cholesterol 11.8 milligrams

Old-Fashioned Oatmeal Rolls

These are best served warm, but Lois's neighbor George claims they're also great cold, split in half, and filled with thinly sliced turkey.

	SMALL RECIPE	MEDIUM RECIPE	LARGE RECIPE
OLD-FASHIONED ROLLED OATS	⅔ cup	1 cup	1⅓ cups
MILK	¾ cup	1 cup	1¼ cups
BUTTER OR MARGARINE	2 tablespoons	3 tablespoons	¼ cup
SUGAR	2 teaspoons	1 tablespoon	4 teaspoons
SALT	½ teaspoon	1 teaspoon	1 teaspoon
ALL-PURPOSE FLOUR	1⅓ cups	2 cups	2⅔ cups
RED STAR BRAND ACTIVE DRY YEAST	1½ teaspoons	1½ teaspoons	2 teaspoons
MELTED BUTTER OR MARGARINE	2 tablespoons	2 tablespoons	3 tablespoons

1. Place all ingredients except melted butter in bread pan, select Dough setting, and press Start.

2. Grease a large baking sheet.

3. When the dough has risen long enough, the machine will beep. Turn off bread machine, remove bread pan, and turn out dough onto a lightly floured countertop or cutting board. Gently roll and stretch dough into an 18-inch rope.

For the Small Recipe
    With a sharp knife, divide dough into 8 pieces.

For the Medium Recipe
    With a sharp knife, divide dough into 12 pieces.

For the Large Recipe
    With a sharp knife, divide dough into 16 pieces.

4. Roll each piece into a ball and flatten slightly; place on prepared baking sheet. With a sharp knife, cut an *X* in the top of each roll.

5. Cover and let rise in a warm oven 30 to 45 minutes until doubled in size. (Hint: To warm oven slightly, turn oven on Warm setting for 1 minute, then turn it off and place covered dough in oven to rise. Remove pan from oven before preheating.)

6. Preheat oven to 425°F. Brush each roll with melted butter. Bake for 12 to 15 minutes until brown. (Note: Rolls will flatten out slightly during baking.)

7. Remove from oven and serve warm.

BAKE CYCLE: Dough

Small recipe yields 8 rolls
Medium recipe yields 1 2 rolls
Large recipe yields 1 6 rolls

NUTRITIONAL INFORMATION PER ROLL
Calories 147 / Fat 4.4 grams / Carbohydrates 22.4 grams / Protein 4.1 grams / Fiber 1.4 grams / Sodium 248 milligrams / Cholesterol .8 milligram

Butterhorn Rolls

*M*ake these rolls just once and they will become one of your favorites. They look impressive, but they're deceptively simple to make because the dough is so easy to handle. They're rich, tender rolls—perfect for company dinners or festive holiday meals.

	SMALL RECIPE	MEDIUM RECIPE	LARGE RECIPE
MILK	½ cup	¾ cup	⅞ cup
EGG	1	1	2
OIL	¼ cup	⅓ cup	½ cup
SALT	½ teaspoon	1 teaspoon	1½ teaspoons
SUGAR	¼ cup	⅓ cup	½ cup
ALL-PURPOSE FLOUR	2 cups	3 cups	4 cups
RED STAR BRAND ACTIVE DRY YEAST	1½ teaspoons	1½ teaspoons	2 teaspoons
MELTED BUTTER OR MARGARINE	1 tablespoon	1½ tablespoons	2 tablespoons

1. Place dough ingredients except melted butter in bread pan, select Dough setting, and press Start.

2. When the dough has risen long enough, the machine will beep. Turn off bread machine, remove bread pan, and turn out dough onto a lightly floured countertop or cutting board. Shape dough into a log.

For the Small Recipe
With a sharp knife, divide dough into 2 pieces; roll each piece into a ball.

For the Medium Recipe
With a sharp knife, divide dough into 3 pieces; roll each piece into a ball.

For the Large Recipe
With a sharp knife, divide dough into 4 pieces; roll each piece into a ball.

3. With a rolling pin, roll each ball, one at a time, into a 9-inch circle. With a sharp knife or pizza cutter, divide each circle into 8 wedges, as if cutting a pizza. Starting at

the wide end, roll up each wedge toward the point. Place rolls on an ungreased baking sheet, point side underneath. Cover and let rise in a warm oven 30 to 45 minutes until doubled in size. (Hint: To warm oven slightly, turn oven on Warm setting for 1 minute, then turn it off and place covered dough in oven to rise. Remove pan from oven before preheating.)

4.   Preheat oven to 375°F. Brush rolls lightly with melted butter. Bake for 12 to 15 minutes until golden. Remove from oven and serve warm.

BAKE CYCLE: Dough

Small recipe yields 16 rolls
Medium recipe yields 24 rolls
Large recipe yields 32 rolls

NUTRITIONAL INFORMATION PER ROLL
Calories 107 / Fat 4.2 grams / Carbohydrates 15.1 grams / Protein 2.2 grams / Fiber .5 gram / Sodium 104 milligrams / Cholesterol 9.2 milligrams

---

Garlic Cheese Rolls

These garlicky rolls are incredibly light and delicious hot out of the oven! We've also found that they go over very well at potluck suppers.

DOUGH

	SMALL RECIPE	MEDIUM RECIPE	LARGE RECIPE
WATER	¾ cup	1 cup	1¼ cups
SALT	1 teaspoon	1½ teaspoons	2 teaspoons
BUTTER OR MARGARINE	1 tablespoon	1½ tablespoons	2 tablespoons
SUGAR	2 tablespoons	3 tablespoons	¼ cup
ALL-PURPOSE FLOUR	2 cups	3 cups	4 cups
NONFAT DRY MILK POWDER	1 tablespoon	2 tablespoons	2 tablespoons
RED STAR BRAND ACTIVE DRY YEAST	1½ teaspoons	1½ teaspoons	2 teaspoons

TOPPING

	SMALL RECIPE	MEDIUM RECIPE	LARGE RECIPE
MELTED BUTTER OR MARGARINE	¼ cup	¼ cup	½ cup
GARLIC CLOVE, CRUSHED	1	1	2
FRESHLY GRATED PARMESAN CHEESE	2 tablespoons	2 tablespoons	¼ cup

1. Place dough ingredients in bread pan, select Dough setting, and press Start.

2. When the dough has risen long enough, the machine will beep. Turn off bread machine, remove bread pan, and turn out dough onto a lightly floured countertop or cutting board. Gently roll and stretch dough into a 24-inch rope.

For the Small Recipe

Grease two 8-inch pie pans. With a sharp knife, divide dough into 16 pieces. (Hint: First cut dough into 8 equal pieces, then cut each of those in half.)

For the Medium Recipe

Grease two 8-inch pie pans. With a sharp knife, divide dough into 24 pieces. (Hint: First cut dough into 12 equal pieces, then cut each of those in half.)

For the Large Recipe

Grease three 8-inch pie pans. With a sharp knife, divide dough into 32 pieces. (Hint: First cut dough into 8 equal pieces, then cut each of those into 4 pieces.)

3. Shape each piece into a ball and place in prepared pie pans. In a small bowl, combine butter and garlic; pour over rolls. Sprinkle with Parmesan cheese.

4. Cover and let rise in a warm oven 30 to 45 minutes until doubled in size. (Hint: To warm oven slightly, turn oven on Warm setting for 1 minute, then turn it off, and place covered dough in oven to rise. Remove pan from oven before preheating.)

5. Preheat oven to 375°F. Bake for 15 minutes until golden. Remove from oven, cut apart, and serve warm.

BAKE CYCLE: Dough

Small recipe yields 16 rolls
Medium recipe yields 24 rolls
Large recipe yields 32 rolls

NUTRITIONAL INFORMATION PER ROLL
Calories 65.3 / Fat 2.2 grams / Carbohydrates 9.8 grams / Protein 1.5 grams / Fiber .3 gram / Sodium 176 milligrams / Cholesterol .4 milligram

---

Egg Buns

This recipe produces a shiny, plump, eggy roll that would look beautiful in a big basket of assorted buns and rolls.

	SMALL RECIPE	MEDIUM RECIPE	LARGE RECIPE
MILK	¼ cup	⅝ cup	1 cup
EGGS	2	2	3
BUTTER OR MARGARINE	¼ cup	⅓ cup	½ cup
SUGAR	2 tablespoons	3 tablespoons	¼ cup
SALT	1 teaspoon	1½ teaspoons	2 teaspoons
ALL-PURPOSE FLOUR	2 cups	3 cups	4 cups
RED STAR BRAND ACTIVE DRY YEAST	1½ teaspoons	1½ teaspoons	2 teaspoons
LIGHTLY BEATEN EGG	1	1	1

1. Place all ingredients except lightly beaten egg in bread pan, select Dough setting, and press Start.

2. When the dough has risen long enough, the machine will beep. Turn off bread machine, remove bread pan, and turn out dough onto a lightly floured countertop or cutting board.

For the Small Recipe

Grease a large baking sheet. Gently roll and stretch dough into an 18-inch rope. With a sharp knife, divide dough into 18 pieces. (Hint: First cut dough into 6 equal pieces, then cut each of those into 3 pieces.)

For the Medium Recipe

Grease a large baking sheet. Gently roll and stretch dough into a 24-inch rope. With a sharp knife, divide dough into 28 pieces. (Hint: First cut dough into 7 equal pieces, then cut each of those into 4 pieces.)

For the Large Recipe

Grease two large baking sheets. Divide dough in half. Gently roll and stretch each half of dough into an 18-inch rope. With a sharp knife, divide each rope into 18 pieces. (Hint: First cut dough into 6 equal pieces, then cut each of those into 3 pieces.)

3. Roll each piece into a ball and place on baking sheet(s). Cover and let rise in a warm oven 30 to 45 minutes until doubled in size. (Hint: To warm oven slightly, turn oven on Warm setting for 1 minute, then turn it off and place covered dough in oven to rise. Remove pan from oven before preheating.)

4. Preheat oven to 375°F. Brush rolls with the beaten egg. Bake for 10 to 12 minutes until brown.

5. Remove from oven and serve either warm or cold.

BAKE CYCLE: Dough

Small recipe yields 18 rolls
Medium recipe yields 28 rolls
Large recipe yields 36 rolls

NUTRITIONAL INFORMATION PER BUN
Calories 76.4 / Fat 2.1 grams / Carbohydrates 12 grams / Protein 2.2 grams / Fiber .4 gram / Sodium 147 milligrams / Cholesterol 19.2 milligrams

---

Caraway Rye Pan Rolls

*T*hese are rich, tender pan rolls—the perfect accompaniment to hearty split pea soup or a pork chop and sauerkraut supper.

	SMALL RECIPE	MEDIUM RECIPE	LARGE RECIPE
WATER	⅔ cup	¾ cup	1¼ cups
SOUR CREAM	⅓ cup	½ cup	⅔ cup
SALT	1½ teaspoons	2 teaspoons	2 teaspoons
SUGAR	2 teaspoons	1 tablespoon	4 teaspoons
ALL-PURPOSE FLOUR	1½ cups	2 cups	3 cups
RYE FLOUR	¾ cup	1 cup	1½ cups
CARAWAY SEEDS	2 teaspoons	1 tablespoon	4 teaspoons
RED STAR BRAND ACTIVE DRY YEAST	1½ teaspoons	1½ teaspoons	2 teaspoons

1.   Place dough ingredients in bread pan, select Dough setting, and press Start.

2.   When the dough has risen long enough, the machine will beep. Turn off bread machine, remove bread pan, and turn out dough onto a floured countertop or cutting board. (Note: This is a very sticky dough, so keep your hands and the countertop well covered with flour.) Gently roll and stretch dough into an 18-inch rope.

For the Small Recipe
Grease one 9-inch round or square cake pan. With a sharp knife, divide dough into 9 pieces; roll each into a ball and place in pan.

For the Medium Recipe
Grease a 9 × 13 × 2-inch pan. With a sharp knife, divide dough into 12 pieces; roll each into a ball and place in pan.

For the Large Recipe
Grease two 9-inch round or square cake pans. With a sharp knife, divide dough into 18 pieces; roll each into a ball and place 9 in each pan.

3.   Cover and let rise in a warm oven 30 to 45 minutes until doubled in size. (Hint: To warm oven slightly, turn oven on Warm setting for 1 minute, then turn it off and place covered dough in oven to rise. Remove pan from oven before preheating.)

4. Preheat oven to 400°F. Bake rolls for 18 minutes until golden.

5. Remove from oven and serve warm.

BAKE CYCLE: Dough

Small recipe yields 9 rolls
Medium recipe yields 1 2 rolls
Large recipe yields 1 8 rolls

NUTRITIONAL INFORMATION PER ROLL
Calories 67 / Fat 1.2 grams / Carbohydrates 12.1 grams / Protein 1.7 grams / Fiber 1 gram / Sodium 181 milligrams / Cholesterol 2.1 milligrams

Scandinavian Rye Rolls

*Y*ou've probably never tasted a roll quite like this. It combines rye, orange, and a light anise flavor.

	SMALL RECIPE	MEDIUM RECIPE	LARGE RECIPE
MILK	⅜ cup	½ cup	⅝ cup
WATER	⅜ cup	½ cup	¾ cup
BUTTER OR MARGARINE	1 tablespoon	1 tablespoon	2 tablespoons
MOLASSES	2 teaspoons	1 tablespoon	4 teaspoons
SALT	½ teaspoon	½ teaspoon	1 teaspoon
GRATED ORANGE RIND	1 tablespoon	1½ tablespoons	2 tablespoons
FENNEL SEEDS	½ teaspoon	1 teaspoon	1 teaspoon
ALL-PURPOSE FLOUR	1⅓ cups	2 cups	2⅔ cups
RYE FLOUR	⅔ cup	1 cup	1⅓ cups
RED STAR BRAND ACTIVE DRY YEAST	1½ teaspoons	1½ teaspoons	2 teaspoons

1. Place dough ingredients in bread pan, select Dough setting, and press Start.

2. When the dough has risen long enough, the machine will beep. Turn off bread machine, remove bread pan, and turn out dough onto a lightly floured countertop or cutting board. Gently roll and stretch dough into a 24-inch rope.

For the Small Recipe
Grease an 8- or 9-inch square baking pan. With a sharp knife, divide dough into 12 pieces; roll each into a ball and place in pan.

For the Medium Recipe
Grease a 9 × 13 × 2-inch baking pan. With a sharp knife, divide dough into 18 pieces. (Hint: First cut dough into 6 equal pieces, then cut each of those into 3 small pieces.) Roll each into a ball and place in pan.

For the Large Recipe
Grease two 8- or 9-inch square baking pans. With a sharp knife, divide dough in half, then cut each half into 12 pieces; roll each into a ball and place in pans.

3. Cover and let rise in a warm oven 30 to 45 minutes until doubled in size. (Hint: To warm oven slightly, turn oven on Warm setting for 1 minute, then turn it off and place covered dough in oven to rise. Remove pan from oven before preheating.)

4. Preheat oven to 350°F. Bake for 20 to 25 minutes until golden.

5. Remove from oven and serve warm.

BAKE CYCLE: Dough

Small recipe yields 12 rolls
Medium recipe yields 18 rolls
Large recipe yields 24 rolls

NUTRITIONAL INFORMATION PER ROLL
Calories 81.8 / Fat .8 gram / Carbohydrates 16.1 grams / Protein 2.3 grams / Fiber 1.3 grams / Sodium 190 milligrams / Cholesterol .3 milligram

---

Buckwheat Biscuits

*T*hese stouthearted biscuits go well with a bowl of soup for lunch or just served warm with homemade apricot jam at breakfast.

	SMALL RECIPE	MEDIUM RECIPE	LARGE RECIPE
BUTTERMILK	1 cup	1¼ cups	2 cups
BUTTER OR MARGARINE	1 tablespoon	2 tablespoons	2 tablespoons
MOLASSES	1 tablespoon	1½ tablespoons	2 tablespoons
SUGAR	1 tablespoon	1½ tablespoons	2 tablespoons
SALT	1 teaspoon	1½ teaspoons	2 teaspoons
ALL-PURPOSE FLOUR	2 cups	3 cups	4 cups
BUCKWHEAT FLOUR	½ cup	¾ cup	1 cup
BAKING SODA	¼ teaspoon	¼ teaspoon	½ teaspoon
RED STAR BRAND ACTIVE DRY YEAST	1½ teaspoons	1½ teaspoons	2 teaspoons
MELTED BUTTER OR MARGARINE	2 tablespoons	3 tablespoons	4 tablespoons

1. Place all ingredients except melted butter in bread pan, select Dough setting, and press Start.

2. When the dough has risen long enough, the machine will beep. Turn off bread machine, remove bread pan, and turn out dough onto a lightly floured countertop or cutting board.

3. With a rolling pin, roll dough to a ½-inch thickness. With a 2-inch biscuit cutter, cut out biscuits. Dip biscuits in melted butter and place on ungreased cookie sheets.

4. Let rise in a warm oven 30 to 45 minutes until doubled in size. (Hint: To warm oven slightly, turn oven on Warm setting for 1 minute, then turn it off and place covered dough in oven to rise. Remove pan from oven before preheating.)

5. Preheat oven to 400°F. Bake for 15 minutes until brown.

6. Remove from oven and serve warm.

BAKE CYCLE: Dough

Small recipe yields 14 to 16 biscuits
Medium recipe yields 20 to 22 biscuits
Large recipe yields 28 to 30 biscuits

NUTRITIONAL INFORMATION PER BISCUIT
Calories 103 / Fat 2.3 grams / Carbohydrates 17.7 grams / Protein 2.7 grams / Fiber .8 gram / Sodium 202 milligrams / Cholesterol .5 milligram

Garlic and Herb Monkey Bread

*T*hese are rich, tender rolls that will spice up any meal. They're perfect for a potluck or a buffet table because they don't require butter, and they take up less space than a basketful of dinner rolls.

	SMALL RECIPE	MEDIUM RECIPE	LARGE RECIPE
WATER	⅜ cup	½ cup	⅝ cup
SOUR CREAM	⅜ cup	½ cup	¾ cup
BUTTER OR MARGARINE	1 tablespoon	1½ tablespoons	2 tablespoons
SUGAR	2 tablespoons	3 tablespoons	¼ cup
SALT	1 teaspoon	1½ teaspoons	2 teaspoons
ALL-PURPOSE FLOUR	2 cups	3 cups	4 cups
RED STAR BRAND ACTIVE DRY YEAST	1½ teaspoons	1½ teaspoons	2 teaspoons
MELTED BUTTER OR MARGARINE	3 tablespoons	4 tablespoons	6 tablespoons
GARLIC CLOVE, MINCED	1	2	2
DRIED THYME	¼ teaspoon	¼ teaspoon	½ teaspoon
DRIED OREGANO	¼ teaspoon	¼ teaspoon	½ teaspoon
DRIED MARJORAM	¼ teaspoon	¼ teaspoon	½ teaspoon

1. Place first 7 ingredients in bread pan, select Dough setting, and press Start.

2. When the dough has risen long enough, the machine will beep. Turn off bread machine, remove bread pan, and turn out dough onto a lightly floured countertop or cutting board. Gently roll and stretch dough into a 24-inch rope.

3. In a small bowl, combine melted butter, garlic, and herbs; set aside.

For the Small Recipe

Butter an 8½ × 4½ × 2½-inch loaf pan. With a sharp knife, divide dough into 30 pieces. (Hint: First cut dough into 10 equal pieces, then cut each of those into 3 small pieces.)

For the Medium Recipe

Butter a 9-inch ring mold or a $9 \times 5 \times 3$-inch loaf pan. With a sharp knife, divide dough into 40 pieces. (Hint: First cut dough into 10 equal pieces, then cut each of those into 4 small pieces.)

For the Large Recipe

Butter two $8\frac{1}{2} \times 4\frac{1}{2} \times 2\frac{1}{2}$-inch loaf pans. With a sharp knife, divide dough in half, then cut each half into 30 pieces. (Hint: First cut each half of dough into 10 equal pieces, then cut each of those into 3 small pieces.)

4. Dip each piece into the herb-butter mixture and place in layers in the ring mold or loaf pan(s). Cover and let rise in a warm oven 30 to 45 minutes until doubled in size. (Hint: To warm oven slightly, turn oven on Warm setting for 1 minute, then turn it off, and place covered dough in oven to rise. Remove pan from oven before preheating.)

5. Preheat oven to 375°F. Bake for 15 to 20 minutes until brown. Immediately turn out of pan onto a plate, then invert onto a serving dish. Serve warm.

BAKE CYCLE: Dough

Small recipe yields 1 loaf
Medium recipe yields 1 loaf
Large recipe yields 2 loaves

NUTRITIONAL INFORMATION PER SERVING ($\frac{1}{12}$ LOAF)
Calories 193 / Fat 6.6 grams / Carbohydrates 29.6 grams / Protein 4.1 grams / Fiber 1.4 grams / Sodium 338 milligrams / Cholesterol 4.3 milligrams

Onion Dill Pan Rolls

F*or a rich, savory dinner roll, try these some night.*

	SMALL RECIPE	MEDIUM RECIPE	LARGE RECIPE
WATER	⅜ cup	⅔ cup	⅝ cup
EGG	1	1	2
COTTAGE CHEESE	½ cup	⅔ cup	1 cup
BUTTER OR MARGARINE	1 tablespoon	1½ teaspoons	2 tablespoons
SUGAR	1½ teaspoons	2 teaspoons	1 tablespoon
SALT	1 teaspoon	1 teaspoon	2 teaspoons
ALL-PURPOSE FLOUR	2 cups	3 cups	4 cups
DRIED MINCED ONION	2 teaspoons	1 tablespoon	4 teaspoons
DRIED DILL	2 teaspoons	1 tablespoon	4 teaspoons
RED STAR BRAND ACTIVE DRY YEAST	1½ teaspoons	1½ teaspoons	2 teaspoons

1.   Place dough ingredients in bread pan, select Dough setting, and press Start.

2.   When the dough has risen long enough, the machine will beep. Turn off bread machine, remove bread pan, and turn out dough onto a lightly floured countertop or cutting board. Gently roll and stretch dough into an 18-inch rope.

For the Small Recipe

Grease an 8- or 9-inch square or round baking pan. With a sharp knife, divide dough into 9 pieces; roll each into a ball and place in pan.

For the Medium Recipe

Grease a 9 × 13 × 2-inch baking pan. With a sharp knife, divide dough into 12 pieces; roll each into a ball and place in pan.

For the Large Recipe

Grease two 8- or 9-inch square or round baking pans. With a sharp knife, divide dough into 18 pieces; roll each into a ball and place in pans.

3. Cover and let rise in a warm oven 10 minutes until doubled in size. (Hint: To warm oven slightly, turn oven on Warm setting for 1 minute, then turn it off and place covered dough in oven to rise. Remove pan from oven before preheating.)

4. Preheat oven to 350°F. Bake for 25 to 30 minutes until lightly browned on top.

5. Remove from oven, cut apart, and serve warm.

BAKE CYCLE: Dough

Small recipe yields 9 rolls
Medium recipe yields 12 rolls
Large recipe yields 18 rolls

NUTRITIONAL INFORMATION PER ROLL
Calories 142 / Fat 1.9 grams / Carbohydrates 25.1 grams / Protein 5.3 grams / Fiber 1 gram / Sodium 248 milligrams / Cholesterol 18.3 milligrams

---

Sweet Rolls,
Breads,
and
Coffee Cakes

Basic Sweet Dough

This is a standard sweet dough that can be used in any recipe in this chapter.

	SMALL RECIPE	MEDIUM RECIPE	LARGE RECIPE
MILK	¼ cup	⅜ cup	⅜ cup
WATER	¼ cup	⅜ cup	⅜ cup
EGG	1	1	2
BUTTER OR MARGARINE	3 tablespoons	4 tablespoons	6 tablespoons
SUGAR	¼ cup	⅓ cup	½ cup
SALT	1 teaspoon	1 teaspoon	2 teaspoons
ALL-PURPOSE FLOUR	2 cups	3 cups	4 cups
RED STAR BRAND ACTIVE DRY YEAST	1½ teaspoons	1½ teaspoons	2 teaspoons

1. Place dough ingredients in bread pan, select Dough setting, and press Start.

2. When the dough has risen long enough, the machine will beep. Turn off bread machine, remove bread pan, and turn out dough onto a lightly floured countertop or cutting board.

3. Follow directions for specific recipe.

BAKE CYCLE: Dough

NUTRITIONAL INFORMATION PER SERVING (1/12 OF RECIPE)
Calories 169 / Fat 3.7 grams / Carbohydrates 29.3 grams / Protein 4.1 grams / Fiber 1 gram / Sodium 235 milligrams / Cholesterol 18.1 milligrams

Basic Not-So-Sweet Dough

T his dough is not quite as sweet and rich as the Basic Sweet Dough. It can be used in any recipe in this chapter.

	SMALL RECIPE	MEDIUM RECIPE	LARGE RECIPE
WATER	½ cup	¾ cup	⅞ cup
EGG	1	1	2
BUTTER OR MARGARINE	2 tablespoons	3 tablespoons	4 tablespoons
SUGAR	1 tablespoon	2 tablespoons	2 tablespoons
SALT	1 teaspoon	1 teaspoon	2 teaspoons
ALL-PURPOSE FLOUR	2 cups	3 cups	4 cups
NONFAT DRY MILK POWDER	1 tablespoon	2 tablespoons	2 tablespoons
RED STAR BRAND ACTIVE DRY YEAST	1½ teaspoons	1½ teaspoons	2 teaspoons

1. Place dough ingredients in bread pan, select Dough setting, and press Start.

2. When the dough has risen long enough, the machine will beep. Turn off bread machine, remove bread pan, and turn out dough onto a lightly floured countertop or cutting board.

3. Follow directions for specific recipe.

BAKE CYCLE: Dough

NUTRITIONAL INFORMATION PER SERVING (¹⁄₁₂ OF RECIPE)
Calories 151 / Fat 2.9 grams / Carbohydrates 26.4 grams / Protein 4.1 grams / Fiber .9 gram / Sodium 223 milligrams / Cholesterol 17.9 milligrams

---

Basic Buttermilk Sweet Dough

*T*his is a rich sweet dough that can be used interchangeably with the other basic sweet doughs in this chapter.

	SMALL RECIPE	MEDIUM RECIPE	LARGE RECIPE
BUTTERMILK	⅝ cup	⅞ cup	⅞ cup
EGG	1	1	2
BUTTER OR MARGARINE	3 tablespoons	4 tablespoons	6 tablespoons
SUGAR	3 tablespoons	¼ cup	6 tablespoons
SALT	1 teaspoon	1 teaspoon	2 teaspoons
ALL-PURPOSE FLOUR	2 cups	3 cups	4 cups
BAKING SODA	¼ teaspoon	¼ teaspoon	½ teaspoon
RED STAR BRAND ACTIVE DRY YEAST	1½ teaspoons	1½ teaspoons	2 teaspoons

1. Place dough ingredients in bread pan, select Dough setting, and press Start.

2. When the dough has risen long enough, the machine will beep. Turn off bread machine, remove bread pan, and turn out dough onto a lightly floured countertop or cutting board.

3. Follow directions for specific recipe.

BAKE CYCLE: Dough

NUTRITIONAL INFORMATION PER SERVING (¹⁄₁₂ OF RECIPE)
Calories 170 / Fat 3.8 grams / Carbohydrates 29 grams / Protein 4.5 grams / Fiber .9 gram / Sodium 266 milligrams / Cholesterol 18.4 milligrams

---

Basic 100% Whole Wheat Sweet Dough

I f you prefer whole wheat doughs, this can be used in any recipe of your choice in this chapter.

	SMALL RECIPE	MEDIUM RECIPE	LARGE RECIPE
MILK	¼ cup	⅜ cup	¼ cup
WATER	¼ cup	⅜ cup	⅝ cup
EGG	1	1	2
BUTTER OR MARGARINE	3 tablespoons	4 tablespoons	6 tablespoons
DARK BROWN SUGAR	3 tablespoons	¼ cup	6 tablespoons
SALT	½ teaspoon	1 teaspoon	1 teaspoon
WHOLE WHEAT FLOUR	2 cups	3 cups	4 cups
RED STAR BRAND ACTIVE DRY YEAST	1½ teaspoons	1½ teaspoons	2 teaspoons

1. Place dough ingredients in bread pan, select Dough setting, and press Start.

2. When the dough has risen long enough, the machine will beep. Turn off bread machine, remove bread pan, and turn out dough onto a lightly floured countertop or cutting board.

3. Follow directions for specific recipe.

BAKE CYCLE: Dough

NUTRITIONAL INFORMATION PER SERVING (1/12 OF RECIPE)
Calories 150 / Fat 3.9 grams / Carbohydrates 26.6 grams / Protein 5 grams / Fiber 3.9 grams / Sodium 237 milligrams / Cholesterol 18.1 milligrams

---

Basic Whole Wheat Sweet Dough

*T*he combination of whole wheat and all-purpose flours make this a lighter version of the 100% whole wheat sweet dough. Use it in your choice of recipes in
this chapter.

	SMALL RECIPE	MEDIUM RECIPE	LARGE RECIPE
MILK	¼ cup	⅜ cup	⅜ cup
WATER	¼ cup	⅜ cup	½ cup
EGG	1	1	2
BUTTER OR MARGARINE	3 tablespoons	4 tablespoons	6 tablespoons
DARK BROWN SUGAR	3 tablespoons	¼ cup	6 tablespoons
SALT	½ teaspoon	1 teaspoon	1 teaspoon
WHOLE WHEAT FLOUR	1 cup	1½ cups	2 cups
ALL-PURPOSE FLOUR	1 cup	1½ cups	2 cups
RED STAR BRAND ACTIVE DRY YEAST	1½ teaspoons	1½ teaspoons	2 teaspoons

1. Place dough ingredients in bread pan, select Dough setting, and press Start.

2. When the dough has risen long enough, the machine will beep. Turn off bread
machine, remove bread pan, and turn out dough onto a lightly floured countertop
or cutting board.

3. Follow directions for specific recipe.

BAKE CYCLE: Dough

NUTRITIONAL INFORMATION PER SERVING (1/12 OF RECIPE)
Calories 161 / Fat 3.8 grams / Carbohydrates 27.7 grams / Protein 4.6 grams / Fiber 2.4 grams /
Sodium 237 milligrams / Cholesterol 18.1 milligrams

Coconut Pecan Rolls

*T**hese are easy to make and a big hit with friends—our favorite combination. The surprise ingredient is canned coconut-pecan cake frosting!*

DOUGH

	SMALL	MEDIUM	LARGE
SWEET DOUGH OF YOUR CHOICE, such as Buttermilk Sweet Dough (page 162)			

1. Place dough ingredients in bread pan, select Dough setting, and press Start.

2. When the dough has risen long enough, the machine will beep. Turn off bread machine, remove bread pan, and turn out dough onto a lightly floured countertop or cutting board. Gently roll and stretch dough into a 20-inch rope.

TOPPING

	SMALL	MEDIUM	LARGE
CANNED COCONUT-PECAN CAKE FROSTING	1 cup	one 16-ounce can	2 cups
CHOPPED PECANS	⅓ cup	½ cup	⅔ cup

For the Small Recipe

Spread frosting for the topping on bottom of an 8- or 9-inch round cake pan; sprinkle pecans evenly on top. With a sharp knife, divide dough into 9 pieces.

For the Medium Recipe

Spread frosting for the topping on bottom of a 9 × 13 × 2-inch pan or two 8- or 9-inch round cake pans; sprinkle pecans evenly on top. With a sharp knife, divide dough into 12 pieces.

For the Large Recipe

Spread frosting for the topping on bottom of two 8- or 9-inch round cake pans; sprinkle pecans evenly on top. With a sharp knife, divide dough into 18 pieces.

3. Roll each piece of dough into a ball and place in prepared pan(s).

4. Cover and let rise in a warm oven 30 to 45 minutes until doubled in size. (Hint: To warm oven slightly, turn oven on Warm setting for 1 minute, then turn it off and place covered dough in oven to rise. Remove pan from oven before preheating.)

5. Preheat oven to 350°F. Bake for 25 to 30 minutes until brown.

6. Remove from oven, invert onto serving dish, and serve warm.

BAKE CYCLE: Dough

Small recipe yields 9 rolls
Medium recipe yields 12 rolls
Large recipe yields 18 rolls

NUTRITIONAL INFORMATION PER ROLL
Calories 358 / Fat 7.1 grams / Carbohydrates 53.1 grams / Protein 4.9 grams / Fiber 1.3 grams / Sodium 348 milligrams / Cholesterol 18.4 milligrams

Jim's Cinnamon Rolls

*N*othing can top the aroma and warm, sweet stickiness of cinnamon rolls, fresh from the oven. What you'll also love about these luscious, light rolls is that the machine does half the work; cinnamon rolls are no longer a major production. The first time Lois made these, her husband, Jim, emphatically declared them his favorite recipe—high praise from one who had been completely noncommittal about our breads until then!

DOUGH

	SMALL	MEDIUM	LARGE
SWEET DOUGH OF YOUR CHOICE, such as Basic Sweet Dough (page 160)			

1. Place dough ingredients in bread pan, select Dough setting, and press Start.

2. When the dough has risen long enough, the machine will beep. Turn off bread machine, remove bread pan, and turn out dough onto a lightly floured countertop or cutting board.

GLAZE

	SMALL	MEDIUM	LARGE
MELTED BUTTER OR MARGARINE	3 tablespoons	5 tablespoons	6 tablespoons
DARK BROWN SUGAR	⅓ cup	½ cup	⅔ cup

For the Small Recipe

Pour melted butter for the glaze into one 9-inch round or square cake pan; sprinkle with brown sugar. With a rolling pin, roll dough into an 8 × 14-inch rectangle.

For the Medium Recipe

Pour melted butter for the glaze into one 9 × 13 × 2-inch pan or two 8- or 9-inch round or square cake pans; sprinkle with brown sugar. With a rolling pin, roll dough into a 9 × 18-inch rectangle.

For the Large Recipe

Pour melted butter for the glaze into two 9-inch round or square cake pans; sprinkle with brown sugar. Divide dough in half. With a rolling pin, roll each ball of dough into an 8 × 14-inch rectangle.

FILLING

	SMALL RECIPE	MEDIUM RECIPE	LARGE RECIPE
MELTED BUTTER OR MARGARINE	1 tablespoon	1 tablespoon	2 tablespoons
GRANULATED SUGAR	1 tablespoon	2 tablespoons	2 tablespoons
GROUND CINNAMON	1½ teaspoons	1 tablespoon	1 tablespoon
DARK BROWN SUGAR	1 tablespoon	2 tablespoons	2 tablespoons
RAISINS (OPTIONAL)	⅓ cup	½ cup	⅔ cup

3. Brush melted butter for the filling on the dough. In a small bowl, combine granulated sugar, cinnamon, brown sugar, and raisins; sprinkle over dough. Starting with long edge, roll up dough; pinch seams to seal. With a knife, lightly mark roll into 1½-inch sections. Slide a 12-inch piece of dental floss or heavy thread underneath. By bringing the ends of the floss up and crisscrossing them at the top of each mark, you can cut through the roll by pulling the strings in opposite directions.

Place rolls cut side up in prepared pan(s), flattening them slightly.* Cover and let rise in a warm oven 30 to 45 minutes until doubled. (Hint: To warm oven slightly, turn oven on Warm setting for 1 minute, then turn it off and place covered dough in oven to rise. Remove pan from oven to preheat.)

4. Preheat oven to 350°F. Bake 25 to 30 minutes until golden brown. Remove from oven and immediately invert rolls onto a large platter or serving dish. Serve warm.

BAKE CYCLE: Dough

Small recipe yields 9 rolls
Medium recipe yields 12 rolls
Large recipe yields 18 rolls

NUTRITIONAL INFORMATION PER ROLL
Calories 302 / Fat 10.6 grams / Carbohydrates 48.1 grams / Protein 4.4 grams / Fiber 1.4 grams / Sodium 274 milligrams / Cholesterol 44.7 milligrams

---

*The rolls can be covered with foil at this point and refrigerated overnight or frozen for 1 month. Before baking, allow rolls to thaw completely and rise in a warm oven for at least 30 minutes.

Mini Cinnamon Rolls

These cinnamon rolls are the perfect addition to a buffet brunch; they're just the right size and there are plenty to go around.

DOUGH

	SMALL	MEDIUM	LARGE
SWEET DOUGH OF YOUR CHOICE, such as Basic Sweet Dough (page 160)			

1. Place dough ingredients in bread pan, select Dough setting, and press Start.

2. When the dough has risen long enough, the machine will beep. Turn off bread machine, remove bread pan, and turn out dough onto a lightly floured countertop or cutting board. Shape dough into a log.

FILLING

	SMALL RECIPE	MEDIUM RECIPE	LARGE RECIPE
MELTED BUTTER OR MARGARINE	2 tablespoons	3 tablespoons	¼ cup
GRANULATED SUGAR	¼ cup	⅓ cup	½ cup
GROUND CINNAMON	1½ teaspoons	2 teaspoons	1 tablespoon

For the Small Recipe

Brush one 9-inch round or square cake pan with a little of the melted butter for the filling. With a rolling pin, roll dough into a 20 × 8-inch rectangle.

For the Medium Recipe

Brush two 9-inch round or square cake pans with a little of the melted butter for the filling. With a sharp knife, divide dough in half. With a rolling pin, roll each piece into a 20 × 5-inch rectangle.

For the Large Recipe

Brush three 9-inch round or square cake pans with a little of the melted butter for the filling. With a sharp knife, divide dough into thirds. With a rolling pin, roll each piece into a 20 × 8-inch rectangle.

3. Brush each rectangle of dough with the rest of the melted butter for the filling. In a small bowl, combine sugar and cinnamon; sprinkle mixture over dough. Starting with long edge, roll up dough tightly; pinch seams to seal. With a knife, lightly mark each roll into 24 pieces. Slide a 12-inch piece of dental floss or heavy thread underneath. By bringing the ends of the floss up and crisscrossing them at the top of each mark, you can cut through the roll by pulling the strings in opposite directions.

Place rolls cut side up in prepared pan(s), flattening them slightly.* Cover and let rise in a warm oven 30 to 45 minutes until doubled. (Hint: To warm oven slightly, turn oven on Warm setting for 1 minute, then turn it off and place covered dough in oven to rise. Remove pan from oven to preheat.)

4. Preheat oven to 350°F. Bake 20 to 25 minutes until brown. Remove from oven, turn out onto plate(s), then invert rolls onto serving dishes. Allow rolls to cool slightly.

ICING

	SMALL RECIPE	MEDIUM RECIPE	LARGE RECIPE
CONFECTIONERS' SUGAR	½ cup	1 cup	1 cup
MILK OR CREAM	1½ to 2 teaspoons	3 to 4 teaspoons	3 to 4 teaspoons
VANILLA EXTRACT	¼ teaspoon	½ teaspoon	½ teaspoon

5. Meanwhile, in a small bowl, combine confectioners' sugar, milk, and vanilla for the icing, using enough milk to make the icing thin enough to drizzle on the rolls. Once the rolls have cooled slightly, drizzle with icing and serve.

BAKE CYCLE: Dough

Small recipe yields 24 rolls
Medium recipe yields 48 rolls
Large recipe yields 72 rolls

NUTRITIONAL INFORMATION PER ROLL
Calories 56 / Fat 1.3 grams / Carbohydrates 10 grams / Protein 1.1 grams / Fiber .3 grams / Sodium 65 milligrams / Cholesterol 4.5 milligrams

---

*The rolls can be covered with foil at this point and refrigerated overnight or frozen for 1 month. Before baking, allow rolls to thaw completely and rise in a warm oven for at least 30 minutes.

Caramel Sticky Buns

*T*hese rolls bake in a thick, syrupy sea of sugar. They'll appeal only to the truly serious sweet-treat lover—a person who can eat brown sugar straight from the box. These buns should be eaten fresh out of the oven because they really don't keep well.

DOUGH

	SMALL	MEDIUM	LARGE
SWEET DOUGH OF YOUR CHOICE, such as Basic Sweet Dough (page 160)			

I. Place dough ingredients in bread pan, select Dough setting, and press Start.

2. When the dough has risen long enough, the machine will beep. Turn off bread machine, remove bread pan, and turn out dough onto a lightly floured countertop or cutting board.

TOPPING

	SMALL RECIPE	MEDIUM RECIPE	LARGE RECIPE
MELTED BUTTER OR MARGARINE	2 tablespoons	2 tablespoons	¼ cup
DARK BROWN SUGAR	½ cup	¾ cup	1 cup
LIGHT OR DARK CORN SYRUP	¼ cup	⅜ cup	½ cup

For the Small Recipe
Brush one 9-inch round or square cake pan with melted butter for the topping. Sprinkle brown sugar over the bottom of the pan. Pour corn syrup over the sugar. With a rolling pin, roll each piece into a 12 × 10-inch rectangle.

For the Medium Recipe
Brush one 9 × 13 × 2-inch pan or two 9-inch round or square cake pans with melted butter for the topping. Sprinkle brown sugar over the bottom of the pan(s). Pour corn syrup over the sugar. With a rolling pin, roll each piece into an 18 × 10-inch rectangle.

For the Large Recipe

With a sharp knife, divide dough in half. Brush two 9-inch round or square cake pans with melted butter for the topping. Sprinkle brown sugar over the bottom of the pans. Pour corn syrup over the sugar. With a rolling pin, roll each piece into a 12 × 10-inch rectangle.

FILLING

	SMALL RECIPE	MEDIUM RECIPE	LARGE RECIPE
MELTED BUTTER OR MARGARINE	1 tablespoon	1 tablespoon	2 tablespoons
DARK BROWN SUGAR	¼ cup	⅓ cup	½ cup
GROUND CINNAMON	1 teaspoon	1 teaspoon	2 teaspoons
RAISINS	¼ cup	⅓ cup	½ cup

3. Brush each piece of dough with melted butter for the filling. In a small bowl, combine brown sugar, cinnamon, and raisins; sprinkle mixture over dough. Starting with long edge, roll up dough tightly; pinch seams to seal. With a knife, lightly mark each roll into 1-inch sections. Slide a 12-inch piece of dental floss or heavy thread underneath. By bringing the ends of the floss up and crisscrossing them at the top of each mark, you can cut through the roll by pulling the strings in opposite directions.

Place rolls cut side up in prepared pan(s), flattening them slightly. Cover and let rise in a warm oven 30 to 45 minutes until doubled. (Hint: To warm oven slightly, turn oven on Warm setting for 1 minute, then turn it off and place covered dough in oven to rise. Remove pan from oven to preheat.)

4. Preheat oven to 325°F. Bake about 45 minutes until brown. Remove from oven and invert onto serving platter. Leave pan on top of rolls 1 to 2 minutes, allowing topping to drip out of pan. Serve warm.

BAKE CYCLE: Dough

Small recipe yields 12 rolls
Medium recipe yields 18 rolls
Large recipe yields 24 rolls

NUTRITIONAL INFORMATION PER BUN
Calories 201 / Fat 3.9 grams / Carbohydrates 39.3 grams / Protein 2.9 grams / Fiber .8 gram / Sodium 189 milligrams / Cholesterol 12 milligrams

Orange Coconut Sweet Rolls

*T**he orange and coconut combine to make these exotic rolls memorable. Serve proudly to your guests.*

DOUGH

	SMALL	MEDIUM	LARGE
SWEET DOUGH OF YOUR CHOICE, SUCH AS Buttermilk Sweet Dough (page 162)			

1. Place dough ingredients in bread pan, select Dough setting, and press Start.

2. When the dough has risen long enough, the machine will beep. Turn off bread machine, remove bread pan, and turn out dough onto a lightly floured countertop or cutting board. Shape dough into a log.

FILLING

	SMALL RECIPE	MEDIUM RECIPE	LARGE RECIPE
MELTED BUTTER OR MARGARINE	1 tablespoon	2 tablespoons	3 tablespoons
FLAKED SWEETENED COCONUT	½ cup	1 cup	1½ cups
GRANULATED SUGAR	¼ cup	½ cup	¾ cup
GRATED ORANGE RIND	of 2 medium oranges	of 3 medium oranges	of 4 medium oranges

3. In a small bowl, combine coconut, sugar, and grated orange rind for the filling; set aside.

For the Small Recipe
Grease one 9-inch round or square cake pan. With a rolling pin, roll dough into a 12 × 8-inch rectangle.

For the Medium Recipe
Grease two 9-inch round or square cake pans. With a sharp knife, divide dough in half. With a rolling pin, roll each piece into a 12 × 8-inch rectangle.

For the Large Recipe

Grease three 9-inch round or square cake pans. With a sharp knife, divide dough into thirds. With a rolling pin, roll each piece into a 12 × 8-inch rectangle.

4. Brush each rectangle of dough with melted butter for the filling; sprinkle filling mixture evenly on top. Starting with long edge, roll up dough tightly; pinch seams to seal. With a knife, lightly mark each roll into 1-inch sections. Slide a 12-inch piece of dental floss or heavy thread underneath. By bringing the ends of the floss up and crisscrossing them at the top of each mark, you can cut through the roll by pulling the strings in opposite directions.

Place rolls cut side up in prepared pan(s), flattening them slightly. Cover and let rise in a warm oven 30 to 45 minutes until doubled. (Hint: To warm oven slightly, turn oven on Warm setting for 1 minute, then turn it off and place covered dough in oven to rise. Remove pan from oven to preheat.)

5. Preheat oven to 350°F. Bake 30 minutes until golden. Remove from oven, turn out onto plate(s), then invert rolls onto serving dishes. Allow rolls to cool slightly.

ICING

	SMALL RECIPE	MEDIUM RECIPE	LARGE RECIPE
CONFECTIONERS' SUGAR	½ cup	1 cup	1 cup
ORANGE JUICE	1 to 2 teaspoons	3 to 4 teaspoons	5 to 6 teaspoons

6. Meanwhile, in a small bowl, combine the sugar and orange juice for the icing, adding enough orange juice to make the icing thin enough to drizzle. When rolls have cooled slightly, drizzle with icing and serve.

BAKE CYCLE: Dough

Small recipe yields 12 rolls
Medium recipe yields 24 rolls
Large recipe yields 36 rolls

NUTRITIONAL INFORMATION PER ROLL
Calories 139 / Fat 3.6 grams / Carbohydrates 24.5 grams / Protein 2.4 grams / Fiber .9 gram / Sodium 153 milligrams / Cholesterol 9.2 milligrams

---

Gooey Orange Rolls

*A*s their name implies, these rolls have a piquant citrus flavor and a bubbly orange sauce. They make an out-of-the-ordinary Sunday brunch treat, one worth repeating for a whole month of Sundays!

DOUGH

	SMALL	MEDIUM	LARGE
SWEET DOUGH OF YOUR CHOICE, such as Basic Sweet Dough (page 160)			

1. Place dough ingredients in bread pan, select Dough setting, and press Start.

2. When the dough has risen long enough, the machine will beep. Turn off bread machine, remove bread pan, and turn out dough onto a lightly floured countertop or cutting board.

TOPPING

	SMALL RECIPE	MEDIUM RECIPE	LARGE RECIPE
FROZEN ORANGE JUICE CONCENTRATE	one 6-ounce can	one 6-ounce can	one 12-ounce can
SUGAR	½ cup	½ cup	1 cup
BUTTER OR MARGARINE	4 tablespoons	4 tablespoons	8 tablespoons
GRATED ORANGE RIND	2 teaspoons	2 teaspoons	4 teaspoons

3. In a small saucepan, combine orange juice and sugar for the topping. Cook on medium heat until sugar dissolves. Add butter and grated orange rind; stir. Cook until the butter melts.

For the Small Recipe

Pour the topping into a 9-inch square or round cake pan. With a rolling pin, roll dough into a 9-inch square.

For the Medium Recipe

Pour the topping into a 9 × 13 × 2-inch square cake pan. With a rolling pin, roll dough into a 12-inch square.

With a sharp knife, divide dough in half. Pour the topping into two 9-inch square or round cake pans. With a rolling pin, roll each piece of dough into a 9-inch square.

FILLING

	SMALL RECIPE	MEDIUM RECIPE	LARGE RECIPE
SUGAR	3 tablespoons	¼ cup	6 tablespoons
GROUND CINNAMON	¾ teaspoon	1 teaspoon	1½ teaspoons
GROUND CLOVES	1 pinch	⅛ teaspoon	⅛ teaspoon
GRATED ORANGE RIND	2 teaspoons	2 teaspoons	4 teaspoons

4. In a small bowl, combine sugar, cinnamon, cloves, and grated orange rind for the filling; sprinkle evenly over dough. Starting at one edge, roll up dough tightly; pinch seam to seal. With a knife, lightly mark each roll into 1-inch sections. Slide a 12-inch piece of dental floss or heavy thread underneath. By bringing the ends of the floss up and crisscrossing them at the top of each mark, you can cut through the roll by pulling the strings in opposite directions.

Place rolls cut side up in prepared pan(s), flattening them slightly. Cover and let rise in a warm oven 30 to 45 minutes until doubled. (Hint: To warm oven slightly, turn oven on Warm setting for 1 minute, then turn it off and place covered dough in oven to rise. Remove pan from oven to preheat.)

5. Preheat oven to 400°F. Bake for 15 to 20 minutes until brown. Remove from oven and immediately invert pan onto a serving platter. Serve warm.

BAKE CYCLE: Dough

Small recipe yields 9 rolls
Medium recipe yields 12 rolls
Large recipe yields 18 rolls

NUTRITIONAL INFORMATION PER ROLL
Calories 267 / Fat 6.6 grams / Carbohydrates 47.6 grams / Protein 4.5 grams / Fiber 1.2 grams / Sodium 282 milligrams / Cholesterol 18.1 milligrams

Cinnamon Bubble Coffee Cake

W*e love this cinnamon-sugar extravagance hot out of the oven, served with a cup of freshly brewed coffee—the perfect way to start a weekend!*

DOUGH

	SMALL	MEDIUM	LARGE
SWEET DOUGH OF YOUR CHOICE, such as Basic Not-So-Sweet Dough (page 161)			

1. Place dough ingredients in bread pan, select Dough setting, and press Start.

2. When the dough has risen long enough, the machine will beep. Turn off bread machine, remove bread pan, and turn out dough onto a floured countertop or cutting board.

For the Small Recipe

Brush an 8½ × 4½ × 2½-inch loaf pan with a little of the melted butter needed for the topping. Gently roll and stretch dough into a 20-inch rope. With a sharp knife, divide dough into 40 pieces and then roll each piece into a ball. (Hint: First cut dough into 10 equal pieces, then cut each of those into 4 small pieces.)

For the Medium Recipe

Brush a 9-inch ring mold with a little of the melted butter needed for the topping. Gently roll and stretch dough into a 24-inch rope. With a sharp knife, divide dough into 60 pieces and then roll each piece into a ball. (Hint: First cut dough into 12 equal pieces, then cut each of those into 5 small pieces.)

For the Large Recipe

Brush two 8½ × 4½ × 2½-inch loaf pans with a little of the melted butter needed for the topping. Cut dough in half. Gently roll and stretch each piece of dough into a 20-inch rope. With a sharp knife, divide each rope into 40 pieces and then roll each piece into a ball. (Hint: First cut dough into 10 equal pieces, then cut each of those into 4 small pieces.)

TOPPING

	SMALL RECIPE	MEDIUM RECIPE	LARGE RECIPE
MELTED BUTTER OR MARGARINE	¼ cup	¼ cup	½ cup
DARK BROWN SUGAR	¾ cup	¾ cup	1½ cups
GROUND CINNAMON	1 teaspoon	1 teaspoon	2 teaspoons

3. In a small bowl, combine brown sugar and cinnamon for the topping; sprinkle ¼ cup of sugar mixture into each of the prepared pan(s). Dip each piece of dough into remaining melted butter, then roll it in the remaining sugar mixture. Place the sugar-coated pieces in the pan(s) in layers.

4. Cover and let rise in a warm oven 30 to 45 minutes until doubled in size. (Hint: To warm oven slightly, turn oven on Warm setting for 1 minute, then turn it off, and place covered dough in oven to rise. Remove pan from oven before preheating.)

5. Preheat oven to 350°F. Bake for 25 to 30 minutes until brown.

6. Remove from oven, turn out onto a plate(s), then invert onto serving platter(s), and serve warm.

BAKE CYCLE: Dough

Small recipe yields 1 coffee cake
Medium recipe yields 1 coffee cake
Large recipe yields 2 coffee cakes

NUTRITIONAL INFORMATION PER SERVING (¹⁄₁₂ OF CAKE)
Calories 228 / Fat 5.8 grams / Carbohydrates 40 grams / Protein 4.2 grams / Fiber 1 gram / Sodium 276 milligrams / Cholesterol 17.9 milligrams

Orange Bubble Loaf

*S*erve this attractive coffee cake at a holiday brunch or on Christmas morning for a surefire crowd pleaser. To eat, pull off sugary, orange-crusted rounds of sweet bread, one at a time.

DOUGH

	SMALL	MEDIUM	LARGE
SWEET DOUGH OF YOUR CHOICE, such as Basic Not-So-Sweet Dough (page 161)			
GRATED LEMON RIND	1 teaspoon	1 teaspoon	2 teaspoons

1. Place dough ingredients, including the grated lemon rind, in bread pan, select Dough setting, and press Start.

2. When the dough has risen long enough, the machine will beep. Turn off bread machine, remove bread pan, and turn out dough onto a floured countertop or cutting board.

For the Small Recipe
Brush an 8½ × 4½ × 2½-inch loaf pan with a little of the melted butter needed for the glaze.

For the Medium Recipe
Brush a 10-inch ring mold with a little of the melted butter needed for the glaze.

For the Large Recipe
Brush two 8½ × 4½ × 2½-inch loaf pans with a little of the melted butter needed for the glaze. Cut dough in half.

GLAZE

	SMALL RECIPE	MEDIUM RECIPE	LARGE RECIPE
MELTED BUTTER OR MARGARINE	¼ cup	¼ cup	½ cup
SUGAR	½ cup	½ cup	1 cup
GRATED ORANGE RIND	3 tablespoons	3 tablespoons	6 tablespoons

3. In a small bowl, combine remaining melted butter, sugar, and grated orange rind for the glaze. Pinch off small pieces of dough about the size of acorns, and roll into balls. Roll each in the glaze and then place in prepared pan(s). Cover and let rise in a warm oven 30 to 45 minutes until doubled in size. (Hint: To warm oven slightly, turn oven on Warm setting for 1 minute, then turn it off and place covered dough in oven to rise. Remove pan from oven before preheating.)

4. Preheat oven to 350°F. Bake for 30 minutes until golden. Remove from oven, turn out onto plate(s), and then invert onto serving platter(s). Serve warm.

BAKE CYCLE: Dough

Small recipe yields 1 coffee cake
Medium recipe yields 1 coffee cake
Large recipe yields 2 coffee cakes

NUTRITIONAL INFORMATION PER SERVING ($\frac{1}{12}$ OF MEDIUM COFFEE CAKE)
Calories 212 / Fat 7.2 grams / Carbohydrates 33.3 grams / Protein 3.6 grams / Fiber .9 gram / Sodium 237 milligrams / Cholesterol 15.5 milligrams

---

Whole Wheat Fruit Roll

A strong whole wheat flavor makes this coffee cake different and surprising. If you omit the icing and use fruit-sweetened (sugarless) preserves, this coffee cake will fall into the "great taste, no guilt" category.

DOUGH

	SMALL	MEDIUM	LARGE
WHOLE WHEAT SWEET DOUGH OF YOUR CHOICE, such as Basic Whole Wheat Sweet Dough (page 163)			

1. Place dough ingredients in bread pan, select Dough setting, and press Start.

2. When the dough has risen long enough, the machine will beep. Turn off bread machine, remove bread pan, and turn out dough onto a floured countertop or cutting board. Shape dough into a log.

For the Small Recipe
Grease a 10 × 15 × 1-inch jelly roll pan or large baking sheet. With a rolling pin, roll dough into a 12 × 8-inch rectangle. With a knife, lightly score the dough lengthwise, dividing it into thirds.

For the Medium Recipe
Grease a 10 × 15 × 1-inch jelly roll pan or large baking sheet. With a rolling pin, roll dough into a 14 × 10-inch rectangle. With a knife, lightly score the dough lengthwise, dividing it into thirds.

For the Large Recipe
Grease two 10 × 15 × 1-inch jelly roll pans or two large baking sheets. Divide dough in half with a sharp knife. With a rolling pin, roll each piece of dough into a 12 × 8-inch rectangle. With a knife, lightly score the dough lengthwise, dividing it into thirds.

	SMALL RECIPE	MEDIUM RECIPE	LARGE RECIPE
ANY FLAVOR FRUIT PRESERVES	1 cup	1½ cups	2 cups

3.   For the filling, spread preserves lengthwise down the center third of the dough. With a sharp knife, cut strips at 1-inch intervals down each side of the dough, from the edge to the filling. Alternately, cross the strips over the filling.

4.   Cover and let rise in a warm oven for 1 hour. (Hint: To warm oven slightly, turn oven on Warm setting for 1 minute, then turn it off and place covered dough in oven to rise. Remove pan from oven to preheat.)

5.   Preheat oven to 350°F. Bake for 25 minutes. Remove from oven, place on serving platter(s), and allow to cool slightly.

ICING

	SMALL RECIPE	MEDIUM RECIPE	LARGE RECIPE
CONFECTIONERS' SUGAR	½ cup	½ cup	1 cup
MILK	2½ teaspoons	2½ teaspoons	5 teaspoons

6.   Meanwhile, in a small bowl, combine sugar and milk for the icing, adding enough milk to make the icing thin enough to drizzle on the coffee cake. Once the coffee cake has cooled slightly, drizzle icing on top and serve.

BAKE CYCLE: Dough

Small recipe yields 1 coffee cake
Medium recipe yields 1 coffee cake
Large recipe yields 2 coffee cakes

NUTRITIONAL INFORMATION PER SERVING (1/12 OF CAKE)
Calories 279 / Fat 4 grams / Carbohydrates 58.8 grams / Protein 5.3 grams / Fiber 4.3 grams / Sodium 242 milligrams / Cholesterol 18.1 milligrams

Celia and Ginny's Raspberry-Cream Coffee Cake with Almonds

Every year, Linda's Aunt Celia and Cousin Ginny made an award-winning raspberry jam from hand-picked Oregon raspberries. Of course, its goodness was enhanced by memories of many happy family breakfasts at their table. Thoughts of those times and that special jam inspired this coffee cake, which rates all the superlatives—simply scrumptious, incredibly edible, and outrageously delicious!

DOUGH

	SMALL RECIPE	MEDIUM RECIPE	LARGE RECIPE
WATER	½ cup	¾ cup	¾ cup
EGG	1	1	2
BUTTER OR MARGARINE, SOFTENED	½ cup	⅔ cup	1 cup
SUGAR	1 tablespoon	1½ tablespoons	2 tablespoons
SALT	¼ teaspoon	½ teaspoon	½ teaspoon
ALL-PURPOSE FLOUR	2 cups	3 cups	4 cups
RED STAR BRAND ACTIVE DRY YEAST	1½ teaspoons	1½ teaspoons	2 teaspoons

1. Place dough ingredients in bread pan, select Dough setting, and press Start.

2. When the dough has risen long enough, the machine will beep. Turn off bread machine, remove bread pan, and turn out dough onto a floured countertop or cutting board. Shape dough into a log.

For the Small Recipe

With a sharp knife, divide dough in half. With a rolling pin, roll each half into a 9-inch square. Gently place 1 of the squares in an ungreased 9-inch square pan.

For the Medium Recipe

With a sharp knife, divide dough in half. With a rolling pin, roll each half into a 9 × 13-inch rectangle. Gently place 1 of the rectangles in an ungreased 9 × 13 × 2-inch pan.

For the Large Recipe

With a sharp knife, divide dough into 4 pieces. With a rolling pin, roll each piece into a 9-inch square. Gently place a square in each of 2 ungreased 9-inch square pans.

FILLING

	SMALL RECIPE	MEDIUM RECIPE	LARGE RECIPE
RASPBERRY JAM	3 tablespoons	5 tablespoons	6 tablespoons
CREAM CHEESE, SOFTENED	8 ounces	11 ounces	16 ounces
EGG	1	1	2
SUGAR	½ cup	⅔ cup	1 cup

TOPPING

	SMALL RECIPE	MEDIUM RECIPE	LARGE RECIPE
SLICED ALMONDS	¼ cup	⅓ cup	½ cup
SUGAR	1 tablespoon	1½ tablespoons	2 tablespoons

3. Spread the raspberry jam over dough in the pan.

4. In a medium bowl, combine the cream cheese, egg(s), and sugar; beat with an electric mixer until well blended. With a spatula, carefully spread cream cheese mixture over the layer of jam. Place the other piece of dough on top of the cream cheese layer. Sprinkle the almonds and sugar over all.

5. Cover and let rise in a warm oven for 20 to 30 minutes until almost doubled. (Hint: To warm oven slightly, turn oven on Warm setting for 1 minute, then turn it off and place covered dough in oven to rise. Remove pan from oven to preheat.)

6. Preheat oven to 350°F. Bake for 40 to 45 minutes until the filling has set. Remove from oven; serve warm or allow to cool slightly and serve at room temperature.

BAKE CYCLE: Dough

Small recipe yields 1 coffee cake
Medium recipe yields 1 coffee cake
Large recipe yields 2 coffee cakes

NUTRITIONAL INFORMATION PER SERVING ($\frac{1}{12}$ OF CAKE)
Calories 332 / Fat 14.3 grams / Carbohydrates 44.5 grams / Protein 6.9 grams / Fiber 1.3 grams / Sodium 225 milligrams / Cholesterol 63.9 milligrams

---

Apple Strudel

This recipe is easier than it looks and well worth a try.

DOUGH

	SMALL RECIPE	MEDIUM RECIPE	LARGE RECIPE
MILK	½ cup	½ cup	¾ cup
EGG	1	2	2
BUTTER OR MARGARINE	½ cup	¾ cup	1 cup
SUGAR	¼ cup	⅓ cup	½ cup
SALT	½ teaspoon	1 teaspoon	1 teaspoon
ALL-PURPOSE FLOUR	2 cups	3 cups	4 cups
RED STAR BRAND ACTIVE DRY YEAST	1½ teaspoons	1½ teaspoons	2 teaspoons

1. Place dough ingredients in bread pan, select Dough setting, and press Start.

2. When the dough has risen long enough, the machine will beep. Turn off bread machine, remove bread pan, and turn out dough onto a heavily floured countertop or cutting board.

For the Small Recipe
With a rolling pin, roll dough into one large 16 × 10-inch rectangle or two 8 × 10-inch rectangles.

For the Medium Recipe
With a rolling pin, roll dough into one large 20 × 12-inch rectangle or two 10 × 12-inch rectangles.

For the Large Recipe
With a sharp knife, cut dough in half. With a rolling pin, roll each half into 16 × 10-inch rectangles or divide again and roll into four 8 × 10-inch rectangles.

3. Butter a 10 × 15 × 1-inch jelly-roll pan or large baking sheet with edges (to avoid spillage during baking).

FILLING

	SMALL RECIPE	MEDIUM RECIPE	LARGE RECIPE
PEELED, CORED, THINLY SLICED GRANNY SMITH APPLES	2 cups	3 cups	4 cups
ALL-PURPOSE FLOUR	1 tablespoon	1½ tablespoons	2 tablespoons
RAISINS	⅓ cup	½ cup	⅔ cup
DARK BROWN SUGAR	⅓ cup	½ cup	⅔ cup
GROUND CINNAMON	1 teaspoon	1 teaspoon	2 teaspoons

4. In a large bowl, combine apples, flour, raisins, sugar, and cinnamon. Spread mixture on each piece of dough to within 1 inch of the edges. Starting from the long edge, carefully roll up dough; pinch edges and ends to seal. Place strudel-rolls seam side down on prepared pan. Shape into large crescents by curving ends slightly toward each other.

5. Cover and let rise in a warm oven about 45 minutes until doubled in size. (Hint: To warm oven slightly, turn oven on Warm setting for 1 minute, then turn it off and place covered dough in oven to rise. Remove pan from oven before preheating.)

6. Preheat oven to 350°F. Bake for 35 to 40 minutes until brown. Remove from oven and place on rack to cool.

ICING

	SMALL RECIPE	MEDIUM RECIPE	LARGE RECIPE
CONFECTIONERS' SUGAR	⅓ cup	½ cup	⅔ cup
MILK	2 teaspoons	2½ teaspoons	3 teaspoons

6. In a small bowl, combine the sugar and milk for the icing, adding enough milk to make the icing thin enough to drizzle on the strudel. Once the strudel has cooled, drizzle icing on top and serve.

BAKE CYCLE: Dough

Small recipe yields 1 large or 2 small strudels
Medium recipe yields 1 large or 2 small strudels
Large recipe yields 2 large or 4 small strudels

NUTRITIONAL INFORMATION PER SERVING ($\frac{1}{12}$ OF MEDIUM STRUDEL)
Calories 319 / Fat 10 grams / Carbohydrates 52.8 grams / Protein 5.2 grams / Fiber 2 grams / Sodium 341 milligrams / Cholesterol 36 milligrams

Irene's Bavarian Coffee Cake

*O*ur friend Irene thought this was the best of all the breads and coffee cakes we asked coworkers to taste-test. Once you make it, you'll understand why. Not only is it velvety rich and spicy, this coffee cake is amazingly quick and easy to create. We think it could also be served for dessert following a light meal.

DOUGH

	SMALL	MEDIUM	LARGE
SWEET DOUGH OF YOUR CHOICE, such as Basic Sweet Dough (page 160)			

1. Place dough ingredients in bread pan, select Dough setting, and press Start.

2. When the dough has risen long enough, the machine will beep. Turn off bread machine, remove bread pan, and turn out dough onto a floured countertop or cutting board.

For the Small Recipe

Grease a 9-inch round or square cake pan. With a rolling pin, roll dough into a 9-inch square or circle to fit pan.

For the Medium Recipe

Grease a 9 × 13 × 2-inch pan. With a rolling pin, roll dough into a 9 × 13-inch rectangle.

For the Large Recipe

Grease two 9-inch round or square cake pans. With a sharp knife, divide dough in half. With a rolling pin, roll each piece of dough into a 9-inch square or circle to fit pans.

3. Place dough in prepared pan(s). Cover and let rise in a warm oven 30 to 45 minutes until doubled in size. (Hint: To warm oven slightly, turn oven on Warm setting for 1 minute, then turn it off and place covered dough in oven to rise. Remove pan from oven before preheating.)

TOPPING

	SMALL RECIPE	MEDIUM RECIPE	LARGE RECIPE
SUGAR	¼ cup	⅓ cup	½ cup
GROUND CINNAMON	¾ teaspoon	1 teaspoon	1½ teaspoons
HEAVY CREAM	⅔ cup	1 cup	1⅓ cups

4. With 2 fingers, punch deep holes all over the dough. In a small bowl, combine sugar and cinnamon; sprinkle mixture evenly over dough. Drizzle cream evenly on top.

5. Preheat oven to 350°F. Bake for 25 to 30 minutes until a tester inserted in the middle of the cake comes out clean. Remove from oven and serve warm.

BAKE CYCLE: Dough

Small recipe yields one 1 coffee cake
Medium recipe yields 1 coffee cake
Large recipe yields 2 coffee cakes

NUTRITIONAL INFORMATION PER SERVING (1⁄12 OF CAKE)
Calories 216 / Fat 9.6 grams / Carbohydrates 28.9 grams / Protein 3.7 grams / Fiber .8 gram / Sodium 192 milligrams / Cholesterol 36.2 milligrams

Aunt Bertha's Moravian Sugar Cake

*T*his is a treat from the Old Country. When Linda took this coffee cake to work to share at break, Janet, a coworker, took one bite and exclaimed, "It's Aunt Bertha's coffee cake!" She was thrilled because it brought back fond memories of a long-lost family recipe. It seemed only fitting to name this in honor of Janet's aunt Bertha.

DOUGH

	SMALL RECIPE	MEDIUM RECIPE	LARGE RECIPE
INSTANT POTATO FLAKES	⅓ cup	½ cup	⅔ cup
WATER	⅝ cup	⅝ cup	⅞ cup
EGG	1	2	2
BUTTER OR MARGARINE	⅓ cup	½ cup	⅔ cup
SUGAR	⅓ cup	½ cup	⅔ cup
SALT	½ teaspoon	1 teaspoon	1 teaspoon
VANILLA EXTRACT	½ teaspoon	1 teaspoon	1 teaspoon
ALL-PURPOSE FLOUR	2 cups	3 cups	4 cups
RED STAR BRAND ACTIVE DRY YEAST	2 teaspoons	2 teaspoons	2½ teaspoons

I. Place dough ingredients in bread pan, select Dough setting, and press Start.

2. When the dough has risen long enough, the machine will beep. Turn off bread machine, remove bread pan, and turn out dough onto a floured countertop or cutting board.

For the Small Recipe
Grease a 9 × 13 × 2-inch pan.

For the Medium Recipe
Grease a 15 × 10 × 1-inch jelly-roll pan or a large, rimmed baking sheet.

For the Large Recipe

Grease two 9 × 13 × 2-inch pans. With a sharp knife, divide dough in half.

3. Place dough in prepared pan(s), gently stretching it and pressing it evenly into the pan(s). Cover and let rise in a warm oven 30 to 45 minutes until doubled in size. (Hint: To warm oven slightly, turn oven on Warm setting for 1 minute, then turn it off and place covered dough in oven to rise. Remove pan from oven before preheating.)

TOPPING

	SMALL RECIPE	MEDIUM RECIPE	LARGE RECIPE
LIGHT BROWN SUGAR	⅔ cup	1 cup	1⅓ cups
GROUND CINNAMON	1½ teaspoons	2 teaspoons	1 tablespoon
MELTED BUTTER OR MARGARINE	⅓ cup	½ cup	⅔ cup

4. In a small bowl, combine brown sugar and cinnamon for the topping. With 2 fingers, punch deep holes all over the dough. Sprinkle sugar mixture evenly over dough. Drizzle melted butter on top.

5. Preheat oven to 350°F. Bake for 20 to 25 minutes until golden brown. Remove from oven and place on a serving plate.

ICING

	SMALL RECIPE	MEDIUM RECIPE	LARGE RECIPE
CONFECTIONERS' SUGAR	½ cup	¾ cup	1 cup
MILK	3 teaspoons	4 teaspoons	6 teaspoons

6. In a small bowl, combine the sugar and milk for the icing, adding enough milk to make the icing thin enough to drizzle on the coffee cake.

7. Serve coffee cake warm without icing, or allow coffee cake to cool slightly, drizzle icing on top, and serve.

BAKE CYCLE: Dough

Small recipe yields 1 coffee cake
Medium recipe yields 1 coffee cake
Large recipe yields 2 coffee cakes

NUTRITIONAL INFORMATION PER SERVING ($\frac{1}{12}$ OF CAKE)
Calories 362 / Fat 12.7 grams / Carbohydrates 58 grams / Protein 4.8 grams / Fiber 1.2 grams / Sodium 388 milligrams / Cholesterol 35.6 milligrams

---

Portuguese Sweet Bread

This is a very sweet coffee cake bread with a hint of lemon. It is delightful with afternoon tea.

	SMALL RECIPE	MEDIUM RECIPE	LARGE RECIPE
INSTANT POTATO FLAKES	2 tablespoons	3 tablespoons	¼ cup
SWEETENED CONDENSED MILK	3 tablespoons	¼ cup	6 tablespoons
WATER	⅓ to ½ cup	½ to ⅝ cup	⅔ to ¾ cup
EGG	1	2	2
BUTTER OR MARGARINE	3 tablespoons	4 tablespoons	6 tablespoons
SUGAR	¼ cup	⅓ cup	½ cup
SALT	½ teaspoon	1 teaspoon	1 teaspoon
VANILLA EXTRACT	½ teaspoon	½ teaspoon	1 teaspoon
LEMON EXTRACT	⅛ teaspoon	¼ teaspoon	¼ teaspoon
BREAD FLOUR	2 cups	3 cups	4 cups
GROUND NUTMEG	1 pinch	1 pinch	⅛ teaspoon
RED STAR BRAND ACTIVE DRY YEAST	3 teaspoons	3 teaspoons	3½ teaspoons
EGG WHITE, LIGHTLY BEATEN	1	1	1

1. Place all ingredients except egg white in bread pan, using the least amount of liquid listed in the recipe. Select Dough setting and press Start.

2. Observe the dough as it kneads. After 5 to 10 minutes, if it appears dry and stiff, or if your machine sounds as if it's straining to knead it, add more liquid 1 tablespoon at a time until dough forms a smooth, soft, pliable ball that is slightly tacky to the touch.

3. When the dough has risen long enough, the machine will beep. Turn off bread machine, remove bread pan, and turn out dough onto a lightly floured countertop or cutting board.

For the Small and Medium Recipes

Grease one 8- or 9-inch pie tin.

For the Large Recipe

Grease two 8- or 9-inch pie tins. With a sharp knife, divide dough in half.

4. Gently roll and stretch each piece of dough into a 30-inch rope of even thickness from one end to the other. Starting at one end and working to the other, gently twist the rope(s). Place one end of the twisted rope of dough in the center of the prepared pie tin(s); carefully coil the rest of the rope around the center, filling the pan.

5. Cover and let rise in a warm oven at least 1 hour until doubled. (Hint: To warm oven slightly, turn oven on Warm setting for 1 minute, then turn it off and place covered dough in oven to rise. Remove pan from oven before preheating.)

6. Preheat oven to 325°F. Brush dough with egg white. Bake for 50 to 60 minutes until brown.

7. Remove from oven, cool on rack in pan. When cool, remove from pan, thinly slice, and serve.

BAKE CYCLE: Dough

Small and medium recipes yield 1 loaf
Large recipe yields 2 loaves

NUTRITIONAL INFORMATION PER SLICE
Calories 169 / Fat 3.9 grams / Carbohydrates 28.3 grams / Protein 4.6 grams / Fiber .9 gram / Sodium 214 milligrams / Cholesterol 32.3 milligrams

---

Squaw Bread

W hen dining out, we've always enjoyed this sweet whole wheat and rye bread. Don't overlook the first step. Puree the liquids and sweeteners in the blender before adding them to the bread pan.

	SMALL RECIPE	MEDIUM RECIPE	LARGE RECIPE
MILK	⅜ cup	⅝ cup	⅞ cup
WATER	⅜ to ½ cup	⅝ to ¾ cup	⅞ to 1 cup
OIL	1½ tablespoons	2 tablespoons	3 tablespoons
HONEY	1 tablespoon	1½ tablespoons	2 tablespoons
RAISINS	1½ tablespoons	2 tablespoons	3 tablespoons
DARK BROWN SUGAR	1½ tablespoons	2 tablespoons	3 tablespoons
BREAD FLOUR	1 cup	1½ cups	2 cups
WHOLE WHEAT FLOUR	¾ cup	1¼ cups	1½ cups
RYE FLOUR	½ cup	¾ cup	1 cup
VITAL WHEAT GLUTEN (OPTIONAL)	2 tablespoons	3 tablespoons	4 tablespoons
RED STAR BRAND ACTIVE DRY YEAST	1½ teaspoons	2 teaspoons	2½ teaspoons

I. In a blender on high speed, liquefy the milk, water, oil, honey, raisins, and brown sugar. Combine mixture with rest of ingredients in bread pan, select Medium Crust setting then the Whole Wheat cycle and press Start.

2. Observe the dough as it kneads. After 5 to 10 minutes, if it appears dry and stiff, or if your machine sounds as if it's straining to knead it, add more liquid 1 tablespoon at a time until dough forms a smooth, soft, pliable ball that is slightly tacky to the touch.

3. After the baking cycle ends, remove bread from pan, place on cake rack, and allow to cool 1 hour before slicing.

CRUST: Medium
BAKE CYCLE: Whole Wheat
OPTIONAL BAKE CYCLES: Standard; Sweet Bread

NUTRITIONAL INFORMATION PER SLICE
Calories 146 / Fat 2.5 grams / Carbohydrates 27.7 grams / Protein 3.9 grams / Fiber 2.7 grams / Sodium 160 milligrams / Cholesterol .4 milligram

Sally Lunn Bread

*H*ere's an egg bread so sweet it almost tastes like a pound cake. We can picture it on a silver tray with a bowl of strawberries and a pitcher of cream.

	SMALL RECIPE	MEDIUM RECIPE	LARGE RECIPE
HEAVY CREAM	⅛ cup	¼ cup	¼ cup
WATER	⅛ to ¼ cup	¼ to ⅜ cup	¼ to ⅜ cup
EGGS	2	3	4
SALT	½ teaspoon	1 teaspoon	1 teaspoon
BUTTER OR MARGARINE, CUT IN PIECES	¼ cup	⅓ cup	½ cup
SUGAR	3 tablespoons	¼ cup	6 tablespoons
ALL-PURPOSE FLOUR	2 cups	3 cups	4 cups
RED STAR BRAND ACTIVE DRY YEAST	1½ teaspoons	2 teaspoons	2½ teaspoons

I. Place all ingredients in bread pan, using the least amount of liquid listed in the recipe. Select Light Crust setting then the Sweet Bread cycle and press Start.

2. Observe the dough as it kneads. After 5 to 10 minutes, if it appears dry and stiff, or if your machine sounds as if it's straining to knead it, add more liquid 1 tablespoon at a time until dough forms a smooth, soft, pliable ball that is slightly tacky to the touch.

3. After the baking cycle ends, remove bread from pan, place on cake rack, and allow to cool 1 hour before slicing.

CRUST: Light
BAKE CYCLE: Sweet Bread
OPTIONAL BAKE CYCLES: Whole Wheat; Standard

NUTRITIONAL INFORMATION PER SLICE
Calories 181 / Fat 7.2 grams / Carbohydrates 24.3 grams / Protein 4.3 grams / Fiber .8 gram / Sodium 218 milligrams / Cholesterol 51.1 milligrams

---

Margaret's Buttermilk Raisin Bread

*T*his bread earns rave reviews from all tasters. It's very moist and tender, and delicious toasted. Our friend Margaret loved it at first taste. In fact, shortly after that, she purchased a bread machine. It really is that good.

	SMALL RECIPE	MEDIUM RECIPE	LARGE RECIPE
BUTTERMILK	⅝ to ¾ cup	⅞ to 1 cup	1 to 1⅛ cups
EGG	1	1	2
BUTTER OR MARGARINE	4 tablespoons	5 tablespoons	6 tablespoons
SUGAR	2 tablespoons	3 tablespoons	¼ cup
SALT	1 teaspoon	1 teaspoon	2 teaspoons
BREAD FLOUR	2 cups	3 cups	4 cups
BAKING SODA	¼ teaspoon	¼ teaspoon	½ teaspoon
RAISINS	½ cup	⅔ cup	1 cup
RED STAR BRAND ACTIVE DRY YEAST	1½ teaspoons	1½ teaspoons	2 teaspoons

1. Place all ingredients in bread pan, using the least amount of liquid listed in the recipe. Select Light Crust setting, then the Sweet cycle, and press Start.

2. Observe the dough as it kneads. After 5 to 10 minutes, if it appears dry and stiff, or if your machine sounds as if it's straining to knead it, add more liquid 1 tablespoon at a time until dough forms a smooth, soft, pliable ball that is slightly tacky to the touch.

3. After the baking cycle ends, remove bread from pan, place on cake rack, and allow to cool 1 hour before slicing.

CRUST: Light
BAKE CYCLE: Sweet
OPTIONAL BAKE CYCLES: Standard; Raisin/Nut

NUTRITIONAL INFORMATION PER SLICE
Calories 167 / Fat 3.8 grams / Carbohydrates 29.5 grams / Protein 4.1 grams / Fiber 1.2 grams / Sodium 237 milligrams / Cholesterol 15.8 milligrams

Raisin Bread

*O*n *a hot summer's evening, a chilled fruit salad and a slice of this delicate bread are perfect together.*

	SMALL RECIPE	MEDIUM RECIPE	LARGE RECIPE
MILK	⅞ to 1 cup	1⅛ to 1¼ cups	1¾ to 1⅞ cups
BUTTER OR MARGARINE	1 tablespoon	2 tablespoons	2 tablespoons
DARK BROWN SUGAR	2 tablespoons	3 tablespoons	¼ cup
SALT	1 teaspoon	1 teaspoon	2 teaspoons
BREAD FLOUR	2 cups	3 cups	4 cups
GROUND CINNAMON	1½ teaspoons	2 teaspoons	1 tablespoon
GRATED NUTMEG	1 pinch	1 pinch	⅛ teaspoon
RAISINS	⅓ cup	½ cup	⅔ cup
RED STAR BRAND ACTIVE DRY YEAST	1½ teaspoons	1½ teaspoons	2 teaspoons

I.   Place all ingredients in bread pan, using the least amount of liquid listed in the recipe. Select Light Crust setting, then the Sweet cycle, and press Start.

2.   Observe the dough as it kneads. After 5 to 10 minutes, if it appears dry and stiff, or if your machine sounds as if it's straining to knead it, add more liquid 1 tablespoon at a time until dough forms a smooth, soft, pliable ball that is slightly tacky to the touch.

3.   After the baking cycle ends, remove bread from pan, place on cake rack, and allow to cool 1 hour before slicing.

CRUST: Light

BAKE CYCLE: Sweet

OPTIONAL BAKE CYCLES: Standard; Raisin/Nut

NUTRITIONAL INFORMATION PER SLICE
Calories 147 / Fat 1.8 grams / Carbohydrates 29.2 grams / Protein 3.7 grams / Fiber 1.2 grams / Sodium 185 milligrams / Cholesterol .8 milligram

Oatmeal Spice Bread

O ur husbands love this delicious, spicy breakfast bread. Try it toasted and spread with cream cheese. (Note: The small loaf is baked on the Rapid Bake setting.)

	SMALL RECIPE	MEDIUM RECIPE	LARGE RECIPE
OLD-FASHIONED ROLLED OATS	½ cup	1 cup	1¼ cups
WATER	⅞ to 1 cup	1¼ to 1⅜ cups	1¾ to 1⅞ cups
OIL	1 tablespoon	3 tablespoons	¼ cup
DARK BROWN SUGAR	3 tablespoons	¼ cup	6 tablespoons
SALT	1 teaspoon	1½ teaspoons	2 teaspoons
BREAD FLOUR	2 cups	3 cups	4 cups
GROUND CINNAMON	¾ teaspoon	1 teaspoon	1½ teaspoons
GRATED NUTMEG	¼ teaspoon	½ teaspoon	½ teaspoon
GROUND GINGER	¼ teaspoon	½ teaspoon	½ teaspoon
GROUND CLOVES	⅛ teaspoon	¼ teaspoon	¼ teaspoon
RAISINS	¼ cup	½ cup	¾ cup
RED STAR BRAND ACTIVE DRY YEAST	1½ teaspoons	1½ teaspoons	2 teaspoons

For the Small Recipe

I.   Place all ingredients in bread pan, using the least amount of liquid listed in the recipe. Select Light Crust setting, then the Rapid Bake cycle, and press Start.

For the Medium and Large Recipes

I.   Place all ingredients in bread pan, using the least amount of liquid listed in the recipe, select Light Crust setting, and press Start.

2.   Observe the dough as it kneads. After 5 to 10 minutes, if it appears dry and stiff, or if your machine sounds as if it's straining to knead it, add more liquid 1 tablespoon at a time until dough forms a smooth, soft, pliable ball that is slightly tacky to the touch.

3. After the baking cycle ends, remove bread from pan, place on cake rack, and allow to cool 1 hour before slicing.

CRUST: Light

BAKE CYCLE: Rapid Bake for small recipe; Standard for medium and large recipes

OPTIONAL BAKE CYCLES: Raisin/Nut

NUTRITIONAL INFORMATION PER SLICE
Calories 180 / Fat 3.6 grams / Carbohydrates 33 grams / Protein 4 grams / Fiber 1.8 grams / Sodium 232 milligrams / Cholesterol 0 milligrams

Specialty
Breads

Whole Wheat Hamburger and Hot Dog Buns

*T*hese are definitely 5-star hamburger buns. You'll never go back to the store-bought version once you've tried these.

	SMALL RECIPE	MEDIUM RECIPE	LARGE RECIPE
WATER	⅝ cup	1 cup	1⅛ cups
EGG	1	1	2
SALT	½ teaspoon	¾ teaspoon	1 teaspoon
SHORTENING	3 tablespoons	¼ cup	6 tablespoons
SUGAR	3 tablespoons	¼ cup	6 tablespoons
ALL-PURPOSE FLOUR	1⅓ cups	2 cups	2⅔ cups
WHOLE WHEAT FLOUR	⅔ cup	1 cup	1⅓ cups
RED STAR BRAND ACTIVE DRY YEAST	2 teaspoons	3 teaspoons	4 teaspoons

I. Place dough ingredients in bread pan, select Dough setting, and press Start.

2. When the dough has risen long enough, the machine will beep. Turn off bread machine, remove bread pan, and turn out dough onto a lightly floured countertop or cutting board.

For the Small Recipe

With a sharp knife, divide dough into 7 pieces for hamburger buns or 8 pieces for hot dog buns.

For the Medium Recipe

With a sharp knife, divide dough into 10 pieces for hamburger buns or 12 pieces for hot dog buns.

For the Large Recipe

With a sharp knife, divide dough into 14 pieces for hamburger buns or 16 pieces for hot dog buns.

3. Grease a baking sheet. Roll pieces of dough into balls and flatten for hamburger buns or shape into 6-inch rolls for hot dog buns. Place on prepared baking sheet.

Cover and let rise in a warm oven 30 to 45 minutes until doubled in size. (Hint: To warm oven slightly, turn oven on Warm setting for 1 minute, then turn it off and place covered dough in oven to rise. Remove pan from oven before preheating.)

4. Preheat oven to 400°F. Bake for 12 to 15 minutes until golden brown. Remove from oven and cool on cake racks. When ready to use, split buns in half horizontally. These will keep in a plastic bag in the freezer for 3 to 4 weeks.

BAKE CYCLE: Dough

Small recipe yields 7 hamburger or 8 hot dog buns
Medium recipe yields 1 0 hamburger or 1 2 hot dog buns
Large recipe yields 1 4 hamburger or 1 6 hot dog buns

NUTRITIONAL INFORMATION PER HAMBURGER BUN
Calories 206 / Fat 6.1 grams / Carbohydrates 32.9 grams / Protein 5.1 grams / Fiber 2.4 grams / Sodium 168 milligrams / Cholesterol 30.4 milligrams

---

NUTRITIONAL INFORMATION PER HOT DOG BUN
Calories 179 / Fat 5.8 grams / Carbohydrates 27.3 grams / Protein 4.4 grams / Fiber 2 grams / Sodium 142 milligrams / Cholesterol 26.6 milligrams

---

Onion Rolls

The distinctive taste of freshly sautéed onions makes these rolls infinitely better than anything bought in a package. They're dynamite with sliced deli meats, cheese, and mustard.

DOUGH

	SMALL RECIPE	MEDIUM RECIPE	LARGE RECIPE
BUTTER OR MARGARINE	3 tablespoons	4 tablespoons	6 tablespoons
MINCED FRESH ONION	½ cup	¾ teaspoon	1 cup
WATER	½ cup	¾ cup	¾ cup
EGG	1	1	2
SUGAR	1 teaspoon	1½ teaspoons	2 teaspoons
SALT	¾ teaspoon	1 teaspoon	1½ teaspoons
NONFAT DRY MILK POWDER	1½ tablespoons	2 tablespoons	3 tablespoons
ALL-PURPOSE FLOUR	2 cups	3 cups	4 cups
RED STAR BRAND ACTIVE DRY YEAST	1½ teaspoons	1½ teaspoons	2 teaspoons

1. In a small skillet over medium heat, melt butter then add onion. Sauté onion about 10 minutes until tender but not browned.

2. Remove pan from heat and allow onion to cool slightly.

For the Small Recipe

Reserve 2 tablespoons of the onion mixture. Place remaining onion mixture and the rest of dough ingredients in bread pan, select Dough setting, and press Start.

When the dough has risen long enough, the machine will beep. Turn off bread machine, remove bread pan, and turn out dough onto a heavily floured countertop or cutting board. Gently roll and stretch dough into a 12-inch rope. With a sharp knife, divide dough into 7 pieces.

For the Medium Recipe

Reserve ¼ cup of the onion mixture. Place remaining onion mixture and the rest of dough ingredients in bread pan, select Dough setting, and press Start.

When the dough has risen long enough, the machine will beep. Turn off bread machine, remove bread pan, and turn out dough onto a heavily floured countertop or cutting board. Gently roll and stretch dough into a 12-inch rope. With a sharp knife, divide dough into 10 pieces.

For the Large Recipe

Reserve 6 tablespoons of the onion mixture. Place remaining onion mixture and the rest of dough ingredients in bread pan, select Dough setting, and press Start.

When the dough has risen long enough, the machine will beep. Turn off bread machine, remove bread pan, and turn out dough onto a heavily floured countertop or cutting board. Gently roll and stretch dough into a 12-inch rope. With a sharp knife, divide dough into 14 pieces.

3. Grease a large baking sheet. Roll each piece of dough into a ball and then flatten slightly. Place rolls on prepared sheet.

TOPPING

	SMALL RECIPE	MEDIUM RECIPE	LARGE RECIPE
EGG	1	1	1
SALT	½ teaspoon	½ teaspoon	½ teaspoon

4. In a small bowl, beat together egg and salt for the topping. Brush egg mixture over each roll. Spread approximately 1 teaspoon of reserved onion mixture on each roll.

5. Let rise in a warm oven about 30 to 45 minutes until doubled in size. (Hint: To warm oven slightly, turn oven on Warm setting for 1 minute, then turn it off and place covered dough in oven to rise. Remove pan from oven before preheating.)

6. Preheat oven to 375°F. Bake for 20 minutes until rolls are golden and onion is brown. Remove from oven and place on racks to cool.

BAKE CYCLE: Dough

Small recipe yields 7 rolls
Medium recipe yields 1 0 rolls
Large recipe yields 1 4 rolls

NUTRITIONAL INFORMATION PER ROLL
Calories 193 / Fat 4.9 grams / Carbohydrates 31 grams / Protein 5.7 grams / Fiber 1.3 grams / Sodium 394 milligrams / Cholesterol 42.8 milligrams

---

Special Ed-ible Pretzels

For years, Linda's Special Ed students have made these incredible soft, doughy pretzels once a week for the high school faculty and staff. They've now perfected a touch and technique that far surpass the skills of those who taught them. So, if your first batches fall short of perfection, we know some very patient kids who would encourage you not to give up hope. For all of us, determination and practice are the keys to success.

	SMALL RECIPE	MEDIUM RECIPE	LARGE RECIPE
WATER	¾ cup	1 cup	1¼ cups
OIL	1½ tablespoons	2 tablespoons	3 tablespoons
SUGAR	2 teaspoons	1 tablespoon	4 teaspoons
ALL-PURPOSE FLOUR	2 cups	3 cups	4 cups
RED STAR BRAND ACTIVE DRY YEAST	2 teaspoons	2 teaspoons	2½ teaspoons
WATER	10 cups	10 cups	10 cups
BAKING SODA	2½ tablespoons	2½ tablespoons	2½ tablespoons
COARSE SALT	to taste	to taste	to taste

1. Place first five ingredients in bread pan, select Dough setting, and press Start.

2. When the dough has risen long enough, the machine will beep. Turn off bread machine, remove bread pan, and turn out dough onto an oiled countertop or cutting board. Gently roll and stretch dough into a 12-inch rope.

For the Small Recipe
Heavily grease a large baking sheet. With a sharp knife, divide dough into 4 or 5 equal pieces.

For the Medium Recipe
Heavily grease 1 or 2 large baking sheets. With a sharp knife, divide dough into 6 or 7 equal pieces.

For the Large Recipe
Heavily grease 2 large baking sheets. With a sharp knife, divide dough into 8 to 10 equal pieces.

3. Gently roll and stretch each piece into a 14-inch rope. Shape into a pretzel by bringing both ends of the rope up toward the top and crossing them (forming something that looks like a bunny's head with ears). Twist those "ears" once, then bring them toward you to rest on the base of the pretzel (the bunny's "chin"), pressing them down slightly. Set aside on the oiled countertop, cover with a cotton dish towel, and let rise until almost doubled, about 20 minutes.

4. Meanwhile, in a 3- or 4-quart nonreactive pot, combine the water and the baking soda. Bring to a boil over high heat, then reduce heat to a gentle simmer.

5. Preheat oven to 425°F.

6. Being careful not to deflate the pretzel, gently lift one onto a slotted spatula and lower into the simmering water. After 20 seconds, turn it over in the water. After another 20 seconds, remove from water with slotted spatula. (With a little experience, you can simmer 2 or 3 at a time.) Allow to drain on a clean broiler pan or cake rack.

7. Place pretzels on prepared baking sheet(s); sprinkle with coarse salt to taste.

8. Bake for 15 to 20 minutes until golden brown. Remove from oven and immediately remove pretzels from baking sheet(s); place on racks to cool. These are best served warm, the same day; they do not keep well.

BAKE CYCLE: Dough

Small recipe yields 4 or 5 pretzels
Medium recipe yields 6 or 7 pretzels
Large recipe yields 8 to 10 pretzels

NUTRITIONAL INFORMATION PER PRETZEL
Calories 238 / Fat 4.4 grams / Carbohydrates 42.7 grams / Protein 5.8 grams / Fiber 1.7 grams / Sodium 845 milligrams / Cholesterol 0 milligrams

---

Cocktail Rye Loaves

*T*hese are soft, flavorful, small loaves—perfect for hors d'oeuvres. Slice thinly, spread with pâté, and enjoy.

	SMALL RECIPE	MEDIUM RECIPE	LARGE RECIPE
WATER	⅞ cup	1⅛ cups	1½ cups
SHORTENING	2 teaspoons	1 tablespoon	4 teaspoons
DARK BROWN SUGAR	1 tablespoon	1½ tablespoons	2 tablespoons
SALT	1 teaspoon	1½ teaspoons	2 teaspoons
BREAD FLOUR	1⅓ cups	2 cups	2⅔ cups
RYE FLOUR	⅔ cup	1 cup	1⅓ cups
CARAWAY SEEDS	1 teaspoon	1½ teaspoons	2 teaspoons
RED STAR BRAND ACTIVE DRY YEAST	2 teaspoons	2 teaspoons	2½ teaspoons
CORNMEAL	small handful	small handful	small handful

1.   Place all ingredients except cornmeal in bread pan, select Dough setting, and press Start.

2.   When the dough has risen long enough, the machine will beep. Turn off bread machine, remove bread pan, and turn out dough onto a floured countertop or cutting board.

3.   Shape dough into a log. Dust a baking sheet with cornmeal.

For the Small Recipe
With a sharp knife, divide dough into 2 pieces.

For the Medium Recipe
With a sharp knife, divide dough into 3 pieces.

For the Large Recipe
With a sharp knife, divide dough into 4 pieces.

4.   Roll each piece into a narrow 12-inch-long loaf. Place on prepared baking sheet and with a sharp knife, slash the dough down the center from one end to the other.

5. Cover and let rise in a warm oven 10 minutes. (Hint: To warm oven slightly, turn oven on Warm setting for 1 minute, then turn it off and place covered dough in oven to rise. Remove pan from oven before preheating.)

6. Preheat oven to 375°F. Bake for 20 to 25 minutes until golden brown.

7. Remove from oven and cool on rack.

BAKE CYCLE: Dough

Small recipe yields 2 loaves
Medium recipe yields 3 loaves
Large recipe yields 4 loaves

NUTRITIONAL INFORMATION PER SERVING ($\frac{1}{14}$ OF RECIPE)
Calories 107 / Fat 1.3 grams / Carbohydrates 20.8 grams / Protein 2.7 grams / Fiber 1.7 grams / Sodium 230 milligrams / Cholesterol 0 milligrams

Shareen's Whole Wheat Pita Bread

*W*e find ourselves making these whole wheat pitas quite often. Their whole-some goodness, relatively few calories, and ease of preparation make them a pleasant, light alternative to the heavier whole-grain breads. Linda's niece Shareen rates these pitas as her all-time favorite. They're so delicious, she likes eating them plain.

	SMALL RECIPE	MEDIUM RECIPE	LARGE RECIPE
WATER	⅞ cup	1⅛ cups	1¾ cups
OIL	2 teaspoons	1 tablespoon	4 teaspoons
SUGAR	1 teaspoon	1½ teaspoons	2 teaspoons
SALT	1 teaspoon	1 teaspoon	2 teaspoons
WHOLE WHEAT FLOUR	2 cups	3 cups	4 cups
RED STAR BRAND ACTIVE DRY YEAST	1½ teaspoons	1½ teaspoons	2 teaspoons

1. Place dough ingredients in bread pan, select Dough setting, and press Start.

2. When the dough has risen long enough, the machine will beep. Turn off bread machine, remove bread pan, and turn out dough onto a lightly floured countertop or cutting board. Gently roll and stretch dough into a 12-inch rope.

For the Small Recipe
With a sharp knife, divide dough into 6 pieces.

For the Medium Recipe
With a sharp knife, divide dough into 8 pieces.

For the Large Recipe
With a sharp knife, divide dough into 12 pieces.

3. Roll each piece into a smooth ball. With a rolling pin, roll each ball into a 6- to 7-inch circle. Set aside on lightly floured countertop; cover with a cotton dish towel. Let pitas rise about 30 minutes until slightly puffy.

4. Position oven rack in middle of oven; preheat oven to 500°F. Place 2 or 3 pitas on a wire cake rack. Place cake rack directly on oven rack; bake pitas 4 to 5 minutes

until puffed and tops begin to brown. Remove from oven and immediately place pitas in a sealed brown paper bag or cover with a damp cotton dish towel until soft.

5.   Once the pitas are softened, either cut in half, or split open the top edge for half or whole pitas. They can be stored in a plastic bag for several days or in the freezer for 1 to 2 months.

BAKE CYCLE: Dough

Small recipe yields 6 pitas
Medium recipe yields 8 pitas
Large recipe yields 1 2 pitas

NUTRITIONAL INFORMATION PER PITA
Calories 172 / Fat 2.6 grams / Carbohydrates 33.5 grams / Protein 6.4 grams / Fiber 5.9 grams / Sodium 269 milligrams / Cholesterol 0 milligrams

---

TIPS FOR SUCCESS
1. The pitas puff up during baking owing to steam, so avoid using too much flour while rolling them out. Keep the unrolled balls covered to prevent them from drying out.
2. Those that don't puff up perfectly during baking were probably torn or creased in handling. Handle the pitas with care while rolling and transferring from counter to cake rack.
3. Avoid overbaking—they'll turn crisp and brittle. You'll end up with something resembling a tortilla chip rather than pita bread.
4. Don't give up if your pitas don't all turn out perfectly the first time. With a little practice and patience, you'll be turning out pita bread like a pro!

Peppy's Pita Bread

*B*e sure and peek in the oven while these bake. It's like magic, watching the dough puff up into little balloons! The result is pita bread that far surpasses anything you can buy in the market.

	SMALL RECIPE	MEDIUM RECIPE	LARGE RECIPE
WATER	¾ cup	1⅛ cups	1⅜ cups
OIL	2 teaspoons	1 tablespoon	4 teaspoons
SUGAR	1 teaspoon	1½ teaspoons	2 teaspoons
SALT	1 teaspoons	1 teaspoons	2 teaspoons
ALL-PURPOSE FLOUR	2 cups	3 cups	4 cups
RED STAR BRAND ACTIVE DRY YEAST	1½ teaspoons	1½ teaspoons	2 teaspoons

1.   Place dough ingredients in bread pan, select Dough setting, and press Start.

2.   When the dough has risen long enough, the machine will beep. Turn off bread machine, remove bread pan, and turn out dough onto a lightly floured countertop or cutting board. Gently roll and stretch dough into a 12-inch rope.

For the Small Recipe
   With a sharp knife, divide dough into 6 pieces.

For the Medium Recipe
   With a sharp knife, divide dough into 8 pieces.

For the Large Recipe
   With a sharp knife, divide dough into 12 pieces.

3.   Roll each piece into a smooth ball. With a rolling pin, roll each ball into a 6- to 7-inch circle. Set aside on lightly floured countertop; cover with a cotton dish towel. Let pitas rise about 30 minutes until slightly puffy.

4.   Position oven rack in middle of oven; preheat oven to 500°F. Place 2 or 3 pitas on a wire cake rack. Place cake rack directly on oven rack; bake pitas 4 to 5 minutes until puffed and tops begin to brown. Remove from oven and immediately place pitas in a sealed brown paper bag or cover with a damp cotton dish towel until soft.

5. Once the pitas are softened, either cut in half or split open the top edge for half or whole pitas. They can be stored in a plastic bag for several days or in the freezer for 1 to 2 months.

BAKE CYCLE: Dough

Small recipe yields 6 pitas
Medium recipe yields 8 pitas
Large recipe yields 12 pitas

NUTRITIONAL INFORMATION PER PITA
Calories 190 / Fat 2.2 grams / Carbohydrates 36.6 grams / Protein 5 grams / Fiber 1.4 grams / Sodium 268 milligrams / Cholesterol 0 milligrams

---

TIPS FOR SUCCESS: See page 214.

Christin's Oatmeal Pita Bread

*A*s we experimented with various breads for this chapter, baking pita bread for the first time was probably one of our biggest thrills. We laughed at how they puffed up in the oven; we thought we'd created a true culinary oddity. When they turned out to be as good as, if not better than, any pita bread we'd ever eaten, we were ecstatic! So if you feel like having some fun in your kitchen, try making these chewy oatmeal pita pockets. Invite friends or family to join you; young children, in particular, are quite impressed.

	SMALL RECIPE	MEDIUM RECIPE	LARGE RECIPE
OLD-FASHIONED ROLLED OATS	½ cup	1 cup	1¼ cups
WATER	⅞ cup	1¼ cups	1⅝ cups
OIL	1 tablespoon	1½ tablespoons	2 tablespoons
SUGAR	1 teaspoon	1½ teaspoons	2 teaspoons
SALT	1 teaspoon	1 teaspoon	1½ teaspoons
ALL-PURPOSE FLOUR	2 cups	3 cups	4 cups
RED STAR BRAND ACTIVE DRY YEAST	1½ teaspoons	1½ teaspoons	2 teaspoons

1.   Place dough ingredients in bread pan, select Dough setting, and press Start.

2.   When the dough has risen long enough, the machine will beep. Turn off bread machine, remove bread pan, and turn out dough onto a lightly floured countertop or cutting board. Gently roll and stretch dough into a 12-inch rope.

For the Small Recipe
   With a sharp knife, divide dough into 7 pieces.

For the Medium Recipe
   With a sharp knife, divide dough into 10 pieces.

For the Large Recipe
   With a sharp knife, divide dough into 14 pieces.

3.   Roll each piece into a smooth ball. With a rolling pin, roll each ball into a 6- to 7-inch circle. Set aside on lightly floured countertop; cover with a cotton dish towel. Let pitas rise about 30 minutes until slightly puffy.

4. Position oven rack in middle of oven; preheat oven to 500°F. Place 2 or 3 pitas on a wire cake rack. Place cake rack directly on oven rack; bake pitas 4 to 5 minutes until puffed and tops begin to brown. Remove from oven and immediately place pitas in a sealed brown paper bag or cover with a damp cotton dish towel until soft.

5. Once the pitas are softened, either cut in half or split open the top edge for half or whole pitas. They can be stored in a plastic bag for several days or in the freezer for 1 to 2 months.

BAKE CYCLE: Dough

Small recipe yields 7 pitas
Medium recipe yields 1 0 pitas
Large recipe yields 1 4 pitas

NUTRITIONAL INFORMATION PER PITA
Calories 189 / Fat 2.9 grams / Carbohydrates 34.7 grams / Protein 5.3 grams / Fiber 2 grams / Sodium 214 milligrams / Cholesterol 0 milligrams

---

TIPS FOR SUCCESS: See page 214.

Lavosh (Armenian Flatbread)

*T*his recipe produces a thin, semicrisp cracker bread that is popular in Eastern
European countries. You can soften the cracker by wrapping it in damp cotton
dish towels for an hour or so. When it is bendable, spread with a curry mayonnaise
and add layers of meat, tomato, cucumber, and lettuce, all sliced paper thin. Roll it
up, cut it into 4-inch-wide sandwiches, and you have a fabulous and unusual late-
night snack for a card party.

	SMALL RECIPE	MEDIUM RECIPE	LARGE RECIPE
WATER	¾ cup	1 cup	1¼ cups
SHORTENING	3 tablespoons	¼ cup	6 tablespoons
SUGAR	2 teaspoons	1 tablespoon	4 teaspoons
SALT	1 teaspoon	1½ teaspoons	2 teaspoons
ALL-PURPOSE FLOUR	2 cups	3 cups	4 cups
RED STAR BRAND ACTIVE DRY YEAST	1½ teaspoons	1½ teaspoons	2 teaspoons
MILK	2 tablespoons	3 tablespoons	¼ cup
SESAME SEEDS	to taste	to taste	to taste

1. Place all ingredients except milk and sesame seeds in bread pan, select Dough
setting, and press Start.

2. When the dough has risen long enough, the machine will beep. Turn off bread
machine, remove bread pan, and turn out dough onto a lightly floured countertop
or cutting board.

3. Shape dough into a log. Grease 2 baking sheets or pizza pans. Preheat oven to
400°F.

For the Small Recipe

With a sharp knife, divide dough into either 3 pieces for large crackers or 8
pieces for small crackers.

For the Medium Recipe

With a sharp knife, divide dough into either 4 pieces for large crackers or 10
pieces for small crackers.

For the Large Recipe

With a sharp knife, divide dough into either 6 pieces for large crackers or 16 pieces for small crackers.

4.   With a rolling pin, roll each piece into a circle that is paper thin. To pick up and move the dough, wrap it around the rolling pin, then gently unroll it onto prepared baking sheets or pizza pans. With a fork, prick the surface of each cracker several times. Brush crackers with milk and sprinkle sesame seeds on top.

5.   Bake 10 to 12 minutes until lightly browned.

6.   Remove from oven; cool crackers on wire rack. Once cooled, wrap in foil and store at room temperature.

BAKE CYCLE: Dough

Small recipe yields 3 large or 8 small crackers
Medium recipe yields 4 large or 10 small crackers
Large recipe yields 6 large or 16 small crackers

NUTRITIONAL INFORMATION PER SMALL CRACKER
Calories 190 / Fat 5.6 grams / Carbohydrates 30.1 grams / Protein 4.2 grams / Fiber 1.1 grams / Sodium 323 milligrams / Cholesterol .2 milligram

---

Soft Bread Sticks

T*hese thick and chewy breadsticks belong in a tall glass on a checkered table-cloth with a big bowl of minestrone soup and "Volare" playing in the background.*

DOUGH

	SMALL RECIPE	MEDIUM RECIPE	LARGE RECIPE
WATER	¾ cup	1 cup	1¼ cups
EGG YOLK	1	1	2
OLIVE OIL	1½ tablespoons	2 tablespoons	3 tablespoons
SUGAR	1 tablespoon	1½ tablespoons	2 tablespoons
SALT	1½ teaspoons	2 teaspoons	2 teaspoons
ALL-PURPOSE FLOUR	2 cups	3 cups	4 cups
RED STAR BRAND ACTIVE DRY YEAST	1½ teaspoons	1½ teaspoons	2 teaspoons

1.   Place dough ingredients in bread pan, select Dough setting, and press Start.

2.   When the dough has risen long enough, the machine will beep. Turn off bread machine, remove bread pan, and turn out dough onto a heavily floured countertop or cutting board.

3.   Gently roll and stretch dough into a 20-inch rope. Grease 2 baking sheets. Preheat oven to 350°F.

For the Small Recipe
With a sharp knife, divide dough into 24 pieces. (Hint: First cut the dough into 12 equal pieces, then cut each of those in half.)

For the Medium Recipe
With a sharp knife, divide dough into 32 pieces. (Hint: First cut the dough into 8 equal pieces, then cut each of those into 4 small pieces.)

For the Large Recipe
With a sharp knife, divide dough into 48 pieces. (Hint: First cut the dough into 12 equal pieces, then cut each of those into 4 small pieces.)

4. Roll each piece of dough into an 8-inch stick;* place on prepared baking sheets.

TOPPING

	SMALL RECIPE	MEDIUM RECIPE	LARGE RECIPE
EGG WHITE	1	1	1
WATER	1 tablespoon	1 tablespoon	1 tablespoon
SESAME SEEDS, POPPYSEEDS, OR COARSE SALT	to taste	to taste	to taste

5. In a small bowl, combine egg white with water for the topping and brush egg mixture over each bread stick. Sprinkle with sesame seeds, poppyseeds, or salt, according to your preference.

6. Bake for 20 to 25 minutes. Remove from oven; remove bread sticks from pans and cool on cake racks.

7. Once cool, store at room temperature in plastic bags. They will stay fresh for 3 to 4 days.

BAKE CYCLE: Dough

Small recipe yields 24 bread sticks
Medium recipe yields 32 bread sticks
Large recipe yields 48 bread sticks

NUTRITIONAL INFORMATION PER BREAD STICK
Calories 55 / Fat 1.1 grams / Carbohydrates 9.6 grams / Protein 1.5 grams / Fiber .4 gram / Sodium 135 milligrams / Cholesterol 6.7 milligrams

*For crisper, thinner bread sticks, roll dough into 16-inch sticks.

Teddy Bears

*T*hese rolls are great sellers at bake sales, cute for parties, and a special treat for young children. Each one has its own personality; it's fun to give them names. You can use any white or whole-grain bread dough.

DOUGH

	SMALL	MEDIUM	LARGE
BREAD DOUGH OF YOUR CHOICE, such as DeDe's Buttermilk Bread (page 18)			

1. Place dough ingredients in bread pan, select Dough setting, and press Start.

2. When the dough has risen long enough, the machine will beep. Turn off bread machine, remove bread pan, and turn out dough onto a floured countertop or cutting board. Shape dough into a log.

For the Small Recipe
   With a sharp knife, divide dough into 4 pieces.

For the Medium Recipe
   With a sharp knife, divide dough into 6 pieces.

For the Large Recipe
   With a sharp knife, divide dough into 8 pieces.

3. Grease a large baking sheet. Taking 1 piece of dough, with a sharp knife, divide it in half. Roll 1 of the halves into a smooth ball; place on cookie sheet for bear's body. Divide the other half in half again. Roll 1 of those pieces into another smooth ball; place on cookie sheet for the bear's head. Divide remaining piece of dough into 6

small pieces. Roll each one into a tiny ball and place on the cookie sheet for the bear's 2 ears, arms, and legs. (You can pinch off a very tiny piece of dough from one of them and roll it into a small nose for the bear's head.) Repeat these steps with the remaining dough.

TOPPING

	SMALL RECIPE	MEDIUM RECIPE	LARGE RECIPE
EGG, LIGHTLY BEATEN	1	1	2
RAISINS	12	18	24

4.   Brush each bear with egg. Place raisins for eyes and belly button.

5.   Let rise slightly in warm oven 10 minutes. (Hint: To warm oven slightly, turn oven on Warm setting for 1 minute, then turn it off and place covered dough in oven to rise. Remove pan from oven before preheating.)

6.   Preheat oven to 375°F. Bake for 15 minutes until golden brown. Remove from oven; remove bears from pan and cool on cake rack.

BAKE CYCLE: Dough

Small recipe yields 4 bears
Medium recipe yields 6 bears
Large recipe yields 8 bears

NUTRITIONAL INFORMATION PER BEAR
Calories 297 / Fat 2.9 grams / Carbohydrates 59.3 grams / Protein 7.9 grams / Fiber 2.1 grams / Sodium 569 milligrams / Cholesterol 35.5 milligrams

---

English Muffins

*Y*our friends and family will marvel over your cooking skills when you present a plate of these for their enjoyment. (There's no need to tell them how truly simple they are to bake.) You'll appreciate the humble, fresh taste of these English muffins if you've ever tried some of the packaged varieties.

	SMALL RECIPE	MEDIUM RECIPE	LARGE RECIPE
WATER	½ cup	¾ cup	¾ cup
EGG	1	1	2
OIL	2 tablespoons	3 tablespoons	¼ cup
MALT VINEGAR	2 teaspoons	1 tablespoon	4 teaspoons
SUGAR	2 teaspoons	1 tablespoon	4 teaspoons
SALT	1 teaspoon	1 teaspoon	1½ teaspoons
BREAD FLOUR	2 cups	3 cups	4 cups
RED STAR BRAND ACTIVE DRY YEAST	1½ teaspoons	1½ teaspoons	2 teaspoons
CORNMEAL	as needed	as needed	as needed

1. Place all ingredients except cornmeal in bread pan, select Dough setting, and press Start.

2. When the dough has risen long enough, the machine will beep. Turn off bread machine, remove bread pan, and turn out dough onto a lightly floured countertop or cutting board.

3. With a rolling pin, roll dough out to a ⅜-inch thickness. Using a 3-inch muffin cutter (or a cleaned 8-ounce pineapple can with both top and bottom removed), cut out muffins. Reroll the scraps one time and cut out 2 or 3 more muffins.

4. Place muffins on a baking sheet sprinkled with cornmeal. Turn muffins to coat both sides with cornmeal. Cover and let rise on countertop until almost doubled, 30 to 60 minutes.

5. Heat an ungreased griddle or electric frying pan to medium-high (375°F). Very gently place muffins on griddle and cook for 5 minutes, then reduce heat to low

(275°F) and cook 10 minutes more. Increase the heat again to medium-high, gently turn the muffins, and repeat the cooking process, reducing the heat again after 5 minutes.

6. Remove muffins from griddle and cool on cake racks. Split in half with a fork, toast, and serve with butter. Any leftovers can be frozen in a plastic bag.

BAKE CYCLE: Dough

Small recipe yields 8 or 9 muffins
Medium recipe yields 1 0 to 1 2 muffins
Large recipe yields 1 4 to 1 6 muffins

NUTRITIONAL INFORMATION PER MUFFIN
Calories 155 / Fat 4.1 grams / Carbohydrates 25 grams / Protein 3.9 grams / Fiber .9 gram / Sodium 184 milligrams / Cholesterol 17.7 milligrams

---

Cinnamon, Whole Wheat, and
Raisin English Muffins

*O*ne of these muffins, with its whole-grain nutty flavor, cinnamon-and-raisin *sweetness, and full-bodied texture, makes a very satisfying morning meal.*

	SMALL RECIPE	MEDIUM RECIPE	LARGE RECIPE
MILLER'S BRAN	2 tablespoons	3 tablespoons	¼ cup
MILK	⅜ cup	½ cup	¾ cup
WATER	⅜ cup	½ cup	⅞ cup
HONEY	1½ tablespoons	2 tablespoons	3 tablespoons
SALT	½ teaspoon	1 teaspoon	1 teaspoon
WHOLE WHEAT FLOUR	1⅓ cups	2 cup	2⅔ cups
BREAD FLOUR	⅔ cup	1 cup	1⅓ cups
BAKING SODA	½ teaspoon	½ teaspoon	1 teaspoon
GROUND CINNAMON	1 teaspoon	1 teaspoon	2 teaspoons
RAISINS	¼ cup	⅓ cup	½ cup
RED STAR BRAND ACTIVE DRY YEAST	1½ teaspoons	1½ teaspoons	2 teaspoons
CORNMEAL	as needed	as needed	as needed

1.   Place all ingredients except cornmeal in bread pan, select Dough setting, and press Start.

2.   When the dough has risen long enough, the machine will beep. Turn off bread machine, remove bread pan, and turn out dough onto a lightly floured countertop or cutting board.

3.   With a rolling pin, roll dough out to a ⅜-inch thickness. Using a 3-inch muffin cutter (or a cleaned 6½-ounce tuna can with both top and bottom removed), cut out muffins. Reroll the scraps one time and cut out 2 or 3 more muffins.

4.   Place muffins on a baking sheet sprinkled with cornmeal. Turn muffins to coat both sides with cornmeal. Cover and let rise on countertop until almost doubled, 30 to 60 minutes.

5. Heat an ungreased griddle or electric frying pan to medium-high (375°F). Very gently place muffins on griddle and cook for 5 minutes, then reduce heat to low (275°F) and cook 10 minutes more. Increase the heat again to medium-high, gently turn the muffins, and repeat the cooking process, reducing the heat again after 5 minutes.

6. Remove muffins from griddle and cool on cake racks. Split in half with a fork, toast, and serve with butter. Any leftovers can be frozen in a plastic bag.

BAKE CYCLE: Dough

Small recipe yields 8 or 9 muffins
Medium recipe yields 10 to 12 muffins
Large recipe yields 14 to 16 muffins

NUTRITIONAL INFORMATION PER MUFFIN
Calories 136 / Fat .7 gram / Carbohydrates 30 grams / Protein 4.6 grams / Fiber 3.4 grams / Sodium 185 milligrams / Cholesterol .4 milligram

---

Focaccia

Focaccia is a flat, rustic Italian herb bread that travels beautifully in a picnic basket along with some sliced cold cuts, an antipasto tray, and a bottle of good Italian red wine. This savory loaf also makes a great appetizer.

DOUGH

	SMALL RECIPE	MEDIUM RECIPE	LARGE RECIPE
WATER	¾ cup	1 cup	1⅜ cups
OLIVE OIL	1 tablespoon	1½ tablespoons	2 tablespoons
SALT	½ teaspoon	1 teaspoon	1 teaspoon
ALL-PURPOSE FLOUR	2 cups	3 cups	4 cups
DRIED OREGANO	1 teaspoon	2 teaspoons	2 teaspoons
RED STAR BRAND ACTIVE DRY YEAST	1½ teaspoons	1½ teaspoons	2 teaspoons

1. Place dough ingredients in bread pan, select Dough setting, and press Start.

2. When the dough has risen long enough, the machine will beep. Turn off bread machine, remove bread pan, and turn out dough onto a heavily floured countertop or cutting board.

For the Small Recipe

Oil a 12- or 14-inch pizza pan. With your hands, gently stretch and press dough to fit evenly into pan.

For the Medium Recipe

Oil a 10 × 15 × 1-inch jelly-roll pan. With your hands, gently stretch and press dough to fit evenly into pan.

For the Large Recipe

With a sharp knife, cut dough in half. Oil two 12- or 14-inch pizza pans. With your hands, gently stretch and press dough to fit evenly into pans.

3. Cover and let rise in a warm oven 30 to 45 minutes until doubled in size. (Hint: To warm oven slightly, turn oven on Warm setting for 1 minute, then turn it off and place covered dough in oven to rise. Remove pan from oven before preheating.)

4. Preheat oven to 400°F.

	SMALL RECIPE	MEDIUM RECIPE	LARGE RECIPE
OLIVE OIL	2 tablespoons	3 tablespoons	¼ cup
GARLIC CLOVE, MINCED	1	1	2
FRESHLY GRATED PARMESAN CHEESE	⅓ cup (1½ ounces)	½ cup (2 ounces)	⅔ cup (3 ounces)
CHOPPED FRESH PARSLEY	3 tablespoons	¼ cup	6 tablespoons

5.   With 2 fingers, poke holes all over the dough. In a medium bowl, combine oil and garlic; drizzle over top of dough. Sprinkle with cheese and parsley.

6.   Bake for 25 to 30 minutes. Remove from oven; cool on cake rack or cut into squares and serve warm.

7.   Once cool, wrap in plastic. The focaccia will stay fresh for 2 to 3 days stored at room temperature.

BAKE CYCLE: Dough

Small recipe yields 1 loaf
Medium recipe yields 1 loaf
Large recipe yields 2 loaves

NUTRITIONAL INFORMATION PER 1 SERVING (¹⁄₁₂ OF LOAF)
Calories 176 / Fat 6.4 grams / Carbohydrates 24.3 grams / Protein 4.8 grams / Fiber 1.1 grams / Sodium 242 milligrams / Cholesterol 2.6 milligrams

Sausage and Pepper Bread

*P*lanning on hosting a Super Bowl party? Here's a hearty, savory sandwich loaf to serve at halftime with a big pot of homemade soup.

DOUGH

	SMALL	MEDIUM	LARGE
BREAD DOUGH OF YOUR CHOICE, such as Egg Bread (page 19)			

1. Place dough ingredients in bread pan, select Dough setting, and press Start.

FILLING

	SMALL RECIPE	MEDIUM RECIPE	LARGE RECIPE
HOT ITALIAN SAUSAGE	1 pound	1½ pounds	2 pounds
BUTTER OR MARGARINE	3 tablespoons	4 tablespoons	6 tablespoons
GARLIC CLOVE, MINCED	1	1	2
EGG, BEATEN	1	1	2
DRIED OREGANO	½ teaspoon	1 teaspoon	1 teaspoon
DRIED BASIL	½ teaspoon	1 teaspoon	1 teaspoon
GRATED MOZZARELLA CHEESE	1 cup (4 ounces)	1½ cups (6 ounces)	2 cups (8 ounces)
FINELY CHOPPED RED OR GREEN BELL PEPPER	⅔ cup	1 cup	1⅓ cups

2. Meanwhile, remove casings from sausages and discard. In a small skillet over medium heat, brown the sausage, crumbling it as it cooks. When brown, remove from pan and drain well on paper towels; set aside to cool.

3. In a small saucepan over low heat, melt butter and stir in garlic; set aside.

4. When the dough has risen long enough, the machine will beep. Turn off bread machine, remove bread pan, and turn out dough onto a heavily floured countertop or cutting board. Grease a large baking sheet or jelly-roll pan.

For the Small Recipe

With a rolling pin, roll dough into a 9 × 12-inch rectangle.

For the Medium Recipe

With a rolling pin, roll dough into a 9 × 18-inch rectangle.

For the Large Recipe

With a sharp knife, cut dough in half. With a rolling pin, roll each piece of dough into a 9 × 12-inch rectangle.

5. Brush top of dough with half of the garlic butter. Combine sausage, egg, oregano, basil, cheese, and bell pepper; spread over dough. Starting with the long edge, roll up; pinch seam and ends to seal. Place seam side down on prepared pan. Brush entire surface of roll with remaining garlic butter.

6. Preheat oven to 375°F. Bake for 30 to 40 minutes until brown. Remove from oven and allow to cool for 2 minutes.

7. Slice into 3-inch pieces and serve warm.

BAKE CYCLE: Dough

Small recipe yields 4 slices
Medium recipe yields 6 slices
Large recipe yields 8 slices

NUTRITIONAL INFORMATION PER SLICE
Calories 853 / Fat 47.4 grams / Carbohydrates 61.9 grams / Protein 41.4 grams / Fiber 2.2 grams / Sodium 1941 milligrams / Cholesterol 211 milligrams

---

Max's Clogging Bread

A good friend brought us this recipe and we adapted it for the bread machine. Now the book just wouldn't be complete without it. Share a bottle of wine and a loaf of this aromatic bread with friends and soon everyone will feel like clogging the taps right off their shoes, just like our friend Max!

DOUGH

	SMALL RECIPE	MEDIUM RECIPE	LARGE RECIPE
WATER	¾ cup	1 cup	1¼ cups
SALT	1 teaspoon	1½ teaspoons	2 teaspoons
SUGAR	2 teaspoons	1 tablespoon	4 teaspoons
ALL-PURPOSE FLOUR	2 cups	3 cups	4 cups
FINELY CHOPPED FRESH ONION	¼ cup	⅓ cup	½ cup
RED STAR BRAND ACTIVE DRY YEAST	2 teaspoons	2 teaspoons	2½ teaspoons

1. Place dough ingredients in bread pan, select Dough setting, and press Start.

2. When the dough has risen long enough, the machine will beep. Turn off bread machine, remove bread pan, and turn out dough onto a lightly floured countertop or cutting board.

3. Oil a baking sheet with olive oil. Preheat oven to 400°F.

TOPPING

	SMALL	MEDIUM	LARGE
OLIVE OIL, COARSE KOSHER SALT, and DRIED ROSEMARY	to taste	to taste	to taste

4. Rub some olive oil onto your hands. Place dough on oiled sheet and, with oiled hands, flatten it into a 1-inch-thick circle or oblong shape. Sprinkle with salt and rosemary to taste. With the edge of a clean ruler or the blunt edge of a long knife,

make several deep creases spaced 1 inch apart from one side of the loaf to the other. Cover and let rise in a warm oven 30 to 45 minutes until doubled in size. (Hint: To warm oven slightly, turn oven on Warm setting for 1 minute, then turn it off and place covered dough in oven to rise. Remove pan from oven before preheating.)

5.   Bake for 20 to 25 minutes until golden. Remove from oven and serve warm with butter.

BAKE CYCLE: Dough

NUTRITIONAL INFORMATION PER SLICE
Calories 112 / Fat 1.3 grams / Carbohydrates 21.7 grams / Protein 2.9 grams / Fiber .9 gram / Sodium 305 milligrams / Cholesterol 0 milligrams

---

Ham, Broccoli, and Cheese Calzone

With a little imagination, you can create endless variations of this basic recipe. The leftovers (if you're lucky enough to have any) can be frozen; they'll come in handy on days when you have to put something on the dinner table in 10 minutes.

DOUGH

	SMALL	MEDIUM	LARGE
BREAD DOUGH OF YOUR CHOICE, such as Pizza Dough (page 237)			

1. Place dough ingredients in bread pan, select Dough setting, and press Start.

2. When the dough has risen long enough, the machine will beep. Turn off bread machine, remove bread pan, and turn out dough onto a heavily floured countertop or cutting board. Shape dough into a log.

For the Small Recipe
With a sharp knife, divide dough into 6 pieces.

For the Medium Recipe
With a sharp knife, divide dough into 9 pieces.

For the Large Recipe
With a sharp knife, divide dough into 12 pieces.

3. Grease a baking sheet. Preheat oven to 400°F.

FILLING

	SMALL RECIPE	MEDIUM RECIPE	LARGE RECIPE
FROZEN, CHOPPED BROCCOLI, THAWED AND DRAINED	2 cups	3 cups	4 cups
RICOTTA CHEESE	1 cup (8 ounces)	1½ cups (12 ounces)	scant 2 cups (15 ounces)
GRATED MOZZARELLA CHEESE	1 cup (4 ounces)	1½ cups (6 ounces)	2 cups (8 ounces)
GARLIC CLOVES, MINCED	2	3	4
PEPPER	to taste	to taste	to taste
THIN SLICES OF HAM	6	9	12

4. In a medium bowl, combine broccoli, cheeses, garlic, and pepper; set aside.

5. With a rolling pin, roll each piece of dough into into a 6-inch circle. On one half of each circle, place folded slice of ham, then spread ½ cup of broccoli mixture on top of ham. Fold other half of dough over filling. Seal well by pressing edges together with the tines of a fork. Brush each calzone with melted butter (see below).

TOPPING

	SMALL RECIPE	MEDIUM RECIPE	LARGE RECIPE
MELTED BUTTER OR MARGARINE	2 tablespoons	3 tablespoons	4 tablespoons
SPAGHETTI SAUCE	1 cup	1½ cups	2 cups
FRESHLY GRATED PARMESAN CHEESE	to taste	to taste	to taste

6. Bake for 30 to 35 minutes until golden brown. Remove from oven. Serve warm with spaghetti sauce and grated Parmesan cheese on the side.

BAKE CYCLE: Dough

Small recipe yields 6 calzone
Medium recipe yields 9 clazone
Large recipe yields 1 2 calzone

NUTRITIONAL INFORMATION PER CALZONE
Calories 407 / Fat 16.1 grams / Carbohydrates 46.2 grams / Protein 19.5 grams / Fiber 3.6 grams / Sodium 805 milligrams / Cholesterol 28.1 milligrams

Pizza Dough

N *ow you can have delicious homemade pizza in the wink of an eye! And
should you change your mind at the last minute, you can keep the dough in
an oiled plastic bag for several days in the refrigerator.*

	SMALL RECIPE	MEDIUM RECIPE	LARGE RECIPE
WATER	⅝ to ¾ cup	⅞ to 1 cup	1⅛ to 1¼ cups
OLIVE OIL	1½ tablespoons	2 tablespoons	3 tablespoons
SALT	½ teaspoon	1 teaspoon	1 teaspoon
SUGAR	2 teaspoons	1 tablespoon	4 teaspoons
ALL-PURPOSE FLOUR	2 cups	3 cups	4 cups
RED STAR BRAND ACTIVE DRY YEAST	2 teaspoons	2 teaspoons	2½ teaspoons

1.   Place dough ingredients in bread pan, select Dough setting, and press Start.

2.   When the dough has risen long enough, the machine will beep. Turn off bread
machine, remove bread pan, and turn out dough onto a lightly floured countertop
or cutting board. Form dough into a mound and allow it to rest for 10 minutes.

For the Small Recipe
Grease one 14-inch pizza pan. With your hands, gently stretch and press dough
to fit evenly into pan. Pinch dough around the edges to form a small rim.

For the Medium Recipe
Grease one deep-dish or two 12-inch pizza pans. If using two pans, cut dough in
half with a sharp knife. With your hands, gently stretch and press dough to fit
evenly into pan(s). Pinch dough around the edges to form a small rim.

For the Large Recipe
Grease two 12- or 14-inch pizza pans. With a sharp knife, divide dough in half.
With your hands, gently stretch and press dough to fit evenly into pans. Pinch
dough around the edges of each to form a small rim.

3.   Spread your favorite pizza sauce on top of the dough, then add toppings of your
choice, except the cheese. Preheat oven to 450°F.

4. Bake for 15 to 20 minutes. Sprinkle with cheese during the last 5 minutes of baking. When cheese melts, remove from oven, slice into wedges, and serve hot. (Note: For a lighter, chewier crust, reduce the oven temperature to 400°F.)

BAKE CYCLE: Dough

Small recipe yields one thin-crust 14-inch pizza
Medium recipe yields one deep-dish pizza or two 12-inch pizzas
Large recipe yields two 12- or 14-inch pizzas

NUTRITIONAL INFORMATION PER SLICE (⅛ OF PIZZA)
Calories 119 / Fat 2.2 grams / Carbohydrates 21.3 grams / Protein 2.9 grams / Fiber .8 gram / Sodium 153 milligrams / Cholesterol 0 milligrams

---

Croutons

Here's a basic recipe for easy-to-make croutons with several variations:
Trim crusts from leftover slices of bread. (White, whole wheat, rye, pumpernickel, herb, and vegetable breads are best; the sweeter fruit breads are not compatible with the seasonings.) Spread each slice with softened butter or margarine; cut into 1/2-inch cubes. Place on a large baking sheet with a rim. Sprinkle with garlic powder and Italian seasoning to taste. Bake in a 350°F oven for 25 to 30 minutes, turning once with a large spatula. Remove from oven, allow to cool in pan, and store in a covered container indefinitely.

VARIATIONS

1. Sprinkle with Parmesan cheese before baking.
2. Omit Italian seasoning; substitute dried dill.
3. Substitute diet margarine for the butter.
4. Omit butter and garlic powder. Place a little minced garlic in some olive oil; drizzle over bread cubes before baking. You can also sprinkle bread cubes with Parmesan cheese before baking.
5. Rather than buttering bread cubes and baking them in the oven, melt some butter in a large skillet; add seasonings and bread cubes. Sauté until golden brown. (Note: This method uses a good deal more butter.)

Chili Burgers

*Y*ou *can make these "burgers" as mild or as spicy as you desire. For a mild flavor, choose plain Monterey Jack cheese; for a little heat, select a mild green chili pepper cheese; for the most intense heat, try jalapeño pepper cheese.*

DOUGH

	SMALL RECIPE	MEDIUM RECIPE	LARGE RECIPE
MILK	¼ cup	⅜ cup	⅜ cup
WATER	¼ cup	⅜ to ½ cup	⅜ cup
EGG	1	1	2
SALT	1 teaspoon	1½ teaspoons	2 teaspoons
SHORTENING	2 tablespoons	3 tablespoons	¼ cup
SUGAR	2 tablespoons	3 tablespoons	¼ cup
ALL-PURPOSE FLOUR	2 cups	3 cups	4 cups
RED STAR BRAND ACTIVE DRY YEAST	2 teaspoons	2 teaspoons	2½ teaspoons

I. Place dough ingredients in bread pan, select Dough setting, and press Start.

FILLING

	SMALL RECIPE	MEDIUM RECIPE	LARGE RECIPE
GROUND BEEF	1 pound	1 pound	2 pounds
LARGE ONION, CHOPPED	½ onion	¾ onion	1 onion
CHILI POWDER	1½ teaspoons	2 teaspoons	1 tablespoon
SALT	½ teaspoon	½ teaspoon	1 teaspoon
PEPPER	¼ teaspoon	¼ teaspoon	½ teaspoon
GRATED MONTEREY JACK CHEESE, MILD GREEN CHILI PEPPER CHEESE, OR JALAPEÑO PEPPER CHEESE	1 cup (4 ounces)	1½ cups (6 ounces)	2 cups (8 ounces)
15-OUNCE CAN CHILI BEANS, DRAINED	1	2	2
MELTED BUTTER OR MARGARINE	2 tablespoons	2 tablespoons	3 tablespoons

2. Meanwhile, in a large skillet, cook ground beef and onion over medium heat until meat is no longer pink. Drain off all grease. Reduce heat to low, return skillet to heat, and add chili powder, salt, pepper, cheese, and beans. Stir gently until beans are heated through, about 5 minutes. Remove skillet from heat; set aside.

3. When the dough has risen long enough, the machine will beep. Turn off bread machine, remove bread pan, and turn out dough onto a lightly floured countertop or cutting board. Gently roll and stretch dough into a 12-inch rope.

For the Small Recipe
With a sharp knife, divide dough into 12 pieces.

For the Medium Recipe
With a sharp knife, divide dough into 18 pieces.

For the Large Recipe
With a sharp knife, divide dough into 24 pieces.

4. Grease a baking sheet. Preheat oven to 400°F.

5. With a rolling pin, roll each piece into a 5-inch circle. Place ⅓ cup of filling mixture in the center of each circle. Pull the edges up to meet in the center and pinch dough together well to seal. Place on prepared baking sheet, sealed side down.

6. Bake for 15 to 20 minutes until brown. Remove from oven and brush with melted butter. Serve warm. These freeze well in a plastic bag for up to 3 months. To reheat, place in a 325°F oven for 30 minutes or microwave on High for 1½ to 2 minutes.

BAKE CYCLE: Dough

Small recipe yields 12 burgers
Medium recipe yields 18 burgers
Large recipe yields 24 burgers

NUTRITIONAL INFORMATION PER BURGER
Calories 304 / Fat 13.8 grams / Carbohydrates 29.3 grams / Protein 15.2 grams / Fiber 4.8 grams / Sodium 556 milligrams / Cholesterol 48.3 milligrams

---

Suggested Uses

As we sampled and shared the breads in this book, we also learned that some breads were better suited for sandwiches than others, some were more impressive for gift giving, and others were perfect for snacks or toasting. We thought it would be helpful to include this list of suggested uses for our breads. You can also refer to it when you're looking for those wonderful aromatic breads that say "welcome" when company's coming or breads that will wake you in the morning.

SANDWICH BREADS

Brown Bagger's White Bread
DeDe's Buttermilk Bread
Egg Bread
Linda's Easy Potato Bread
"San Francisco" Sourdough French
    Bread
Basic Whole Wheat Bread
Heavenly Whole Wheat Bread
Madeleine's Neighborly Bread
Shredded-Wheat Bread
Lou's Beer Bread
Miller's Bran Bread
Cracked-Wheat Bread
Lois's Rye Bread
Lorraine's Buttermilk Rye Bread

Michael's Onion Rye
Sauerkraut Rye Bread
Dilly Deli Rye
Black Forest Pumpernickel
Rick's Seven-Grain Bread
Multigrain Buttermilk Bread
Marilyn's Everyday Health Bread
Whole Wheat Soda Bread
Olde English Barley Bread
Wheat and Barley Bread
Shayna's Millet Bread
Sunflower Bread
Carrot-Herb Bread
Orange Bread

BREAKFAST BREAD OR TOAST

Midnight-Sun Bread
English Toasting Bread
Heavenly Whole Wheat Bread
Debbie's Honey Whole Wheat Bread

San Diego Sunshine
Apple Butter Wheat Bread
Daily Bread
Whole Wheat Sunflower Bread

Miller's Bran Bread
Citrus Rye
Briscoe's Irish Brown Bread
Irish Soda Bread
Sweet Oatmeal Bread
Honey 'n Oats Bread
Dennis's Blarney-Stone Bread
Buckwheat Bread
Sunny California Bread
Aloha Bread
Sunday Morning Apricot Bread
Johnny Appleseed Bread
Banana Oatmeal Bread
Apple Oatmeal Bread with Raisins

Granola Date Bread
Mixed Fruit Bread
Orange Bread
Eric and Janey's Poppyseed Peach
    Bread
Buckwheat Biscuits
Squaw Bread
Margaret's Buttermilk Raisin Bread
Oatmeal Spice Bread
English Muffins
Cinnamon, Whole Wheat, and Raisin
    English Muffins
Any sweet rolls or coffee cakes

SNACKING BREADS

Daily Bread
"San Francisco" Sourdough French
    Bread
San Diego Sunshine
Herb Bread
L & L Bakers' Dill Bread
Midnight-Sun Bread
Debbie's Honey Whole Wheat Bread
Apple Butter Wheat Bread
Whole Wheat Sunflower Bread
Cheddar Rye Bread
Swedish Limpa Rye Bread
Dilly Deli Rye
Vollkornbrot
Russian Black Bread
Zuni Indian Bread
Irish Soda Bread
Sweet Oatmeal Bread
Cheri's Orange Millet Bread

Sunny California Bread
Sunflower Bread
Carrot-Herb Bread
Broccoli-Cheese Bread
Onion Soup Bread
Jalapeño-Cheese Bread
Autumn Harvest Bread
Zucchini-Carrot Bread
Zucchini Wheat Bread
Crunchy-Munchy Bread
Banana Oatmeal Bread
Marmalade and Oats Bread
Sally Lunn Bread
Special Ed-ible Pretzels
Cocktail Rye Loaves
Pita Breads
Lavosh
Max's Clogging Bread

GIFT BREADS

DeDe's Buttermilk Bread
Irish Potato Bread
L & L Bakers' Dill Bread
"San Francisco" Sourdough French
    Bread
San Diego Sunshine
Whole Wheat Sunflower Bread
Lorraine's Buttermilk Rye Bread
Black Forest Pumpernickel
Zuni Indian Bread
Irish Soda Bread
Dennis's Blarney-Stone Bread
Sunny California Bread
Crunchy Carrot Bread
Elliot and Sara's Red Pepper Bread
Jalapeño-Cheese Bread

Sunday Morning Apricot Bread
Granola Date Bread
Marmalade and Oats Bread
Peaches and Spice Bread
Sweet Leilani Bread
Butterhorn Rolls
Jim's Cinnamon Rolls
Mini Cinnamon Rolls
Apple Strudel
Orange Bubble Loaf
Portuguese Sweet Bread
Shareen's Whole Wheat Pita Bread
Christin's Oatmeal Pita Bread
Teddy Bears
Croutons

DINNER PARTY BREADS

Authentic French Bread
Tangy Buttermilk Cheese Bread
Herb Bread
L & L Bakers' Dill Bread
Anita's Italian Herb Bread
"San Francisco" Sourdough French
    Bread
Buttermilk Cracked-Wheat Bread
Lois's Rye Bread
Vollkornbrot
Morris and Evelyn's Old World
    Pumpernickel

Sunflower Bread
Tomato Bread
Onion Soup Bread
Jalapeño-Cheese Bread
I Yam What I Yam Bread
Raisin Bread
Cocktail Rye Loaves
Bread Sticks
Focaccia
Max's Clogging Bread
Any dinner rolls

STUFFING / CROUTONS / BREAD CRUMBS

Basic White Bread
Egg Bread
Herb Bread
L & L Bakers' Dill Bread
Basic Whole Wheat Bread
Lois's Rye Bread
Michael's Onion Rye
Citrus Rye

Morris and Evelyn's Old World
    Pumpernickel
Carrot-Herb Bread
Tomato Bread
Elliot and Sara's Red Pepper Bread
Onion Soup Bread
Jalapeño-Cheese Bread

MOST AROMATIC BREADS

Herb Bread
Tangy Buttermilk Cheese Bread
L & L Bakers' Dill Bread
Anita's Italian Herb Bread
San Diego Sunshine
Michael's Onion Rye
Sauerkraut Rye Bread
Sunny California Bread

Broccoli-Cheese Bread
Tomato Bread
Onion Soup Bread
Jalapeño-Cheese Bread
Autumn Harvest Bread
Crunchy-Munchy Bread
Peaches and Spice Bread
Oatmeal Spice Bread

ON A DELAYED TIMER

Anadama Bread
Heavenly Whole Wheat Bread
San Diego Sunshine
Apple Butter Wheat Bread
Shredded-Wheat Bread
Bulgur Wheat Bread
His Favorite Rye Bread
Michael's Onion Rye
Swedish Limpa Rye Bread
Sauerkraut Rye Bread
Black Forest Pumpernickel
Morris and Evelyn's Old World
    Pumpernickel

Russian Black Bread
Marilyn's Everyday Health Bread
Sweet Oatmeal Bread
Wheat and Barley Bread
Cheri's Orange Millet Bread
Crunchy Carrot Bread
Elliot and Sara's Red Pepper Bread
Autumn Harvest Bread
Zucchini-Carrot Bread
Johnny Appleseed Bread
Apple Oatmeal Bread with Raisins
Oatmeal Spice Bread

Index